THE
HISTORY
OF THE
DEVIL

THE
HISTORY
OF THE
DEVIL

ANCIENT & MODERN

in

TWO PARTS

by

DANIEL DEFOE

With a new Introduction
by
Richard G. Landon

ROWMAN AND LITTLEFIELD
TOTOWA, NEW JERSEY

THIS EDITION FIRST PUBLISHED IN THE
UNITED STATES 1972
*by Rowman and Littlefield, Totowa,
New Jersey*

PR
3404
.H5
1972

ISBN 0 87471 102 9

THIS REPRINT TAKEN FROM THE
1819 EDITION
by T. Kelly, London

This edition published by kind permission of the
copyright holders,
EP Publishing Limited,
Wakefield, Yorkshire, England

Printed in Great Britain by
Scolar Press Limited, Menston, Yorkshire

INTRODUCTION

by RICHARD G. LANDON

Rare Books and Special Collections Department
University of Toronto

The History of the Devil, or, as it was titled for the first edition *The Political History of the Devil*, was first published in 1726. Rather surprisingly it proved one of Defoe's most popular works of non-fiction. A second edition, with the amended title and a new preface, but otherwise made up from the same sheets as the first edition, appeared in 1727, the third edition (reset) was published in 1734, the fourth in 1739 and at least eight more editions appeared in England during the eighteenth century. In the nineteenth century the book was regularly reprinted and many editions appeared in the U.S.A. It is interesting to note the number of editions published in the provincial cities of England in relation to the accounts of the Devil collected by county folklore researchers during the nineteenth century. French translations were published in 1729 and 1730 and there are at least two eighteenth-century German editions (1733 and 1748).

This edition, published in London and Exeter, is somewhat unusual in that it contains, besides an engraved title page, four plates engraved by Wallis. One (the frontispiece) is a rendering of Raphael's 'Satan Chained', the other three are all drawn by G. M. Brighty. These plates appear to have originally been engraved for an 1814 edition published by Bailey of London but were not actually used in that edition. They first appear in the 1819 edition although the three inserted in the text are all dated 1815. The page numbers on each plate refer to the position they should have occupied in the 1814 edition and thus do not conform to this edition. Rather they are positioned to correspond with the passage they are meant to illustrate.

The evident popularity of *The History of the Devil* (in the prefaces to each new edition before 1750 much is made of the large impressions which have been sold out) is even more surprising when one considers that its point of view is philosophically old-fashioned and runs counter to the prevailing 'natural philosophy' represented by the writings of Richard Cumberland, Shaftesbury and Hutcheson. Neither is its expression akin to the iconoclastic concepts of Mandeville.

The History of the Devil is closely related to two other works by Defoe; *A System of Magick*, also published in 1726, and *An Essay on the History and Reality of Apparitions*, published in 1727. It can also be compared with an earlier book, *A True Relation of the Apparition of One Mrs. Veal* (1705). Two other works on the supernatural attributed to Defoe, *The History of the Life and Adventures of Mr. Duncan Campbell*, (1720) and *The Friendly Daemon* (1726), both of which deal with the curious deaf and dumb Highlander with second sight known as Duncan Campbell, are now considered by some Defoe scholars not to have been written by Defoe, and considerable proof exists that their real author was William Bond.[1] A similar authorial controversy surrounds *The Dumb Philosopher* (1719)[2], the story of Dickory Cronke, a Cornish tinner who having been dumb for fifty-eight years, suddenly began to speak just before his death.

The History of the Devil did not appear under Defoe's name in 1726 (indeed very few of Defoe's five hundred odd works appeared under his name which has been partially responsible for some of the most confusing bibliographical problems in English literature), but enough external and internal evidence exists to accurately and authoritatively assign the book to Defoe. It was attributed to him within twenty years of his death[3] and Defoe himself, as he often did, provided some internal clues. A

---

[1] See Rodney M. Baine. *Daniel Defoe and the Supernatural.* Athens (Ga.): University of Georgia Press, 1968. pp. 137–180.

[2] See Baine, p. 181–197.

[3] In Theophilus Cibber's *Lives of the Poets of Great Britain and Ireland.* (1753).

poem on the origin of evil, beginning 'Thou sin of witchcraft! first born child of crime' had already appeared as by Defoe in *Jure Divino*, published in 1706, and in 'A Vision of the Angelick World', appended to his *Serious Reflections during the Life and Suprizing Adventures of Robinson Crusoe* (1720) Defoe forecast and puffed in advance *The History of the Devil*[4]. In *A System of Magick* there are two references to *The History of the Devil* (p. 53 and p. 57). This evidence, considered cumulatively, firmly establishes Defoe's authorship and ties together the three works on the supernatural of the middle 1720s.

Defoe was basically a writer in the Puritan tradition and indeed is often discussed as if he was an intellectual contemporary of Bunyan and Milton. His consistent moral point of view, which was grounded in the Puritan belief in God's direct intervention in the affairs of man, can be shown to pervade the whole corpus of his work and despite attempts by his contemporaries and many later commentators to present him solely as a Whig businessman and political time-server whose principles swayed with the winds of political change, there exists a remarkable philosophical consistency throughout both his fiction and non-fiction. Calvinistic theology, tempered with the rationalism of Locke, and the use of 'natural law' or 'laws of

[4] Defoe. *Serious reflections.* . . . (1720). p. 271.

reason', based on the writings of Grotius, Hobbes and Locke, seem to have been important influences on his work and are especially apposite when interpreting works like *The History of the Devil*[5]. The belief in the direct intervention of God in the world of man engendered a corollary notion that the Devil also was able to participate in and directly influence life on earth. While God attempted to guide man the Devil attempted to seduce and ensnare him. This basic Protestant belief, with its attendant interpretation of unusual events as signs and portents had, during Defoe's life, fallen into some disrepute as a result of the attacks of freethinkers and scientists (e.g. Anthony Collin's *Discourse of the Grounds and Reasons of the Christian Religion* (1724). Educated men had become more sceptical about the traditional explanations concerning the causes of what seemed supernatural events and what we choose to call the 'Age of Reason' was in its formative stage.

Defoe was concerned with putting supernatural phenomena into what he considered a proper perspective. He could be just as sceptical as the most advanced freethinker in the sense that he was willing to subject the supernatural to the rigours of rational thought and interpretation. He had no patience with the gullibility of people who would accept and base

[5] For a study of this aspect of Defoe's life and work see Maximillian E. Novak's *Defoe and the Nature of Man*. Oxford University Press, 1963.

their actions on the prognostications of astrologers, palmists and the con-men who played upon mass superstition. Defoe had a great deal of common-sense. However, two forms of divination he appeared to accept, at least partially, as having some validity were bibliomancy and second-sight and examples of both appear regularly in his writings (the use of bibliomancy in Robinson Crusoe is particularly notable).

In *The History of the Devil* Defoe was attempting to treat a supernatural phenomenon as if it was real and thus capable of being subjected to an historical and logical enquiry. There is certainly an element of irony in the book and something of the rather oblique satire directed at the writers who subjected the Bible and the commentaries of the church fathers to logical criticism shows itself in the examples Defoe chooses to illustrate his narrative. He divides his 'history' into two sections; the ancient history of the Devil and his modern history. The first part includes the expulsion of the Devil from Heaven and his history to the time of the creation of man. Defoe accepted the essential angelic nature of the Devil and in his *Essay on . . . Apparitions* explains that 'the word angel is to be understood of good angels for the devils are also angels'[6]. This part of the

---

[6] Defoe. *An Essay on the History and Reality of Apparitions* in *Novels and Miscellaneous Works* (Oxford, 1840–41) vol. XIII, p. 127.

book also contains the famous attack on Milton and his *Paradise Lost*. 'In a word', Defoe asserts, 'Mr. Milton has indeed made a fine poem; but it is the Devil of a History'. He goes on to take Milton to task over his treatment of Christ, his description of Hell and other 'historical' matters. Defoe was apparently unwilling, as are many modern students, to suspend his disbelief when reading *Paradise Lost*. He was very quick to pick up the Arianism implicit in Milton's treatment of Christ, a doctrinal complaint levelled against Milton almost since the first appearance of the poem. Defoe is quite vituperative about Milton in many parts of *The History of the Devil* and the vehemence of his criticism is but one of the curious features of the work.

In the second section of *The History of the Devil* Defoe describes what he refers to on the title page as the Devil's 'more private conduct down to the present times' and here he is able to lay about him with a will, castigating Tories, financial speculators, rakes, corrupt ministers, and all the evils he could identify in his own society. Especially he attacks the Roman Catholic Church, trotting out the old arguments concerning the relationships between certain Popes and the Devil and regularly refers to the Pope as the 'Whore of Babylon'. The Church perhaps gained some measure of revenge by having *The History of the Devil* put on the *Index of Prohibited Books* in 1744. Financial frauds such as the Mississippi Bubble and the South Sea scheme are, to Defoe, plainly manifestations of the Devil's influence on earth and wherever greed and corruption exist one will find the Devil's hand at work. He ridicules, at some length, contemporary ideas about the Devil's appearance, particularly the notion of the 'cloven hoof'. (There is a slight irony implicit in the fact that many editions of *The History of the Devil* appeared with a frontispiece showing the Devil enthroned in state, with his 'cloven hoof' plainly sticking out from under his gown. In this edition (page 25) a plate illustrating his 'cloven foot and saucer eyes' is inserted.) Defoe cites oracles as an example of one of the Devil's methods of controlling men, and Merlin and Mother Shipton are called forth as instances of the Devil at work.

Defoe was also concerned to point out the very real power that the Devil possessed and was willing to attribute to the dark spirit a considerable degree of intelligence. Silly notions of the Devil's physical appearance he is anxious to dispel and indeed states right at the beginning of the book that 'children and old women have told themselves so many frightful things of the Devil, and have formed ideas of him in their minds, in so many horrible and monstrous shapes, that really it was enough to fright the Devil himself to meet himself in the dark, dressed up in the several figures which imagination has formed for him in the minds of men'. Defoe envisaged the Devil as more of a psychological force; a state of mind brought about by human imperfection which is exploited by satanic forces. He does, however, comment that the Devil generally assumes the female form to enter the world. Many interesting cases of the various ways men are tempted and influenced by the Devil are given and here Defoe assumes his role as a 'super journalist' reporting interesting events with verve and imagination. In one instance he is told of a man who is haunted by the Devil through the device of beautiful naked ladies being introduced into his bed every night and offering their favours to him. As he was a man of virtuous life and a high moral sense his nightly visitations disturbed him greatly and he asked Defoe to suggest a remedy. All Defoe could suggest was that he 'bring his mind to such a stated habit of virtue, as to prevent its assenting to any wicked motion even in sleep', but this course of treatment seems to have been effective. Defoe does, however, make the point that dreams are one of the Devil's most effective means of influencing men.

Defoe also, interestingly, cites the story of the first printed books brought to Paris by John Faustus, who sold them as manuscripts. When the learned doctors on the faculty of the University looked closely at the books and discovered that the texts were exactly the same, even to the point of reproducing spelling mistakes, they concluded that they had been produced through the agency of the Devil. Faustus was threatened with hanging and, in order to save himself, was forced to reveal the secret of printing with moveable type. This story is part of the Koster legend and shows something of Defoe's very wide reading in curious sources. The story is cited in *The History of the Devil* as an example of how ignorant men will attribute anything they do not understand to supernatural forces.

The History of the Devil, while not one of Defoe's major works, is an important part of his canon. It displays his astoundingly wide general knowledge and the range of his curiosity. It discusses themes which occur and recur throughout his major fiction and well illustrates not only his versatility but also the consistency of his concept of man's position in the universe. 'Natural man', described as 'mixt up of a nature convertible and pervertible, capable indeed of infinite excellence, and consequently of eternal felicity; but subject likewise to Corruption and Degeneracy, and consequently to eternal Misery' is Crusoe, Moll Flanders, Colonel Jack, . . . and Daniel Defoe.

JUNE 1972

SATAN CHAINED.

Painted by RAPHAEL.

Engraved by T. WALLIS.

LONDON.
Publish'd By Thomas Kelly, Paternoster Row.

THE HISTORY OF THE

OF THE

DEVIL

Ancient & Modern

IN TWO PARTS,

T. Eldridge sculp

Drawn by G. M. Brighty *Engrav'd by C. Wallis*

SATAN EXPELL'D FROM HEAVEN.

" UNABLE TO SUPPORT THE HATED SIGHT

" EXPAND SEREPHIC WINGS AND SWIFT AS LIGHT.

" SEEK FOR NEW SAFETY IN ETERNAL NIGHT

Page 45

EXETER:

Publish'd by DAVIES & ELDRIDGE, April 1ᵗʰ 1815.

SATAN'S DEVICES;

OR, THE

POLITICAL HISTORY

OF

THE DEVIL:

ANCIENT AND MODERN.

In Two Parts.

PART I.

HIS ORIGINAL; A STATE OF HIS CIRCUMSTANCES; HIS CONDUCT,
PUBLIC AND PRIVATE; THE VARIOUS TURNS OF HIS AF-
FAIRS, FROM ADAM DOWN TO THIS PRESENT TIME.

PART II.

THE VARIOUS METHODS HE TAKES TO CONVERSE WITH MANKIND;
WITH THE MANNER OF HIS MAKING WITCHES, WIZARDS, AND
CONJURORS; AND HOW THEY SELL THEIR SOULS TO HIM.

The whole interspersed with many of the

DEVIL'S ADVENTURES.

TO WHICH IS ADDED,

A DESCRIPTION OF THE DEVIL'S DWELLING,

VULGARLY CALLED

HELL.

BY THE CELEBRATED DANIEL DE FOE.

A new Edition, with Engravings.

Bad as he is, the Devil may be abus'd,
Be falsely charg'd, and causelessly accus'd;
When men, unwilling to be blam'd alone,
Shift off the crimes on him which are their own.

LONDON:

PRINTED FOR T. KELLY, No. 17, PATERNOSTER ROW.

Sold by William Davies, Gandy Street, Exeter; and by
all other Booksellers.

1819.

Printed by Weed and Rider, Little Britain, London.

PREFACE.

THE subject of this history is singular, and it has been handled after a singular manner: The wise part of the world has been pleased with it, the merry part has been diverted with it, and the ignorant part has been taught by it; none but the malicious part of the world has been offended at it. Who can wonder, then, that when the Devil is not pleased, his friends should be angry?

The strangest thing of it all is, to hear Satan complain that the story is handled profanely: But who can think it strange that his advocates should be, what he was from the beginning?

The author affirms, and has good vouchers for it, in the opinion of such whose judgment passes with him for an authority, the whole tenor of the work is solemn, calculated to promote serious religion, and capable of being improved in a religious manner. But he does not think that we are bound never to speak of the Devil but with an air of terror, as if we were always afraid of him.

It is evident the Devil, as subtle and as frightful as he is, has acted the ridiculous and foolish part, as much as most of God's creatures, and daily does so.　And he cannot believe it is any sin to expose him for a foolish Devil as he is, or shew him to the world that he may be laughed at.

Those who think the subject not handled with gravity enough, have all the room given them in the world to handle it better; and as the author professes he is far from thinking his piece perfect, they ought not to be angry that he gives them leave to mend it.

He has had the satisfaction to please some readers, and to see good men approve it; and for the rest, as my Lord Rochester says, in another case,

" He counts their censure fame."

As for a certain reverend gentleman, who is pleased gravely to dislike the work, he hopes rather for the author's sake than the Devil's, he only says, Let the performance be how it will, and the author what he will, it is apparent he has not yet preached away all his hearers.

It is enough to me, says the author, that the Devil himself is not pleased with my work, and less with the design of it; let the Devil and all his fellow-complainers stand on one side, and the honest, well-meaning, charitable world, who approve my work, on the other, and I'll tell noses with Satan, if he dares.

CONTENTS

Part the First

CHAPTER I.

BEING an introduction to the whole work.

CHAPTER II.

Of the word Devil, as it is a proper name to the Devil, and any or all his host, angels, &c.

CHAPTER III.

Of the original of the Devil, who he is, what he was before his expulsion out of heaven, and in what state he was from that time to the creation of man.

CHAPTER IV.

Of the name of the Devil, his original, and the nature of his circumstances since he has been called by that name.

CHAPTER V.

Of the station Satan had in heaven before he fell; the nature and original of his crime, and some of Mr. Milton's mistakes about it.

CHAPTER VI.

What became of the Devil and of his host of fallen spirits after their being expelled from heaven, and his wandering condition till the creation; with some of Mr. Milton's absurdities on that subject.

CHAPTER VII.

Of the number of Satan's host; how they came first to know of the new-created worlds, now in being, and their measures with mankind upon the discovery.

CHAPTER VIII.

Of the power of the Devil at the time of the creation of this world; whether it has not been further straitened and limited since that time, and what shifts and stratagems he is obliged to make use of to compass his designs upon mankind.

CHAPTER IX.

Of the progress of Satan in carrying on his conquest over mankind, from the fall of Eve to the deluge.

CHAPTER X.

Of the Devil's second kingdom, and how he got footing in the renewed world by his victory over Noah and his race.

CHAPTER XI.

Of God's calling a church out of the midst of a degenerate world, and of Satan's new measures upon that incident: how he attacked them immediately, and his success in those attacks.

Part the Second

CHAPTER I.

The Introduction.

CHAPTER II.

Of hell, as it is represented to us, and how the Devil is to be understood, as being personally in hell, when at the same time we find him at liberty ranging over the world.

CHAPTER III.

Of the manner of Satan's acting and carrying on his affairs in this world, and particularly of his ordinary workings in the dark, by possession and agitation.

CHAPTER IV.

Of Satan's agents or missionaries, and their actings upon the minds of men in his name.

CHAPTER V.

Of the Devil's management in the Pagan hierarchy by omens, entrails, augurs, oracles, and such like pageantry of hell; and how they went off the stage at last by the introduction of true religion.

CHAPTER VI.

Of the extraordinary appearances of the Devil, and particularly of the Cloven-Foot.

CHAPTER VII.

Whether is most hurtful to the world, the Devil walking about without his Cloven-Foot, or the Cloven-Foot walking about without the Devil.

CHAPTER VIII.

Of the Cloven-Foot walking about the world without the Devil, viz. of witches making bargains for the Devil, and particularly of selling the soul to the Devil.

CHAPTER IX.

Of the tools the Devil works with, viz. witches, wizards or warlocks, conjurors, magicians, diviners, astrologers, interpreters of dreams, tellers of fortunes; and above all the rest, his particular modern privy-counsellors, called wits and fools.

CHAPTER X.

Of the various methods the Devil takes to converse with mankind.

CHAPTER XI.

Of divination, sorcery, the black-art, pawawing, and such like pretenders to devilism, and how far the Devil is or is not concerned in them.

THE CONCLUSION.

Of the Devil's last scene of liberty, and what may be supposed to be his end; with what we are to understand of his being tormented for ever and ever.

THE

HISTORY

OF

THE DEVIL, &c.

CHAPTER I.

Being an Introduction to the whole work.

I DOUBT not but the title of this book will amuse some of my reading friends a little at first: they will make a pause, perhaps, as they do at a witch's prayer, and be some time resolving whether they had best look into it or no, lest they should really raise the Devil by reading his story.

Children and old women have told themselves so many frightful things of the Devil, and have formed ideas of him in their minds in so many horrible and monstrous shapes, that really it were enough to fright the Devil himself to meet himself in the dark, dressed up in the several figures which imagination has formed for him in the minds of men ; and as for themselves, I cannot think by any means that the Devil would terrify them half so much, if they were to converse face to face with him.

It must certainly, therefore, be a most useful undertaking to give a true history of this Tyrant of the Air,

1.   B

this God of the World, this terror and aversion of mankind, which we call Devil; to shew what he *is*, and what he *is not*, where he *is*, and where he *is not*; when he is *in us*, and when he *is not*; for I cannot doubt but that the Devil is really and *bona fide* in a great many of our honest weak-headed friends, when they themselves know nothing of the matter.

Nor is the work so difficult as some may imagine. The Devil's history is not so hard to come at, as it seems to be: his original and the first rise of his family is upon record; and as for his conduct, he has acted indeed in the dark, as to method, in many things; but in general, as cunning as he is, he has been fool enough to expose himself in some of the most considerable transactions of his life, and has not shewn himself a politician at all. Our old friend Machiavel outdid him in many things; and I may in the process of this work, give an account of several of the sons of Adam, and some societies of them too, who have outwitted the Devil, nay, who have out-sinned the Devil, and that I think may be called out-shooting him in his own bow.

It may, perhaps, be expected of me in this history, that since I seem inclined to speak favourably of Satan, to do him justice, and to write his story impartially, I should take some pains to tell you what religion he is of; and even this part may not be so much a jest, as at first sight you may take it to be; for Satan has something of religion in him, I assure you; nor is he such an unprofitable Devil that way, as some may suppose him to be; for though, in reverence to my brethren, I will not reckon him among the Clergy; no, not so much as a gifted brother, yet I cannot deny, but that he often

OF THE DEVIL. 11

~~~~~~
Introduction to the whole work.
~~~~~~

preaches, and if it be not profitable to his hearers, it is as much their fault as it is out of his design.

It has, indeed, been suggested, that he has taken orders, and that a certain pope, famous for being an extraordinary favourite of his, gave him both institution and induction; but as this is not upon record, and therefore we have no authentic document for the probation, I shall not affirm it for a truth, for I would not slander the Devil.

It is said, also, and I am apt to believe it, that he was very familiar with that holy father Pope Silvester II. and some charge him with personating Pope Hildebrand on an extraordinary occasion, and himself sitting in the chair apostolic, in a full congregation; and you may hear more of this hereafter: But as I do not meet with Pope Diabolus among the list, in all Father Platina's lives of the popes, so I am willing to leave it as I find it.

But to speak to the point, and a nice point it is, I acknowledge; namely, what religion the Devil is of; my answer will indeed be general, yet not at all ambiguous, for I love to speak positively and with undoubted evidence.

1. He is a believer. And if, in saying so, it should follow, that even the Devil has more religion than some of our men of fame can at this time be charged with, I hope my Lord ———, and his Grace the ——— of ———, and some of the upper class in the Red-hot Club will not wear the coat, however well it may sit to their shapes; or challenge the satire, as if it were pointed at them, because it is due

to them. In a word, whatever their lordships are, I can assure them that the Devil is no infidel.

2. He fears God. We have such abundant evidence of this in sacred history, that if I were not at present, in common with a few others, talking to an infidel sort of gentlemen, with whom those remote things called Scriptures are not allowed in evidence, I might say it was sufficiently proved; but I doubt not in the process of this undertaking to shew, that the Devil really fears God, and that after another manner than ever he feared St. Francis or St. Dunstan; and if that be proved, as I take upon me to advance, I shall leave it to judgment, who is the better Christian, the Devil who believes and trembles, or our modern gentry of ———, who believe neither God nor Devil.

Having thus brought the Devil within the pale, I shall leave him among you for the present; not but that I may examine in its order, who has the best claim to his brotherhood, the Papists or the Protestants; and among the latter the Lutherans or the Calvinists; and so descending to all the several denominations of churches, see who has less of the Devil in them, and who more; and whether less or more, the Devil has not a seat in every synagogue, a pew in every church, a place in every pulpit, and a vote in every synod; even from the Sanhedrim of the Jews, to our friends at the Bull and Mouth, &c. from the greatest to the less.

It will, I confess, come very much within the compass

of this part of my discourse, to give an account, or at least to make an essay towards it, of the share the Devil has had in the spreading religion in the world; and especially in dividing and subdividing opinions in religion; perhaps, to eke it out and make it reach the farther; and also to shew how far he is or has made himself a missionary of the famous clan *de propaganda fide*; it is true we find him heartily employed in almost every corner of the world *ad propagandum errorem:* But that may require a history by itself.

As to his propagating religion, it is a little hard indeed, at first sight, to charge the Devil with propagating religion, that is to say, if we take it literally, and in the gross: but if you take it as the Scots insisted to take the oath of fidelity, viz. with an explanation, it is plain Satan has very often a share in the method, if not in the design, of propagating the Christian faith: For example :

I think I do no injury at all to the Devil, to say that he had a great hand in the old Holy War, as it was ignorantly and enthusiastically called ; stirring up the Christian princes and powers of Europe to run a madding after the Turks and Saracens, and make war with those innocent people above a thousand miles off, only because they entered into God's heritage when he had forsaken it; grazed upon his ground when he had fairly turned it into a common, and laid it open for the next comer; spending their nation's treasure, and embarking their kings and people (I say) in a war above a thousand miles off, filling their heads with that religious madness, called in those days Holy Zeal, to recover the *terra sancta*, the sepulchres of Christ and the saints, and, as they called it falsely, the Holy City, though true religion says it was the accursed city, and not worth spending one drop of blood for.

This religious bubble was certainly of Satan, who as he craftily drew them in, so, like a true Devil, he left them in the lurch when they came there, faced about to the Saracens, animated the immortal Saladin against them, and managed so dexterously that he left the bones of about thirteen or fourteen hundred thousand Christians there, as a trophy of his infernal politics. And after the Christian world had run *a la santa terra*, or in English, a sauntering about a hundred years, he dropt it to play another game more foolish, but ten times wickeder than that which went before it, namely, turning the Crusadoes of the Christians one against another; and, as Hudibras said, in another case,

> " Made them fight like mad or drunk
> " For Dame Religion as for Punk."

Of this you have a complete account in the history of the Pope's decrees against the Count de Thoulouse, and the Waldenses and Albigenses, with the crusadoes and massacres which followed upon them, wherein, to do the Devil's politics some justice, he met with all the success he could desire; the zealots of that day executed his infernal orders most punctually, and planted religion in those countries in a glorious and triumphant manner, upon the destruction of an infinite number of innocent people, whose blood has fattened the soil for the growth of the Catholic faith, in a manner very particular, and to Satan's full satisfaction.

I might, to complete this part of his history, give you the detail of his progress in these first steps of his alliances with Rome; and add a long list of massacres, wars, and expeditions in behalf of religion, which he has had the honour to have a visible hand in; such as the Parisian massacre, the Flemish war under the Duke d'Alva, the Smithfield fires in the Marian days, in England, and the massacres in Ireland; all which would most effectually convince us, that the Devil has not been idle in his business: but I may meet with these again in my way; it is enough while I am upon the generals only, to mention them thus in a summary way: I say it is enough to prove, that the Devil has really been as much concerned as any body, in the methods taken by some people for propagating the Christian religion in the world.

Some have rashly, and I had almost said maliciously, charged the Devil with the great triumphs of his friends the Spaniards in America, and would place the conquests of Mexico and Peru to the credit of his account.

But I cannot join with them in this at all. I must say, I believe the Devil was innocent of that matter: my reason is, because Satan was never such a fool as to spend his time or his politics, or embark his allies, to conquer nations who were already his own: that would be Satan against Beelzebub, a making war upon himself, and at least doing nothing to the purpose.

If they should charge him, indeed, with deluding Philip II. of Spain into that preposterous attempt called the *Armada Anglice*, (the Spanish Invasion,) I should indeed more readily join with them: But whether he did it weakly, in hope, which was indeed not likely, that it should succeed; or wickedly, to destroy that great fleet of the Spaniards, and draw them within the reach of his own dominions, the elements: this being a question which authors differ exceedingly about, I shall leave it to decide itself.

But the greatest piece of management, which we find the Devil has concerned himself in of late, in the matter of religion, seems to be that of the mission into China; and here indeed Satan has acted his master-piece: It was no doubt much for his service, that the Chinese should have no insight into matters, of religion I mean, that we call Christian: and, therefore, though Popery and the Devil are not at so much variance as some may imagine, yet he did not think it safe to let the general system of Christianity be heard of among them in China. Hence when the name of the Christian religion had but been received with some seeming approbation in the country of Japan, Satan immediately, as if alarmed at the thing, and dreading what the consequences of it might be, armed the Japanese against it with such fury, that they expelled it at once.

It was much safer to his designs, when, if the story be not fiction, he put that Dutch witticism into the mouths of the States commanders, when they came to Japan; who having more wit than to own themselves Christians in such a place as that, when the question was put to them, answered negatively, that they were not, but that they were of another religion, called Hollanders.

However, it seems the diligent Jesuits outwitted the Devil in China, and, as I said above, over-shot him in his own bow; for the mission being in danger by the Devil and the Chinese emperor's joining together, of being wholly expelled there too, as they had been in Japan, they cunningly fell in with the ecclesiastics of the country, and joining the priestcraft of both religions together, they brought Jesus Christ and Confucius to be so reconcilable, that the Chinese and the Roman idolatry appeared capable of a confederacy, of going on hand in hand together, and consequently of being very good friends.

This was a master-piece indeed, and, as they say, almost frighted Satan out of his wits; but he being a ready manager, and particularly famous for serving himself of the rogueries of the priests, faced about immediately to the mission, and making a virtue of necessity, clapt in, with all possible alacrity, with the proposal;* so the Jesuits and he formed a hotch-potch of religion, made up of Popery and Paganism, and calculated to leave the latter rather worse than they found it, blending the faith of Christ and the philosophy or morals of Confucius together, and formally christening them by the name of religion; by which means the politic interest of the mission was preserved; and yet Satan lost not one inch of ground with the Chinese, no, not by the planting the gospel itself, such as it was, among them.

Nor has it been such disadvantage to him that this plan or scheme of new-modelled religion would not go down at Rome, and that the Inquisition damned it with bell, book, and candle; distance of place served his new allies, the missionaries, in the stead of a protection from

---

* He never refused setting his hand to any opinion, which he thought it for his interest to acknowledge.

1.   C

the Inquisition; and now and then a rich present well placed, found them friends in the congregation itself; and where any nuncio with his impudent zeal pretended to take such a long voyage to oppose them, Satan took care to get him sent back *re infecta*, or inspired the mission to move him off the premises, by methods of their own (that is to say, being interpreted,) to murder him.

Thus the mission has in itself been truly devilish, and the Devil has interested himself in the planting the Christian religion in China.

The influence the Devil has in the politics of mankind, is another especial part of his history, and would require, if it were possible, a very exact description; but here we shall necessarily be obliged to inquire so nicely into the arcana of circumstances, and unlock the cabinets of state in so many courts, canvas the councils of ministers and the conduct of princes so fully, and expose them so much, that it may, perhaps, make a combustion among the great politicians abroad; and in doing that we may come so near home too, that though personal safety and prudentials forbid our meddling with our own country, we may be taken in a double entendre, and fall unpitied for being only suspected of touching truths that are so tender, whether we are guilty or no: On these accounts I must meddle the less with that part, at least for the present.

Be it that the Devil has had a share in some of the late councils of Europe, influencing them this way or that way to his own advantage, What is it to us? For example, What if he has had any concern in the late affair of Thorn? What need we put it upon him, seeing his confederates, the Jesuits, with the assessorial tribunal of Poland take it upon themselves? I shall leave that part to the issue of time. I wish it were as easy to persuade the world that he had no hand in bringing the injured Protestants to leave the justice due to the crimes of Protestant blood, to the arbitrament of a Popish power, who dare say that the Devil must be in it, if justice should be obtained that way: I should rather say, the Devil is in it, or else it would never be expected.

It occurs next to inquire from the premises, whether the Devil has more influence or less in the affairs of the world now, than he had in former ages; and this will depend upon comparing, as we go along, his methods and ways of working in past times, and the modern politics by which he acts in our days; with the differing reception which he has met with among the men of such distant ages.

But there is so much to inquire of about the Devil, before we can bring his story down to our modern times, that we must for the present let them drop, and look a little back to the remoter parts of this history; drawing his picture that people may know him when they meet him, and see who and what he is, and what he has been doing ever since he got leave to act in the high station he appears in.

In the mean time, if I might obtain leave to present an humble petition to Satan, it should be, that he would, according to modern usage, oblige us all, with writing the history of his own times; it would, as well as one that is gone before it, be a devilish good one; for, as to the sincerity of the performance, the authority of the particulars, the justice of the characters, &c., if they were no better vouched, no more consistent with them-

selves, with charity, with truth, and with the honour
of an historian, than the last of that kind which came
abroad among us, it must be a reproach to the Devil
himself to be the author of it.

Were Satan to be brought under the least obligation
to write truth, and that the matters of fact which he
should write, might be depended on, he is certainly
qualified by his knowledge of things to be a complete
historian; nor could the bishop himself, who, by the
way, has given us already the devil of a history, come
up to him: Milton's Pandemonium, though an excellent
dramatic performance, would appear a mere trifling
sing-song business, beneath the dignity of Chevy-Chase:
The Devil could give us a true account of all the civil
wars in heaven; how and by whom, and in what manner he lost the day there, and was obliged to quit the
field: The fiction of his refusing to acknowledge and
submit to the Messiah, upon his being declared Generalissimo of the heavenly forces, which Satan expected
himself, as the eldest officer; and his not being able to
brook another to be put in over his head; I say, that
fine-spun thought of Mr. Milton would appear to be
strained too far, and only serve to convince us that he
(Milton) knew nothing of the matter. Satan knows very
well that the Messiah was not *declared to be the Son of
God with power*, till by and after the *resurrection from
the dead*, and that all power was then given him *in heaven and earth*, and not before; so that Satan's rebellion
must derive from other causes, and upon other occasions, as he himself can doubtless give us an account,
if he thinks fit, and of which we shall speak further in
this work.

What a fine history might this old gentleman write, of the antediluvian world, and of all the weighty affairs, as well of state as of religion, which happened during the fifteen hundred years of the Patriarchal administration!

Who, like him, could give a full and complete account of the deluge, whether it was a mere vindictive, a blast from heaven, wrought by a supernatural power in the way of miracle? Or whether, according to Mr. Burnet's theory, it was a consequence following antecedent causes by the mere necessity of nature; seen in the constitution, natural position, and unavoidable working of things, as by the theory, published by that learned enthusiast, it seems to be?

Satan could easily account for all the difficulties of the theory, and tell us whether, as there was a natural necessity of the deluge, there is not the like necessity and natural tendency to a conflagration at last.

Would the Devil exert himself as an historian, for our improvement and diversion, how glorious an account could he give us of Noah's voyage round the world, in the famous Ark! He could resolve all the difficulties about the building it, the furnishing it, and the laying up provision in it for all the collection of kinds that he had made: he could tell us whether all the creatures came volunteer to him to go into the ark, or whether he went a hunting for several years before, in order to bring them together.

He could give us a true relation how he wheedled the people of the next world into the absurd ridiculous undertaking of building a Babel; how far that stupendous stair-case, which was in imagination to reach up to heaven, was carried, before it was interrupted, and

the builders confounded; how their speech was altered,
how many tongues it was divided into, or whether they
were divided at all; and how many subdivisions or
dialects have been since that, by which means very few
of God's creatures, except the brutes, understand one
another, or care one farthing whether they do or no.

In all these things, Satan, who no doubt would make
a very good Chronologist, could settle every epocha,
correct every calendar, and bring all our accounts of
time to a general agreement; as well the Grecian
olympiads, the Turkish heghira, the Chinese fictitious
account of the world's duration, as our blind Julian and
Gregorian accounts, which have put the world, to this
day, into such confusion, that we neither agree in our
holy-days or working-days, fasts or feasts, nor keep the
same sabbaths in any part of the same globe.

This great antiquary could bring us to a certainty in
all the difficulties of ancient story, and tell us whether
the tale of the siege of Troy, and the rape of Helen,
was a fable of Homer, or a history; whether the fictions
of the poets are formed from their own brain, or founded
in facts; and whether letters were invented by Cadmus
the Phœnician, or dictated immediately from Heaven
at Mount Sinai.

Nay, he could tell us how and in what manner he
wheedled Eve, deluded Adam, put Cain into a passion,
till he made him murder his own brother; and made
Noah, who was about 500 years a preacher of righteousness, turn sot in his old age, dishonour all his ministry,
debauch himself with wine, and, by getting drunk and
exposing himself, become the jest and laughing-stock
of his children, and of all his posterity to this day.

And would Satan, according to the modern practice
of the late Right Reverend Historian, enter into the
characters of the great men of his age, how should we be
diverted with the just history of Adam, in paradise and
out of it; his character, and how he behaved at and after
his expulsion; how Cain wandered in the land of Nod,
what the mark was which God set upon him, whose
daughter his wife was, and how big the city was he built
there, according to a certain poet of noble extraction,

> How Cain in the land of Nod,
>   When the rascal was alone,
> Like an owl in an ivy tod,
>   Built a city as big as Roan.
>
>   Roch.

He could have certainly drawn Eve's picture, told us
every feature in her face, and every inch in her shape,
whether she was a perfect beauty or no, and whether
with the fall she did grow crooked, ugly, ill-natured,
and a scold; as the learned Valdemar suggests to be
the effects of the curse.

Descending to the character of the Patriarchs in
that age, he might, no doubt, give us in particular the
characters of Belus, worshipped under the name of
Baal; with Saturn and Jupiter, his successors; who
they were here, and how they behaved; with all the
Pharaohs of Egypt, the Abimelechs of Canaan, and
the great monarchs of Assyria and Babylon.

Hence, also, he is able to write the lives of all the
heroes of the world, from Alexander of Macedon to
Lewis XIV., and from Augustus to the great king

George; nor could the Bishop himself go beyond him for flattery, any more than the Devil himself could go beyond the Bishop for falsehood:

I could enlarge, with a particular satisfaction, upon the many fine things which Satan, rummaging his inexhaustible store-house of slander, could set down to blacken the characters of good men, and load the best princes of the world with infamy and reproach.

But we shall never prevail with him, I doubt, to do mankind so much service, as resolving all those difficulties would be; for he has an indelible grudge against us, as he believes, and perhaps is assured, that men were at first created by his Sovereign, to the intent that, after a certain state of probation in life, such of them as shall be approved are appointed to fill up those vacancies in the heavenly host, which were made by the abdication and expulsion of him (the Devil) and his angels; so that man is appointed to come in Satan's stead, to make good the breach, and enjoy all those ineffable joys and beatitudes which Satan enjoyed before his fall; no wonder, then, that the Devil swells with envy and rage at mankind in general, and at the best of them in particular; nay, the granting this point is giving an unanswerable reason, why the Devil practises with such unwearied and indefatigable application upon the best men, if possible, to disappoint God Almighty's decree; and that he should not find enough amongst the whole race, to be proper subjects of his clemency, and qualified to succeed the Devil and his host, or fill up the places vacant by the fall. It is true, indeed, the Devil, who we have reason to say is no fool, ought to know better than to suppose that if he should seduce the whole

HISTORY OF THE DEVIL

I SEE HIS CLOVEN FOOT & SAUCER EYES!

Page 45

Drawn by G.M. Brighty.   Engraved by T. Wallis.

EXETER

Published by DAVIES & ELDRIDGE 1815
and J. WALLIS, Berwick Street Soho.
LONDON.

race of mankind, and make them as bad as himself, he could, by that success of his wickedness, thwart or disappoint the determined purposes of heaven ; but that those which are appointed to inherit the thrones, which he and his followers abdicated, and were deposed from, shall certainly be preserved in spite of his devices for that inheritance, and shall have the possession secured to them, notwithstanding all that the Devil and all the host of Hell can do to prevent it.

But, however he knows the certainty of this, and that when he endeavours the seducing the chosen servants of the Most High, he fights against God himself, struggles with irresistible grace, and makes war with infinite power ; undermining the church of God, and that faith in him which is fortified with the eternal promises of Jesus Christ, that the gates of Hell, that is to say, the Devil and all his power, shall not prevail against them ; I say, however, he knows the impossibility there is that he should obtain his ends, yet so blind is his rage, so infatuate his wisdom, that he cannot refrain breaking himself to pieces against this mountain, and splitting against the rock. *Qui Jupiter vult perdere hos dementat.*

But to leave this serious part, which is a little too solemn, for the account of this rebel ; seeing we are not to expect he will write his own history for our information and diversion, I shall see if I cannot write it for him : In order to this, I shall extract the substance of his whole story, from the beginning to our own times, which I shall collect out of what is come to hand, whether by revelation or inspiration, that is nothing to him ; I shall take care so to improve my intelligence, as may make my account of him authentic, and, in a word, such as the Devil himself shall not be able to contradict.

In writing this uncouth story, I shall be freed from the censures of critics, in a more than ordinary manner, upon one account especially; (viz) that my story shall be so just and well grounded, and, after all the good things I shall say of Satan, will be so little to his satisfaction, that the Devil himself will not be able to say, I dealt with the Devil in writing it: I might, perhaps, give you some account where I had my intelligence, and how all the arcana of his management have come to my hands; but pardon me, gentlemen, this would be to betray conversation, and to discover my agents, and you know statesmen are very careful to preserve the correspondences they keep in the enemy's country, lest they expose their friends to the resentment of the power whose councils they betray.

Besides, the learned tell us, that ministers of state make an excellent plea of their not betraying their intelligence, against all party inquiries into the great sums of money pretended to be paid for secret service; and whether the secret service was to bribe people to betray things abroad or at home; whether the money was paid to some body or to no body, employed to establish correspondences abroad, or to establish families and amass treasure at home; in a word, whether it was to serve their country or serve themselves, it has been the same thing, and the same plea has been their protection: Likewise in the important affair which I am upon, it is hoped you will not desire me to betray my correspondents; for you know Satan is naturally cruel and malicious, and who knows what he might do to shew his resentment? at least it might endanger a stop of our intelligence for the future.

And yet, before I have done, I shall make it very plain, that however my information may be secret and difficult, that yet I came very honestly by it, and shall make a very good use of it; for it is a great mistake in those who think that an acquaintance with the affairs of the Devil may not be made very useful to us all : They that know no evil can know no good ; and, as the learned tell us, that a stone taken out of the head of a toad is a good antidote against poison; so a competent knowledge of the Devil, and all his ways, may be the best help to make us defy the Devil and all his works.

CHAPTER II.

Of the word Devil, as it is a proper name to the Devil, and any or all his host, angels, &c.

IT is a question, not yet determined by the learned, whether the word Devil be a singular, that is to say, the name of a person standing by himself, or a noun of multitude; if it be a singular, and so must be used personally only as a proper name, it consequently implies one imperial Devil, monarch or king of the whole clan of Hell; justly distinguished by the term *The Devil*, or, as the Scots call him, the muckle Horn'd Dee'l, or as others, in a wilder dialect, the Devil of Hell, that is to say, the Devil of a Devil; or (better still) as the Scripture expresses it, by way of emphasis, the great Red Dragon, the Devil and Satan.

But if we take this word to be, as above, a noun of multitude, and so to be used *ambo-dexter*, as occasion presents, singular or plural; then the Devil signifies Satan by himself, or Satan with all his legions at his heels, as you please, more or less; and this way of understanding the word, as it may be very convenient for my purpose, in the account I am now to give of the infernal powers, so it is not altogether improper in the nature of the thing: It is thus expressed in Scripture, where the person possessed, Matt. iv. 24. is first said to be possessed of the Devil (singular) and our Saviour asks him, as speaking to a single person, What is thy name? and is answered in the plural and singular together, My name is *Legion*, for we are many.

Nor will it be any wrong to the Devil, supposing him a single person, seeing entitling him to the conduct of all his inferior agents, is what he will take rather for an addition to his infernal glory, than a diminution or lessening of him, in the extent of his fame.

Having thus articled with the Devil for liberty of speech, I shall talk of him sometimes in the singular, as a person, and sometimes in the plural, as an host of devils or of infernal spirits, just as occasion requires, and as the history of his affairs makes necessary.

But before I enter upon any part of his history, the nature of the thing calls me back, and my Lord B———— of ———— in his late famous orations in defence of liberty, summons me to prove that there is such a thing or such a person as the Devil; and in short, unless I can give some evidence, of his existence, as my Lord ———— said very well, I am talking of nobody.

D—n me, Sir, says a graceless comrade of his to a great man, your Grace will go to the Devil.

D—n ye, sir, says the D————, then I shall go no where; I wonder where you intend to go?

Nay, to the D—l too, I doubt, says Graceless, for I am almost as wicked as my Lord Duke.

D. Thou art a silly empty dog, says the D —— and if there is such a place as a Hell, though I believe nothing of it, it is a place for fools, such as thou art.

Gr. I wonder then, what heaven the great wits go to, such as my Lord Duke; I do not care to go there, let it be where it will; they are a tiresome kind of people, there is no bearing them, they'll make a Hell wherever they come.

D. Prithee, hold thy fool's tongue, I tell thee, if there is any such place as we call *no where*, that's all the Heaven or Hell that I know of, or believe any thing about.

Gr. Very good, my Lord;—so that Heaven is no where, and Hell is no where, and the Devil is nobody, according to my Lord Duke.

D. Yes, Sir, and what then?

Gr. And you are to go no where when you die, are you?

D. Yes, you dog, do not you know what that incomparable noble genius my lord Rochester, sings upon the subject, I believe it unfeignedly.

Sings.

After death nothing is,
And nothing death.

Gr. You believe it, my Lord; you mean, you would feign believe it if you could; but since you put that great genius my lord Rochester upon me, let me play him back upon your Grace; I am sure you have read his fine poem upon nothing, in one of the stanzas of which is this beautiful thought,

> And to be part of * thee
> The wicked wisely pray.

D. You are a foolish dog.

Gr. And my Lord Duke is a wise infidel.

D. Why? is it not wiser to believe no Devil, than to be always terrified at him?

Gr. But shall I toss another poet upon you, my Lord?

> If it should so fall out, as who can tell
> But there may be a God, a Heaven and Hell?
> Mankind had best consider well, for fear
> 'T should be too late when their mistakes appear.

D. D—n your foolish poet, that is not my lord Rochester.

Gr. But how must I be damn'd if there is no Devil? Is not your Grace a little inconsistent there? My lord Rochester would not have said that, and't please your Grace.

D. No, you dog, I am not inconsistent at all, and if I

Meant of * nothing.

had the ordering of you, I'd make you sensible of it; I'd make you think yourself damn'd for want of a Devil.

Gr. That is like one of your Grace's paradoxes, such as when you swore by God that you did not believe there was any such thing as a God or Devil; so you swear by nothing, and damn me to no where.

D. You are a critical dog, who taught you to believe these solemn trifles? who taught you to say there is a God?

Gr. Nay, I had a better school-master than my Lord Duke.

D. Why, who was your school-master, pray?

Gr. The Devil, and't please your Grace.

D. The Devil! the Devil he did? What you're going to quote Scripture, are you? Prithee don't tell me of Scripture, I know what you mean, the Devils believe and tremble; why then I have the whip-hand of the Devil, for I hate trembling; and am delivered from it effectually, for I never believed any thing of it, and therefore I don't tremble.

Gr. And there indeed, I am a wickeder creature than the Devil, or even than my Lord Duke, for I believe, and yet don't tremble neither.

D. Nay, if you are come to your penitentials I have done with you.

Gr. And I think I must have done with my Lord Duke, for the same reason.

D. Ay, ay, pray do, I'll go and enjoy myself; I won't throw away the pleasure of my life, I know the consequence of it.

Gr. And I'll go and reform myself, else I know the consequence too.

This short dialogue happened between two men of quality, and both men of wit too ; and the effect was, that the Lord brought the reality of the Devil into the question, and the debate brought the profligate to be a penitent; so in short, the Devil was made a preacher of repentance.

The truth is, God and the Devil, however opposite in their nature, and remote from one another in their place of abiding, seem to stand pretty much upon a level in our faith : For as to our believing the reality of their existence, he that denies one, generally denies both ; and he that believes one, necessarily believes both.

Very few, if any, of those who believe there is a God, and acknowledge the debt of homage which mankind owes to the supreme Governor of the world, doubt the existence of the Devil, except here and there one, whom we call Practical Atheists ; and it is the character of an atheist, if there is such a creature on earth, that, like my Lord Duke, he believes neither God or Devil.

As the belief of both these stands upon a level, and that God and the Devil seem to have an equal share in our faith, so the evidence of their existence seems to stand upon a level too, in many things ; and as they are known by their works in the same particular cases, so they are discovered after the same manner of demonstration.

Nay, in some respects it is equally criminal to deny the reality of them both, only with this difference, that to believe the existence of a God is a debt to nature, and to believe the existence of the Devil is a like debt to rea- son ; one is demonstration from the reality of visible causes, and the other a deduction from the like reality of their effects.

One demonstration of the existence of God, is from the universal well-guided consent of all nations to worship and adore a supreme power; one demonstration of the existence of the Devil, is from the avowed ill-guided consent of some nations, who knowing no other God, make a God of the Devil for want of a better.

It may be true, those nations have no other ideas of the Devil than as of a superior power; if they thought him a supreme power it would have other effects on them, and they would submit to and worship him with a different kind of fear.

But it is plain they have right notions of him as a Devil or evil spirit, because the best reason, and in some places the only reason they give for worshipping him is, that he may do them no hurt; having no notions at all of his having any power, much less any inclination to do them good; so that indeed they make a meer Devil of him, at the same time that they bow to him as God.

All the ages of Paganism in the world have had this notion of the Devil: Indeed in some parts of the world they had also some deities which they honoured above him, as being supposed to be beneficent, kind and inclined, as well as capable to give them good things; for this reason the more polite heathens, such as the Grecians and Romans, had their Lares or household gods, whom they paid a particular respect to; as being their protectors from hobgoblins, ghosts of the dead, evil spirits, frightful appearances, evil genius's and other noxious beings from the invisible world; or to put it into the language of the day we live in, from the Devil, in whatever shape or appearance he might come to them, and from whatever might hurt them; and what was all this

2   E

but setting up Devils against Devils, supplicating one
Devil under the notion of a good spirit, to drive out
and protect them from another, whom they called a bad
spirit, the white Devil against the black Devil?

This proceeds from the natural notions mankind necessarily entertain of things to come; superior or in
ferior, God and the Devil, fill up all futurity in our
thoughts; and it is impossible for us to form any image
in our minds of an immortality and invisible world, but
under the notions of perfect felicity, or extreme misery.

Now as these two respect the eternal state of man after
life, they are respectively the object of our reverence and
affection, or of our horror and aversion; but notwithstanding they are placed thus in a diametrical opposition
in our affections and passions, they are on an evident
level as to the certainty of their existence, and, as I said
above, bear an equal share in our faith.

It being then as certain that there is a Devil, as that
there is a God, I must from this time forward admit
no more doubt of his existence, nor take any more pains
to convince you of it; but speaking of him as a reality
in being, proceed to enquire who he is, and from whence,
in order to enter directly into the detail of his history.

Now not to enter into all the metaphysical trumpery
of the schools, nor wholly to confine myself to the language of the pulpit: where we are told that to think of
God and of the Devil, we must endeavour first to form
ideas of those things which illustrate the description of
rewards and punishment; in the one the eternal presence
of the highest good, and, as a necessary attendant, the
most perfect, consummate, durable bliss and felicity,
springing from the presence of that Being, in whom all

Of the word Devil.

possible beatitude is inexpressibly present, and that in the highest perfection : On the contrary, to conceive of a sublime fallen arch-angel, attended with an innumerable host of degenerate, rebel seraphs, or angels cast out of heaven together; all guilty of inexpressible rebellion, and all suffering from that time, and to suffer for ever the eternal vengeance of the Almighty, in an inconceivable manner; that his presence, though blessed in itself, is to them the most complete article of terror : That they are in themselves perfectly miserable; and to be with whom for ever, adds an inexpressible misery to any state as well as place; and fills the minds of those who are to be, or expect to be banished to them with inconceivable horror and amazement.

But when you have gone over all this, and a great deal more of the like, though less intelligible language, which the passions of men collect to amuse one another with ; you have said nothing if you omit the main article, namely, the personality of the Devil; and till you add to all the rest some description of the company with whom all this is to be suffered, viz. the Devil and his angels.

Now who this Devil and his angels are, what share they have either actively or passively in the eternal miseries of a future state, how far they are agents in or partners of the sufferings of the place, is a difficulty yet not fully discovered by the most learned; nor do I believe it is made less a difficulty by their n.eddling with it.

But to come to the person and original of the Devil, or, as I said before, of Devils ; I allow him to come of an ancient family, for he is from heaven, and more truly than the Romans could say of their idolized Numa, he is of the race of the gods.

That Satan is a fallen angel, a rebel seraph, cast out for his rebellion, is the general opinion, and it is not my business to dispute things universally received; as he was tried, condemned, and the sentence of expulsion executed on him in heaven, he is in this world like a transported felon never to return; his crime, whatever particular aggravations it might have, it is certain, amounted to high-treason against his Lord and Governor, who was also his Maker; against whom he rose in rebellion, took up arms, and in a word, raised a horrid and unnatural war in his dominions; but being overcome in battle, and made prisoner, he and all his host, whose numbers were infinite, all glorious angels like himself, lost at once their beauty and glory with their innocence, and commenced Devils, being transformed by crime into monsters and frightful objects; such as to describe, human fancy is obliged to draw pictures and descriptions in such forms as are most hateful and frightful to the imagination.

These notions, I doubt not, gave birth to all the beauteous images and sublime expressions in Mr. Milton's majestic poem; where, though he has played the poet in a most luxuriant manner, he has sinned against Satan most egregiously, and done the Devil a manifest injury in a great many particulars, as I shall shew in its place. And as I shall be obliged to do Satan justice when I come to that part of his history, Mr. Milton's admirers must pardon me, if I let them see, that though I admire Mr. Milton as a poet, yet that he was greatly out in matters of history, and especially the history of the Devil;

in short, that he has charged Satan falsely in several particulars; and so he has Adam and Eve too: But that I shall leave it till I come to the history of the royal family of Eden; which I resolve to present you with when the Devil and I have done with one another.

But not to run down Mr. Milton neither, whose poetry or his judgment, cannot be reproached without injury to our own; all those bright ideas of his, which make his poem so justly valued, whether they are capable of proof as to the fact, are notwithstanding, confirmation of my hypothesis; and are taken from a supposition of the personality of the Devil, placing him at the head of the infernal host, as a sovereign elevated spirit and monarch of Hell; and as such it is that I undertake to write his history.

By the word Hell I do not suppose, or at least not determine, that his residence, or that of the whole army of Devils, is yet in the same local Hell, to which the divines tell us he shall be at last chained down? or at least that he is yet confined to it, for we shall find he is at present a prisoner at large; of both which circumstances of Satan, I shall take occasion to speak in its course.

But when I call the Devil the Monarch of Hell, I am to be understood as suits to the present purpose; that he is the sovereign of all the race of Hell, that is to say, of all the Devils or spirits of the infernal clan, let their numbers, quality and powers be what they will.

Upon this supposed personality and superiority of Satan, or, as I call it, the sovereignty and government of one Devil above all the rest; I say, upon this notion are formed all the systems of the dark side of futurity, that we can form in our minds : And so general is the opinion of it, that it will hardly bear to be opposed by any other arguments, at least that will bear to be reasoned upon : All the notions of a party of Devils, or making a commonwealth among the black divan, seem to be enthusiastic and visionary, but with no consistency or certainty, and is so generally exploded, that we must not venture so much as to debate the point.

Taking it then as the generality of mankind do, that there is a grand Devil, a superior of the whole black race ; that they all fell, together with their general, Satan, at the head of them ; that though he, Satan, could not maintain his high station in heaven, yet that he did continue his dignity among the rest, who are called his servants, in Scripture, his angels ; that he has a kind of dominion or authority over the rest, and that they were all, how many millions soever in number, at his com-mand ; employed by him in all his hellish designs, and in all his wicked contrivances for the destruction of man, and for the setting up his own kingdom in the world.

Supposing then that there is such a superior master-Devil over all the rest, it remains that we inquire into his character, and something of his history ; in which, though we cannot perhaps produce such authentic do-cuments as in the story of other great monarchs, tyrants, and furies of the world ; yet I shall endeavour to speak some things which the experience of mankind may be apt to confirm, and which the Devil himself will hardly be able to contradict.

It being then granted that there is such a thing or person, call him which we will, as a master-Devil ; that

he is thus superior to all the rest in power and in authority, and that all the other evil spirits are his angels, or
ministers, or officers to execute his commands, and are
employed in his business; it remains to inquire, Whence
he came? How he got hither, into this world? What that
business is which he is employed about? What his present state is, and where and to what part of the creation
of God he is limited and restrained? What the liberties
are he takes or is allowed to take? In what manner he
works, and how his instruments are likewise allowed to
work? What he has done ever since he commenced
Devil, what he is now doing, and what he may yet do before his last and closer confinement? As also, What
he cannot do, and how far we may or may not be said to
be exposed to him, or have not reason to be afraid of
him? These, and whatever else occurs in the history
and conduct of this arch-Devil and his agents, that may
be useful for information, caution or diversion, you may
expect in the process of this work.

I know it has been questioned by some, with more
face than fear, how it consists with a complete victory of the Devil, which they say was at first obtained
by the heavenly powers over Satan, and his apostate
army in heaven, that when he was cast out of his
holy place, and dashed down into the abyss of eternal darkness, as into a place of punishment, a condemned hold, or place of confinement, to be reserved
there to the judgment of the great day: I say, how
it consists with that entire victory, to let him loose
again, and give him liberty, like a thief that has broken
prison, to range about God's creation, and there to
continue his rebellion, commit new ravages and acts

of hostility against God, make new efforts at dethroning the almighty Creator; and in particular to fall upon the weakest of his creatures, man? How Satan being so entirely vanquished, he should be permitted to recover any of his wicked powers, and find room to do mischief to mankind.

Nay they go farther, and suggest bold things against the wisdom of heaven, in exposing mankind, weak in comparison of the immense extent of the Devil's power, to so manifest an overthrow, to so unequal a fight, in which he is sure, if alone in the conflict, to be worsted; to leave him such a dreadful enemy to engage with, and so ill-furnished with weapons to assist him.

These objections I shall give an good as answer to, as the case will admit of in this course, but must adjourn them for the present.

That the Devil is not yet a close prisoner, we have evidence enough to confirm; I will not suggest, that like our Newgate thieves, (to bring little devils ·and great devils together) he is let out by connivance, and has some little latitudes and advantages for mischief, by that means; returning at certain seasons to his confinement again.

This might hold, were it not, that the comparison must suggest, that the power which has cast him down could be deluded, and the under-keepers or jailors, under whose charge he was in custody, could wink at his excursions, and the Lord of the place know nothing of the matter. But this wants farther explanation.

CHAPTER III.

Of the original of the Devil, who he is, and what he was before his expulsion out of heaven, and in what state he was from that time to the creation of man.

TO come to a regular inquiry into Satan's affairs, it is needful we should go back to his original, as far as history and the opinion of the learned world will give us leave.

It is agreed by all writers, as well sacred as prophane, that this creature, we now call a Devil, was originally an angel of light, a glorious seraph; perhaps the choicest of all the glorious seraphs. See how Milton describes his original glory :

> Satan, so call him now, his former name
> Is heard no more in heaven : He of the first,
> If not the first archangel; great in power,
> In favour and pre-eminence.
>
> *lib.* v. *fol.* 140.

And again the same author, and upon the same subject :

> ——— Brighter once amidst the host
> Of angels, than that star the stars among.
>
> *lib.* vii. *fol.* 189.

2   F

The glorious figure which Satan is supposed to make among the thrones and dominions in heaven is such, as we might suppose the highest angel in that exalted train could make; and some think, as above, that he was the chief of the archangels.

Hence that notion, (and not ill founded) namely, that the first cause of his disgrace, and on which ensued his rebellion, was occasioned upon God's proclaiming his Son generalissimo, and with himself supreme ruler in heaven; giving the dominion of all his works of creation, as well already finished, as not then begun, to him; which post of honour (say they) Satan expected to be conferred on himself, as next in honour, majesty and power to God the supreme.

This opinion is followed by Mr. Milton too, as appears in the following lines, where he makes all the angels attending on a general summons, and God the Father making the following declaration to them.

' Hear all ye angels, progeny of light,
' Thrones, dominations, princedoms, virtues, pow'rs!
' Hear my decree, which unrevok'd shall stand.
' This day I have begot whom I declare
' My only Son, and on this holy hill
' Him have anointed, who ye now behold
' At my right hand; your head I him appoint;
' And myself have sworn to him shall bow
' All knees in heav'n, and shall confess him Lord;
' Under his great vice-gerent reign abide
' United, as one individual soul,
' For ever happy: Him who disobeys,
' Me disobeys, breaks union, and that day

' Cast out from God and blessed vision, falls
' Into utter darkness, deep ingulph'd his place
' Ordain'd without redemption, without end.'

Satan, affronted at the appearance of a new essence or
being in heaven, called the Son of God, for God, says
Mr. Milton (tho' erroneously) declared himself at that
time, saying, This day have I begotten him, and that he
should be set up, above all the former powers, of heaven,
of whom Satan (as above) was the chief, and expecting, if
any higher post could be granted, it might be his due ; I
say, affronted at this, he resolv'd

' With all his legions to dislodge, and leave
' Unworship'd unobey'd, the throne supreme
' Contemptuous.————

Par. Lost, lib. v. fol. 140.

But Mr. Milton is grossly erroneous in ascribing those
words, This day have I begotten thee, to that declara·
tion of the Father, before Satan fell, and consequently to
a time before the creation ; whereas, it is by interpreters
agreed to be understood of the incarnation of the Son of
God, or at least of the resurrection : * See Pool upon
Acts xiii. 33.

---

* Mr. Pool's words are these : Some refer the words, This day
have I begotten thee, to the incarnation of the Son of God, others to
the resurrection; our translators lay the stress on the preposition of
which the verb is compounded, and by adding again, (viz) rais'd up
Jesus again, Acts xiii. 33. intended it to be understood of the resurrection; and there is grounds for it, in the context, for the resur-

In a word, Satan withdrew with all his followers malcontent, and chagrine, resolved to disobey this new command, and not yield obedience to the Son.

But Mr. Milton agrees in that opinion, that the number of angels which rebelled with Satan was infinite, and suggests in one place, that they were the greatest half of all the angelic body or seraphic host.

> ' But Satan with his powers,
>   ' An host
> ' Innumerable as the stars of night,
> ' Or stars of morning, dew-drops, which the sun
> ' Impearls on ev'ry leaf and ev'ry flower.

ib. lib. v. fol. 142.

Be their number as it is, numberless millions and legions of millions, that is no part of my present inquiry; Satan then leader, guide and superior, as he was author of the celestial rebellion, is still the great head and master-Devil as before; under his authority they still act, not obeying but carrying on the same insurrection against God, which they begun in heaven; making war still against heaven, in the person of his image and creature man; and though vanquished by the thunder of the Son of God, and cast down headlong from heaven, they have yet reassumed, or rather not lost either the will or the power of doing evil.

---

rection of Christ, is that which St. Paul had propounded in v. 30. of the same chapter, as his theme or argument to preach upon.

Not that Christ at his resurrection began to be the Son of God, but that he was then manifested to be so.

This fall of the angels, with the war in heaven which preceded it, is finely described by Ovid, in his war of the Titans against Jupiter; casting mountain upon mountain, and hill upon hill (Pelion upon Ossa) in order to scale the adamantine walls, and break open the gates of heaven; till Jupiter struck them with his thunder-bolts, and overwhelmed them in the abyss.

Vide Ovid Metam. new Translation, *lib.* 1. *p.* 19.

' Nor were the Gods themselves secure on high,
' For now the giants strove to storm the sky,
' The lawless brood with bold attempt invade
' The Gods, and mountains upon mountains laid.
' But now the bolt enrag'd the Father took,
' Olympus from her deep foundations shook,
' Their structure nodded at the mighty stroke,
' And Ossa's shattered top o'er Pelion broke,
' They're in their own ungodly ruins slain.—

Then again speaking of Jupiter, resolving in council to destroy mankind by the deluge, and giving the reasons of it, to the heavenly host, say thus, speaking of the demi-gods alluding to good men below,

' Think you that they in safety can remain,
' When I myself who o'er immortals reign,
' Who send the lightning and heaven's empire sway,
' The stern * Lycaon practis'd to betray.

ib. p. 10.

---

* Satan.

The original of the Devil.

Since then so much poetic liberty is taken with the Devil, relating to his most early state, and the time before his fall, give me leave to make an excursion of the like kind, relating to his history immediately after the fall, and till the creation of man; an interval which I think much of the Devil's story is to be seen in, and which Mr. Milton has taken little notice of, at least it does not seem completely filled up; after which I shall return to honest prose again, and pursue the duty of an historian.

Satan, with hideous ruin thus supprest
Expell'd the seat of blessedness and rest,
Look'd back and saw the high eternal mound,
Where all his rebel host their outlet found
Restored impregnable: The breach made up,
And garrisons of angels rang'd a top;
In front a hundred thousand thunders roll,
And lightning temper'd to transfix a soul,
Terror of devils. Satan and his host,
Now to themselves as well as station lost,
Unable to support the hated sight,
Expand seraphic wings, and swift as light,
Seek for new safety in eternal night.
   In the remotest gulphs of dark they land,
Here vengeance gives them leave to make their stand,
Not that to steps and measures they pretend,
Councils and schemes their station to defend;
But broken, disconcerted and dismay'd,
By guilt and fright to guilt and fright betray'd;
Rage and confusion ev'ry spirit possess'd,
And shame and horror swell'd in ev'ry breast;

Transforming envy to their essential burns,
And the bright angel to a frightful Devil turns.
Thus Hell began ; the fire of conscious rage
No years can quench, no length of time assuage.
Material fire, with its intensest flame,
Compar'd with this can scarce deserve a name ;
How should it up to immaterials rise,
When we're all flame, we shall all fire despise.
This fire outrageous and its heat intense
Turns all the pain of loss to pain of sense.
The folding flames concave and inward roll,
Act upon spirit, and penetrate the soul:
Not force of Devils can its new powers repel,
Where'er it burns it finds or make a Hell :
For Satan flaming with unquench'd desire
Forms his own Hell, and kindles his own fire,
Vanquish'd, not humbl'd, not in will brought low,
But as his powers decline his passions grow :
The malice, viper-like, takes vent within,
Gnaws its own bowels, and bursts in its own sin :
Impatient of the change he scorns to bow,
And never impotent in power till now ;
Ardent with hate, and with revenge distract,
A will to new attempts, but none to act ;
Yet all seraphic, and in just decree,
Suited to spirit's high sense of misery,
Deriv'd from loss which nothing can repair,
And room for nothing left but mere despair.
Here's finish'd Hell! what fiercer fire can burn !
Enough ten thousand worlds to over-turn.
Hell's but the frenzy of defeated pride,
Seraphic treason's strong impetuous tide,

Where vile ambition disappointed first,
To its own rage, and boundless hatred curst;
The hate's fan'd up to fury, that to flame,
For fire and fury are in kind the same;
These burn unquenchable in every face,
And the word Endless constitutes the place.
O state of being! where being's the only grief,
And the chief torture's to be damn'd to life;
O life! the only thing they have to hate;
The finish'd torment of a future state,
Complete in all the parts of endless misery,
And worse ten thousand times than not to be!
Could but the damn'd the immortal law repeal,
And Devils die, there'd be an end of Hell;
Could they that thing call'd Being annihilate,
There'd be no sorrows in a future state;
The wretch, whose crimes had shut him out on high,
Could be reveng'd on God himself, and die;
Job's wife was in the right, and always we
Might end by death all human misery,
Might have it in our choice, to be or not to be.

CHAPTER IV.

Of the name of the Devil, his original, and the nature of his circumstances since he has been called by that name.

THE Scripture is the first writing on earth where we find the Devil called by his own proper distinguishing denomination, Devil,* or the Destroyer; nor indeed is there any other author of antiquity, or of sufficient authority, which says any thing of that kind about him.

Here he makes his first appearance in the world, and on that occasion he is called the Serpent; but the Serpent, however, since made to signify the Devil, when spoken of in general terms, was but the Devil's representative, or the Devil in *quovis vehiculo*, for that time, clothed in a bodily shape, acting under cover and in disguise; or, if you will, the Devil in masquerade: Nay, if we believe Mr. Milton, the angel Gabriel's spear had such a secret powerful influence, as to make him strip of a sudden, and with a touch to unmask, and stand upright in his naked original shape, meer Devil, without any disguises whatsoever.

Now as we go to the Scripture for much of his history, so we must go there also for some of his names; and he has a great variety of names indeed, as his

---

* The meaning of the word Devil is Destroyer. See Pool upon Acts xiii. 10.

3. G

several mischievous doings guide us to conceive of him.
The truth is, all the antient names given him, of which
the Scripture is full, seem to be originals, derived from
and adapted to the several steps he has taken, and the
several shapes he has appeared in to do mischief in the
world.

> Here he is called the Serpent, Gen. iii. 1.
> The Old Serpent, Rev. xii. 9.
> The Great Red Dragon, Rev. xii. 3.
> The Accuser of the Brethren, Rev. xii. 10.
> The Enemy, Matt. xxiii. 29.
> Satan, Job i. Zech. iii. 1, 2.
> Belial, 2 Cor. vi. 15.
> Beelzebub, Matt. xii. 24.
> Mammon, Matt. vi. 24.
> The Angel of Light, 2 Cor. xi. 14.
> The Angel of the Bottomless-Pit, Rev. ix. 11.
> The Prince of the Power of the Air, Eph. ii. 2.
> Lucifer, Isa. xiv. 12.
> Abaddon, or Apollyon, Rev. ix. 11.
> Legion, Mark v. 9.
> The God of this World, 2 Cor. iv. 4.
> The Foul Spirit, Mark ix. 5.
> The Unclean Spirit, Mark i. 27.
> The Lying Spirit, 2 Chron. xxx.
> The Tempter, Matt. iv. 3.
> The Son of the Morning, Isa. xiv. 12.

But to sum them all up in one, he is called in the
New Testament plain Devil; all his other names are
varied according to the custom of speech, and the dia-

lects of the several nations where he is spoken of: But, in a word, Devil is the common name of the Devil in all the known languages of the earth. Nay, all the mischiefs he is empowered to do, are in Scripture placed to his account, under the particular title of the Devil, not of devils in the plural number, though they are sometimes mentioned too; but, in the singular, it is the identical individual Devil, in and under whom all the little devils, and all the great devils, if such there be, are supposed to act; nay, they are supposed to be governed and directed by him. Thus we are told in Scripture of the works of the Devil, 1 John iii. 8.; of casting out the Devil, Mark i. 34.; of resisting the Devil, James iv. 5.; of our Saviour being tempted of the Devil, Matt. iv. 1.; of Simon Magus, a child of the Devil, Acts xiii. 10. The Devil came down in a great wrath, Rev. xiii. 12. and the like. According to this usage in speech we go on to this day, and all the infernal things we converse with in the world, are fathered upon the Devil, as one undivided simple essence, by how many agents soever working: Every thing evil, frightful in appearance, wicked in its actings, horrible in its manner, monstrous in its effects, is called the Devil; in a word, Devil is the common name for all devils; that is to say, for all evil spirits, all evil powers, all evil works, and even all evil things: Yet 'tis remarkable, the Devil is no Old Testament word, and we never find it used in all that part of the Bible but four times, and then not once in the singular number, and not once to signify Satan as 'tis now understood.

It is true the learned give a great many differing interpretations of the word Devil; the English commentators tell us, it means a destroyer; others, that it signifies a deceiver, and the Greeks derive it from a calumniator or false witness; for we find that Calumny was a goddess, to whom the Athenians built altars and offered sacrifices upon some solemn occasions, and they call her *Diabole*, from whence came the masculine *Diabolos*, which we translate Devil.

Thus we take the name of Devil to signify, not persons only, but actions and habits; making imaginary devils, and transforming that substantial creature called Devil into every thing noxious and offensive: Thus St. Francis being tempted by the Devil in the shape of a bag of money lying in the highway, the Saint having discovered the fraud, whether seeing his cloven-foot hang out of the purse, or whether he distinguished him by his smell of sulphur, or how otherwise, authors are not agreed; but, I say, the Saint having discovered the cheat, and out-witted the Devil, took occasion to preach that eminent sermon to his disciples, where his text was, Money is the Devil.

Nor, upon the whole, is any wrong done to the Devil by this kind of treatment; it only gives him the sovereignty of the whole army of hell, and making all the numberless legions of the bottomless pit servants, or, as the Scripture calls them, angels to Satan the grand Devil; all their actions, performances, and achievements are justly attributed to him, not as the prince of devils only, but the emperor of devils, the prince of all the princes of devils.

Under this denomination then of Devil, all the powers of hell, all the princes of the air, all the black armies of Satan, are comprehended, and in such manner they are to be understood in this whole work; *mutatis mutandis*, according to the several circumstances of which we are to speak of him.

This being premised, and my authority being so good, Satan must not take it ill, if I treat him after the manner of men, and give him those titles which he is best known by among us; for, indeed, having so many, it is not very easy to call him out of his name.

However, as I am obliged, by the duty of an historian, to decency as well as impartiality, so I thought it necessary, before I used too much freedom with Satan, to produce authentic documents, and bring antiquity upon the stage, to justify the manner of my writing, and let you see I shall describe him in no colours, nor call him by any name, but what he has been known by for many ages before me.

And now, though writing to the common understanding of my readers, I am obliged to treat Satan very coarsely, and to speak of him in the common acceptation, calling him plain Devil; a word which, in this mannerly age, is not so sonorous as others might be, and which by the error of the times is apt to prejudice us against his person: Yet it must be acknowledged he has a great many other names and surnames, which he might be known by, of a less obnoxious import than that of Devil, or Destroyer, &c.

Mr. Milton, indeed, wanting titles of honour to give to the leaders of Satan's host, is obliged to borrow several of his Scripture names, and bestow them upon his infernal heroes, whom he makes the generals and leaders of the armies of hell; and so he makes Beelzebub, Lucifer, Belial, Mammon, and some others, to be the names of particular devils, members of Satan's upper house or pandemonium : Whereas, indeed, these are all names proper and peculiar to Satan himself.

The Scripture also has some names of a coarser kind, by which the Devil is understood, as particularly, which is noted already, in the Apocalypse he is called the Great Red Dragon, the Beast, the Old Serpent, and the like: But take it in the Scripture, or where you will in history, sacred and profane, you will find that in general the Devil is, as I have said above, his ordinary name in all languages and in all nations; the name by which he and his works are principally distinguished : also, the Scripture, besides that it often gives him this name, speaks of the works of the Devil, of the subtilty of the Devil, of casting out Devils, of being tempted of the Devil, of being possessed with a Devil, and so many other expressions of that kind, as I have said already, are made use of for us to understand the evil spirit by, that, in a word, Devil is the common name of all wicked spirits : For Satan is no more the Devil, as if he alone was so, and all the rest were a diminutive species, who did not go by that name : But, I say, even in Scripture, every spirit, whether under his dominion or out of his dominion, is called the Devil, and is as much a real Devil, that is to say, a condemned spirit, and employed in the same wicked work as Satan himself.

His name then being thus ascertained, and his existence acknowledged, it should be a little enquired what he is; we believe there is such a thing, such a creature as the Devil, and that he has been, and may still with propriety of speech, and without injustice to his character, be called by his antient name Devil.

But who is he? What is his original? Whence came

he? And what is his present station and condition? For these things and these enquiries are very necessary to his history, nor indeed can any part of his history be complete without them.

That he is of an antient and noble original must be acknowledged, for he is heaven-born, and of angelic race, as has been touched already: If Scripture-evidence may be of any weight in the question, there is no room to doubt the genealogy of the Devil; he is not only spoken of as an angel, but as a fallen angel, one that had been in heaven, had beheld the face of God in his full effulgence of glory, and had surrounded the throne of the Most High; from whence, commencing rebel, and being expelled, he was cast down, down, down, God and the Devil himself only knows where; for indeed we cannot say that any man on earth knows it; and where ever it is, he has ever since man's creation been a plague to him, been a tempter, a deluder, a calumniator, an enemy, and the object of man's horror and aversion.

As his original is heaven-born, and his race angelic, so the angelic nature is evidently placed in a class superior to the human, and this the Scripture is express in also; when speaking of man, it says, he made him a little lower than the angels.

Thus the Devil, as mean thoughts as you may have of him, is of a better family than any of you, nay, than the best gentleman of you all; what he may be fallen to, is one thing, but what he is fallen from, is another; and therefore I must tell my learned and reverend friend J. W. LL.D., when he spoke so rudely of the Devil lately, that in my opinion he abused his betters.

Nor is the Scripture more a help to us in the search

after the Devil's original, than it is in our search after his
nature: It is true, authors are not agreed about his age,
what time he was created, how many years he enjoyed
his state of blessedness before he fell; or how many
years he continued with his whole army in a state of
darkness, and before the creation of man.   'Tis supposed
it might be a considerable space, and that it was a part
of his punishment too, being all the while inactive, unemployed, having no business, nothing to do but gnaw-
ing his own bowels, and rolling in the agony of his own
self-reproaches, being a hell to himself in reflecting on
the glorious state from whence he was fallen.

How long he remained thus, 'tis true, we have no
light into from history, and but little from tradition.
Rabbi Judah says, the Jews were of the opinion that he
remained twenty thousand years in that condition, and
that the world shall continue twenty thousand more, in
which he shall find work enough to satisfy his mischievous desires; but he shews no authority for his
opinion.

Indeed let the Devil have been as idle as they think
he was before, it must be acknowledged that now he is
the most busy, vigilant, and diligent, of all God's creatures, and very full of employment too, such as it is.

Scripture, indeed, gives us light into the enmity there
is between the two natures, the diabolical and the
human; the reason of it, and how and by what means
the power of the Devil is restrained by the Messias: and
to those who are willing to trust to gospel-light, and
believe what the Scriptures say of the Devil, there may
much of his history be discovered, and therefore those
that list may go there for a fuller account of the matter.

But to reserve all Scripture-evidence of these things as a magazine in store for the use of those with whom Scripture-testimony is of force, I must for the present turn to other enquiries, being now directing my story to an age, wherein to be driven to Revelation and Scripture-assertions is deemed giving up the dispute: People now-a-days must have demonstration; and, in a word, nothing will satisfy the age, but such evidence as perhaps the nature of the question will not admit.

It is hard, indeed, to bring demonstrations in such a case as this: *No man hath seen God at any time,* says the Scripture, 1 John iv. 12. So the Devil being a spirit incorporeal, an angel of light, and consequently not visible in his own substance, nature, and form, it may in some sense be said, no man hath seen the Devil at any time. All those pretences of phrensiful and fanciful people, who tell us they have seen the Devil, I shall examine, and perhaps expose, by themselves.

It might take up a great deal of our time here, to enquire whether the Devil has any particular shape or personality of substance, which can be visible to us, felt, heard, or understood, and which he cannot alter; and then, what shapes or appearances the Devil has at any time taken upon him; and whether he can really appear in a body which may be handled and seen, and yet so as to know it to have been the Devil at the time of his appearing; but this also I defer as not of weight in the present enquiry.

We have divers accounts of witches conversing with the Devil; the Devil in a real body, with all the appearance of a body of a man or woman appearing to them; also of having a familiar, as they call it, an

3.   H

Incubus or little devil, which sucks their bodies, runs away with them into the air, and the like : much of this is said, but much more than it is easy to prove, and we ought to give but a just proportion of credit to those things.

As to his borrowed shapes and his subtle transformings, that we have such open testimony of, that there is no room for any question about it; and when I come to that part, I shall be obliged rather to give a history of the fact, than to enter into any dissertation upon the nature and reason of it.

I do not find in any author, whom we can call creditable, that even in those countries where the dominion of Satan is more particularly established, and where they may be said to worship him in a more particular manner, as a devil; which some tell us the Indians in America did, who worshipped the Devil that he might not hurt them; yet, I say, I do not find that even there the Devil appeared to them in any particular constant shape or personality peculiar to himself.

Scripture and history, therefore, giving us no light into that part of the question, I conclude and lay it down, not as my opinion only, but as what all ages seem to concur in, that the Devil has no particular body; that he is a spirit, and that though he may, Proteus like, assume the appearance of either man or beast, yet it must be some borrowed shape, some assumed figure, *pro hac vice*, and that he has no visible body of his own.

I thought it needful to discuss this as a preliminary, and that the next discourse might go upon a certainty in this grand point; namely, that the Devil, however he may for his particular occasions put himself into a great many shapes, and clothe himself, perhaps, with what appearances he pleases, yet that he is himself still a mere spirit; that he retains the seraphic nature, is not visible by our eyes, which are human and organic, neither can he act with the ordinary powers, or in the ordinary manner as bodies do ; and, therefore, when he has thought fit to descend to the meannesses of disturbing and frightening children and old women, by noises and knocking, dislocating the chairs and stools, breaking windows, and such like little ambulatory things, which would seem to be below the dignity of his character, and which, in particular, is ordinarily performed by organic powers; yet even then he has thought fit not to be seen, and rather to make the poor people believe he had a real shape and body, with hands to act, mouth to speak, and the like, than to give proof of it in common to the whole world, by shewing himself, and acting visibly and openly, as a body usually and ordinarily does.

Nor is it any disadvantage to the Devil, that his seraphic nature is not confined or imprisoned in a body or shape, suppose that shape to be what monstrous thing we would; for this would, indeed, confine his actings within the narrow sphere of the organ or body to which he was limited; and though you were to suppose the body to have wings for a velocity of motion equal to spirit, yet if he had not a power of invisibility too, and a capacity of conveying himself undiscovered, into all the secret recesses of mankind, the same secret art or capacity of insinuation, suggestion, accusation, &c. by which his wicked designs are now propagated, and all his other devices assisted, by which he deludes and betrays man-

kind; I say, he would be no more a devil, that is, a destroyer, no more a deceiver, and no more a Satan, that is,
a dangerous arch enemy to the souls of men; nor would
it be any difficulty to mankind to shun and avoid him,
as I shall make plain in the other part of his history.

Had the Devil from the beginning been embodied, as he
could not have been invisible to us, whose souls equally
seraphic are only prescribed by being embodied and en-
cased in flesh and blood as we are; so he would have
been no more a devil to any body but himself.   The
imprisonment in a body, had the powers of that body
been all that we can conceive to make him formidable to
us, would yet have been a hell to him; consider him as
a conquered exasperated rebel, retaining all that fury
and swelling ambition, that hatred of God, and envy at
his creatures which dwells now in his enraged spirit as
a Devil; yet suppose him to have been condemned to
organic powers, confined to corporeal motion, and restrained as a body must be supposed to restrain a spirit;
it must, at the same time, suppose him to be effectually
disabled from all the methods he is now allowed to make
use of, for exerting his rage and enmity against God, any
farther than as he might suppose it to affect his Maker
at second hand, by wounding his glory through the sides
of his weakest creature, man.

He must, certainly, be thus confined, because body
can only act upon body, not upon spirit; no species
being empowered to act out of the compass of its own
sphere: he might have been empowered, indeed, to
have acted terrible and even destructive things upon
mankind, especially if this body had any powers given
it which mankind had not, by which man would be

overmatched, and not be in a condition of self-defence; for example, suppose him to have had wings to have flown in the air; or to be invulnerable, and that no human invention, art, or engine, could hurt, ensnare, captivate, or restrain him.

But this is to suppose the righteous and wise Creator to have made a creature, and not be able to defend and preserve him; or to have left him defenceless to the mercy of another of his own creatures, whom he had given power to destroy him: this, indeed, might have occasioned a general idolatry, and made mankind, as the Americans do to this day, worship the Devil, that he might not hurt them; but it could not have prevented the destruction of mankind, supposing the Devil to have had malice equal to his power: and he must put on a new nature, be compassionate, generous, beneficent, and steadily good in sparing the rival enemy he was able to destroy, or he must have ruined mankind: in short, he must have ceased to have been a Devil, and must have reassumed his original, angelic, heavenly nature; been filled with the principles of love to, and delight in the works of, his Creator, and bent to propagate his glory and interest; or he must have put an end to the race of man, whom it would be in his power to destroy, and oblige his Maker to create a new species, or fortify the old with some kind of defence, which must be invulnerable, and which his fiery darts could not penetrate.

On this occasion, suffer me to make an excursion from the usual style of this work, and with some solemnity to express my thoughts thus:

How glorious is the wisdom and goodness of the great Creator of the world! in thus restraining these seraphic outcasts from the power of assuming human or organic bodies! which could they do, invigorating them with the supernatural powers, which, as seraphs and angels, they now possess and might exert, they would be able even to fright mankind from the face of the earth, and to destroy and confound God's creation; nay, even as they are, were not their power limited, they might destroy the creation itself, reverse and overturn nature, and put the world into a general conflagration: but were those immortal spirits embodied, though they were not permitted to confound nature, they would be able to harass poor, weak, and defenceless man out of his wits, and render him perfectly useless, either to his Maker or himself.

But the dragon is chained, the Devil's power is limited; he has indeed a vastly extended empire, being prince of the air, having, at least, the whole atmosphere to range in, and how far that atmosphere is extended, is not yet ascertained by the nicest observations; I say at least, because we do not yet know how far he may be allowed to make excursions beyond the atmosphere of this globe into the planetary worlds, and what power he may exercise in all the habitable parts of the solar system; nay, of all the other solar systems, which for ought we know, may exist in the mighty extent of created space, and of which you may hear farther in its order.

But let his power be what it will there, we are sure it is limited here, and that in two particulars; first, he is limited as above, from assuming body or bodily shapes with substance; and secondly, from exerting seraphic powers, and acting with that supernatural force which, as an angel, he was certainly vested with before the fall, and which we are not certain is yet taken from him; or, at most, we do not know how much it may or may not be diminished by his degeneracy, and by the blow given him at his expulsion : this we are certain, that be his power greater or less, he is restrained from the exercise of it in this world; and he, who was once equal to the angel who killed 180,000 men in one night, is not able now, without a new commission, to take away the life of one Job, nor touch any thing he had.

But let us consider him then limited and restrained as he is, yet he remains a mighty, a terrible, an immortal being; infinitely superior to man, as well in the dignity of his nature, as in the dreadful powers he retains still about him : it is true the brain-sick heads of our enthusiastics paint him blacker than he is, and, as I have said, wickedly represent him clothed with terrors that do not really belong to him ; as if the power of good and evil was wholly vested in him, and that he was placed in the throne of his Maker, to distribute both punishments and rewards : in this they are much wrong, terrifying and deluding fanciful people about him, till they turn their heads, and fright them into a belief that the Devil will let them alone, if they do such and such good things ; or carry them away with him they know not whither, if they do not; as if the Devil, whose proper business is mischief, seducing and deluding mankind, and drawing them in to be rebels like himself, should threaten to seize upon them, carry them away, and, in a word, fall upon them to hurt them, if they did evil; and, on the contrary, be favourable and civil to them, if they did well.

Thus a poor deluded country fellow in our town,

that had lived a wicked, abominable, debauched life, was frighted with an apparition, as he called it, of the Devil; he fancied that he spoke to him, and telling his tale to a good honest christian gentleman, his neighbour, that had a little more sense than himself; the gentleman asked him if he was sure he really saw the Devil? Yes, yes, sir, says he, I saw him very plain : and so they began the following discourse.

Gent. See him! see the Devil! art thou sure of it, Thomas?

Tho. Yes, yes, I am sure enough of it, master; to be sure 'twas the Devil.

Gent. And how do you know 'twas the Devil, Thomas? had you ever seen the Devil before?

Tho. No, no, I had never seen him before, to be sure; but, for all that, I know 'twas the Devil.

Gent. Well, if you're sure, Thomas, there's no contradicting you; pray, what clothes had he on?

Tho. Nay, sir, don't jest with me, he had no clothes on, he was clothed with fire and brimstone.

Gent. Was it dark or day-light when you saw him?

Tho. O! it was very dark, for it was midnight.

Gent. How could you see him then? did you see by the light of the fire you speak of?

Tho. No, no, he gave no light himself, but I saw him, for all that.

Gent. But was it within doors, or out in the street?

Tho. It was within, it was in my own chamber, when I was going into bed, that I saw him.

Gent. Well, then, you had a candle, hadn't you?

Tho. Yes, I had a candle, but it burnt as blue! and as dim!

Gent. Well, but if the Devil was clothed with fire and brimstone, he must give you some light; there can't be such a fire as you speak of, but it must give a light with it.

Tho. No, no, he gave no light, but I smelt his fire and brimstone; he left a smell of it behind him, when he was gone.

Gent. Well, so you say he had fire, but gave no light: it was a devilish fire, indeed: Did it feel warm? Was the room hot while he was in it?

Tho. No, no, but I was hot enough without it; for it put me into a great sweat with the fright.

Gent. Very well, he was all in fire, you say, but without light or heat ; only, it seems, he stunk of brimstone; pray, what shapes was he in ; what was he like? for you say you saw him?

Tho. O! sir, I saw two great staring saucer-eyes, enough to fright any body out of their wits.

Gent. And was that all you saw?

Tho. No, I saw his cloven-foot very plain, 'twas as big as one of our bullock's that goes to plough.

Gent. So you saw none of his body, but his eyes and his feet? a fine vision indeed!

Tho. Sir, that was enough to send me going.

Gent. Going! what did you run away from him?

Tho. No, but I fled into bed at one jump, and sunk down, and pull'd the bed-clothes quite over me.

Gent. And what did you do that for?

Tho. To hide myself from such a frightful creature.

Gent. Why, if it had really been the Devil, do you think the bed-clothes would have secured you from him?

3.   I

Nature of the Devil's circumstances.

Tho. Nay, I don't know, but in a fright it was all I could do.

Gent. Nay, 'twas as wise as all the rest; but come, Thomas, to be a little serious, pray did he speak to you?

Tho. Yes, yes, I heard a voice, but who it was, the Lord knows.

Gent. What kind of voice was it? was it like a man's voice?

Tho. No, it was a hoarse ugly noise, like the croaking of a frog, and it called me by my name twice, Thomas Dawson, Thomas Dawson.

Gent. Well, did you answer?

Tho. No, not I; I could not have spoke a word for my life; why, I was frighted to death.

Gent. Did it say any thing else?

Tho. Yes, when it saw that I did not speak, it said ' Thomas Dawson, Thomas Dawson, you are a wicked wretch, you lay with Jenny —— last night; if you don't repent, I will take you away alive, and carry you to hell, and you shall be damn'd, you wretch.'

Gent. And was it true, Thomas; did you lie with Jenny —— the night before?

Tho. Indeed, master, why yes, it was true; but I was very sorry afterwards.

Gent. But how should the Devil know it, Thomas?

Tho. Nay, he knows it to be sure; why, they say he knows every thing.

Gent. Well, but why should he be angry at that? he would rather bid you lie with her again, and encourage you to lie with forty whores, than hinder you: This can't be the Devil, Thomas.

Tho. Yes, yes, sir, 'twas the Devil, to be sure.

Gent. But he bid you repent too, you say?

Tho. Yes, he threatened me, if I did not.

Gent. Why, Thomas, do you think the Devil would have you repent?

Tho. Why no, that's true, too, I don't know what to say to that; but what could it be? 'twas the Devil, to be sure, it could be nobody else.

Gent. No, no, 'twas neither the Devil, Thomas, nor any body else, but your own frighted imagination; you had lain with that wench, and being a young sinner of that kind, your conscience terrified you, told you the Devil would fetch you away, and you would be damned; and you were so persuaded it would be so, that you at last imagined he was come for you indeed: that you saw him and heard him; whereas, you may depend upon it, if Jenny S—— will let you lie with her every night, the Devil will hold the candle, or do any thing to forward it, but will never disturb you; he is too much a friend to your wickedness: It could never be the Devil, Thomas; it was only your own guilt frighted you, and that was devil enough too; if you knew the worst of it, you need no other enemy.

Tho. Why, that's true, master, one would think the Devil should not bid me repent, that's true; but certainly 'twas the Devil for all that.

Now Thomas was not the only man that, having committed a flagitious crime, had been deluded by his own imagination, and the power of fancy, to think the Devil was come for him; whereas, the Devil, to give him his due, is too honest to pretend to such things; it is his

business to persuade men to offend, not to repent; and
he professes no other ; he may press men to this or that
action, by telling them it is no sin, no offence, no breach
of God's law, and the like, when really it is both ; but
to press them to repent, when they have offended, that's
quite out of his way; it is none of his business, nor does
he pretend to it ; therefore, let no man charge the Devil
with what he is not concerned in.

But to return to his person: he is, as I have said,
notwithstanding his lost glory, a mighty, a terrible, and
an immortal spirit; he is himself called a Prince, the
Prince of the Power of the Air; the Prince of Darkness,
the Prince of Devils, and the like; and his attending
spirits are called his Angels : So that, however Satan has
lost the glory and rectitude of his nature, by his apostate state, yet he retains a greatness and magnificence,
which places him above our rank, and indeed above our
conception; for we know not what he is, any more than
we know what the blessed angels are; of whom we can
say no more than that they are ministering spirits, &c.
as the Scripture has described them.

Two things, however, may give us some insight into
the nature of the Devil, in the present state he is in;
and these we have a clear discovery of in the whole
series of his conduct from the beginning.

1. That he is the vanquished but implacable enemy of
   God his creator, who has conquered him, and expelled him from the habitations of bliss ; on which
   account he is filled with envy, rage, malice, and all
   uncharitableness; would dethrone God, and over-
   turn the thrones of heaven, if it were in his power.

2. That he is man's irreconcileable enemy; not as he is a man, nor on his own account simply, nor for any advantage he (the Devil) can make by the ruin and destruction of man; but in mere envy at the felicity he is supposed to enjoy as Satan's rival, and as he is appointed to succeed Satan and his angels in the possession of those glories from which they are fallen.

And here I must take upon me to say, Mr. Milton makes a wrong judgment of the reason of Satan's resolution to disturb the felicity of man: He tells us it was merely to affront God his maker, rob him of the glory designed in his new work of creation, and to disappoint him in his main design, namely, the creating a new species of creatures in a perfect rectitude of soul, and after his own image, from whom he might expect a new fund of glory should be raised, and who was to appear as the triumph of the Messiah's victory over the Devil. In all which Satan could not be fool enough not to know that he should be disappointed by the same power which had so eminently counteracted his rage before.

But, I believe, the Devil went upon a much more probable design; and though he may be said to act upon a meaner principle than that of pointing his rage at the personal glory of his Creator; yet I own, that, in my opinion, it was by much the more rational undertaking, and more likely to succeed; and that was, that whereas he perceived this new species of creatures had a sublime as well as a human part, and were made capable of possessing the mansions of eternal beatitude, from whence he (Satan) and his angels were expelled and irretrievably banished: Envy at such a rival moved him by all

possible artifice, for he saw him deprived of capacity to
do it by force, to render him unworthy like himself;
that bringing him to fall into rebellion and disobedience,
he might see his rival damned with him; and those who
were intended to fill up the empty spaces in heaven,
made so by the absence of so many millions of fallen
angels, be cast out into the same darkness with them.

How he came to know that this new species of creatures were liable to such imperfection, is best explained
by the Devil's prying vigilant disposition, judging or
leading him to judge by himself; (for he was as near
being infallible as any of God's creatures had been;) and
then inclining him to try whether it was so or no.

Modern naturalists, especially some who have not so
large a charity for the fair sex, as I have, tells us, that as
soon as ever Satan saw the woman, and looked in her
face, he saw evidently that she was the best formed creature to make a tool of, and the best to make a hypocrite
of, that could be made, and therefore the most fitted for
his purpose.

1. He saw by some thwart lines in her face, (legible,
perhaps, to himself only,) that there was a throne ready
prepared for the sin of pride to sit in state upon, especially if it took an early possession: Eve, you may
suppose, was a perfect beauty, if ever such a thing may
be supposed in the human frame; her figure being so
extraordinary, was the ground-work of his project;
there needed no more than to bring her to be vain of it,
and to conceit that it either was so, or was infinitely
more sublime and beautiful than it really was; and
having thus tickled her vanity, to introduce pride gradually, till at last he might persuade her, that she was

really angelic, or of heavenly race, and wanted nothing but to eat the forbidden fruit, and that would make her something more excellent still.

2. Looking farther into her frame, and with a nearer view to her imperfections, he saw room to conclude that she was of a constitution easy to be seduced, and especially by flattering her; raising a commotion in her soul, and a disturbance among her passions; and accordingly he set himself to work, to disturb her repose, and put dreams of great things into her head; together with something of a nameless kind, which (however some have been ill-natured enough to suggest) I shall not injure the Devil so much as to mention, without better evidence.

3. But, besides this, he found, upon the very first survey of her outside, something so very charming in her mien and behaviour, so engaging as well as agreeable in the whole texture of her person, and withal such a sprightly wit, such a vivacity of parts, such a fluency of tongue, and, above all, such a winning prevailing whine in her smiles, or at least in her tears, that he made no doubt, if he could but once delude her, she would easily be brought to delude Adam, whom he found set not only a great value upon her person, but was perfectly captivated by her charms; in a word, he saw plainly, that if he could but ruin her, he should easily make a devil of her, to ruin her husband, and draw him into any gulf of mischief, were it ever so black and dreadful, that she should first fall into herself. How far some may be wicked enough, from hence, to suggest of the fair sex, that they have been devils to their husbands ever since, I cannot say; I hope they will not be

so unmerciful to discover truths of such fatal consequence, though they should come to their knowledge.

Thus subtle and penetrating has Satan been from the
beginning; and who can wonder that, upon these discoveries made into the woman's inside, he went immediately to work with her, rather than with Adam? Not
but that one would think, if Adam was fool enough to
be deluded by his wife, the Devil might have seen so
much of it in his countenance, as to have encouraged
him to make his attack directly upon him, and not go
round about, beating the bush, and ploughing with the
heifer; setting upon the woman first, and then setting
her upon her husband, who might as easily have been
imposed upon as she.

Other commentators upon this critical text suggest to
us, that Eve was not so pleased with the hopes of being
made a goddess; that the pride of a seraphic knowledge
did not so much work upon her imagination to bring her
to consent, as a certain secret notion infused into her
head by the same wicked instrument, that she should be
wiser than Adam, and should, by the superiority of her
understanding, necessarily have the government over
him; which, at present, she was sensible she had not;
he being master of a particular air of gravity and majesty, as well as of strength, infinitely superior to her.

This is an ill-natured suggestion; but, it must be confessed, the impatient desire of government, which (since
that) appears in the general behaviour of the sex, and
particularly of governing husbands, leaves too much
room to legitimate the supposition.

The expositors, who are of this opinion, add to it,
that this being her original crime, or the particular

temptation to that crime, heaven thought fit to shew his justice, in making her more entire subjection to her husband be a part of the curse, that she might read her sin in the punishment, (viz.) *he shall rule over thee.*

I only give the general hint of these things, as they appear recorded in the annals of Satan's first tyranny, and at the beginning of his government in the world: those that would be more particularly informed, may inquire of him, and know further.

I cannot however but observe here with some regret, how it appears by the consequence, that the Devil was not mistaken when he made an early judgment of Mrs. Eve; and how Satan really went the right way to work, to judge of her: it is certain the Devil had nothing to do but to look in her face, and, upon a near steady view, he might easily see there an instrument for his turn; nor has he failed to make her a tool ever since, by the very methods which he at first proposed; to which perhaps he has made some additions in the corrupting her composition, as well as her understanding; qualifying her to be a complete snare to the poor weaker vessel Man; to wheedle him with her Syren's voice, abuse him with her smiles, delude him with her crocodile tears, and sometimes cock her crown at him, and terrify him with the thunder of her Treble; making the effeminated Male Apple-Eater tremble at the noise of that very tongue, which at first commanded him to sin. For it is yet a debate, which the learned have not decided, whether she persuaded and entreated him, or, like a true she-tyrant, exercised her authority, and obliged him to eat the forbidden fruit.

And therefore a certain author, whose name, for fear

4. K

of the sex's resentment, I conceal, brings her in, calling
to Adam at a great distance, in an imperious haughty
manner, beckoning to him with her hand, thus: ' Here,'
says she, ' you cowardly faint-hearted wretch, take this
branch of heavenly fruit, eat, and be a stupid fool no
longer; eat and be wise; eat and be a god; and know,
to your eternal shame, that your wife has been made
an enlightened goddess before you.'

He tells you Adam hung a little back at first, and
trembled, afraid to trespass: ' What ails the sot,' says
the new termagant; ' what are you afraid of? Did God
forbid you! yes, and why? that we might not be knowing and wise like himself? What reason can there be
that we, who have capacious souls, able to receive
knowledge, should have it withheld? take it, you fool,
and eat; don't you see how I am exalted in soul by it,
and am quite another creature? Take it, I say, or,
if you don't, I'll go and cut down the tree, and you shall
never eat any of it at all, and you shall be still a fool,
and be governed by your wife for ever.'

Thus, if this interpretation of the thing be just, she
scolded him into it; rated him, and brought him to it by
the terror of her voice;—a thing that has retained a
dreadful influence over him ever since: nor have the
greatest of Adam's successors, how light soever some
husbands make of it in this age, been ever able, since
that, to conceal their terror, at the very sound; nay, if
we may believe history, it prevailed even among the
gods; not all the noise of Vulcan's hammers could
silence the clamours of that outrageous whore his goddess; nay, even Jupiter himself led such a life with a
termagant wife, that once, they say, Juno out-scolded

the noise of all his thunders, and was within an ace of brawling him out of heaven. But to return to the Devil.

With these views he resolved, it seems, to attack the woman; and if you consider him as a Devil, and what he aimed at, and consider the fair prospect he had of success, I must confess, I do not see who can blame him, or, at least, how any thing less could be expected from him: But we shall meet with it again by and by.

CHAPTER V.

Of the station Satan had in heaven before he fell; the nature and original of his crime, and some of Mr. Milton's mistakes about it.

THUS far I have gone upon general observation, in this great affair of Satan and his empire in the world: I now come to my title, and shall enter upon the historical part, as the main work before me.

Besides what has been said poetically, relating to the fall, and wandering condition of the Devil and his host, which poetical part I offer only as an excursion, and desire it should be taken so; I shall give you what I think is deduced from good originals on the part of Satan's story, in a few words.

He was one of the created angels, formed by the same omnipotent hand and glorious power, who created the heavens and the earth, and all that is therein: This innumerable heavenly host, as we have reason to believe,

contained angels of higher and lower stations, of greater
and of lesser degree, expressed in the Scripture by
thrones, dominions, and principalities: This, I think,
we have as much reason to believe as we have, that
there are stars in the firmament (or starry heavens) of
greater and of lesser magnitude.

What particular station among the immortal choir of
angels this arch-seraph, this prince of devils, called
Satan, was placed in before his expulsion, that indeed
we cannot come at the knowledge of, at least not with
such an authority as may be depended upon; but as,
from Scripture authority, he is placed at the head of all
the apostate armies, after he was fallen, we cannot think
it in the least assuming to say, that he might be supposed to be one of the principal agents in the rebellion
which happened in heaven, and consequently that he
might be one of the highest in dignity there, before that
rebellion.

The higher his station, the lower, and with the greater
precipitation, was his overthrow; and therefore those
words, though taken in another sense, may very well be
applied to him: *How art thou fallen, O Lucifer!
Son of the morning!*

Having granted the dignity of his person, and the
high station in which he was placed among the heavenly
host, it would come then necessarily to enquire into the
nature of his fall, and, above all, a little into the reason
of it: Certain it is, he did fall, was guilty of rebellion
and disobedience, the just effect of pride; sins, which,
in that holy place, might well be called wonderful.

But what to me is more wonderful, and which, I
think, will be very ill-accounted for, is, How came seeds

of crime to rise in the angelic nature, created in a state of perfect unspotted holiness? How was it first found in a place where no unclean thing can enter? How came ambition, pride, or envy, to generate there? Could there be offence where there was no crime? Could untainted purity breed corruption? Could that nature contaminate and infect, which was always drinking in principles of perfection?

Happy it is to me, that writing the history, not solving the difficulties of Satan's affairs, is my province in this work; that I am to relate the fact, not give reasons for it, or assign causes: if it was otherwise, I should break off at this difficulty; for I acknowledge I do not see through it; neither do I think that the great Milton, after all his fine images and lofty excursions upon the subject, has left it one jot clearer than he found it. Some are of opinion, and among them the great Dr. B—s, that crime broke in upon them at some interval, when they omitted but one moment fixing their eyes and thoughts on the glories of the Divine face, to admire and adore, which is the full employment of angels: but even this, though it goes as high as imagination can carry us, does not reach it, nor, to me, make it one jot more comprehensible than it was before: all I can say to it here is, that so it was, the fact was upon record, and the rejected troops are in being, whose circumstances confess the guilt, and still groan under the punishment.

If you will bear with a poetic excursion upon the subject, not to solve but to illustrate the difficulty, take it in a few lines, thus,

Thou sin of witchcraft! first-born child of crime!
   Produc'd before the bloom of time;
Ambition's maiden sin, in heav'n conceiv'd,
    And who could have believ'd,
Defilement could in purity begin,
And bright eternal day be soil'd with sin!
Tell us, sly penetrating crime,
How cam'st thou there, thou fault sublime?
How didst thou pass the adamantine gate,
    And into spirit thyself insinuate?
From what dark state? from what deep place?
From what strange uncreated race?
Where was thy ancient habitation found,
Before void chaos heard the forming sound?
Wast thou a substance, or an airy ghost,
   A vapour flying in the fluid waste
   Of unconcocted air?
   And how at first didst thou come there?
Sure there was once a time when thou wert not.
By whom wast thou created? and for what?
Art thou a steam from some contagious damp exhal'd?
   How should contagion be entail'd
   On bright seraphic spirits, and in a place,
Where all's supreme, and glory fills the space?
   No noxious vapour there could rise,
   For there no noxious matter lies;
   Nothing that's evil could appear,
Sin never could seraphic glory bear;
The brightness of the eternal face,
Which fills as well as constitutes the place,
Would be a fire too hot for crime to bear,
'Twould calcine sin, or melt it into air.

Satan's station in heaven before his fall.

How then did first defilement enter in?
Ambition, thou first vital seed of sin!
Thou life of death, how cam'st thou there?
   In what bright form didst thou appear?
   In what seraphic orb didst thou arise?
Surely that place admits of no disguise,
   Eternal sight must know thee there,
   And being known, thou soon must disappear.
   But since the fatal truth we know,
   Without the matter whence or manner how,
Thou highest superlative of sin,
   Tell us thy nature, where thou didst begin?
The first degree of thy increase,
   Debauch'd the regions of eternal peace;
And fill'd the breasts of loyal angels there,
With the first treason and infernal war.

Thou art the high extreme of pride,
And dost o'er lesser crimes preside;
Not for the mean attempt of vice design'd,
But to embroil the world, and damn mankind.
   Transforming mischief, now hast thou procur'd,
That loss that's ne'er to be restor'd,
   And made the bright seraphic morning star
In horrid monstrous shapes appear?
   Satan, that while he dwelt in glorious light,
Was always then as pure as he was bright,
That in refulgent rays of glory shone,
Excell'd by eternal light, by him alone,
Distorted now, and stript of innocence,
And banish'd with thee from the high pre-eminence.

How has this splendid seraph chang'd his face,
Transform'd by thee, and like thy monstrous race?
Ugly as is the crime for which he fell,
Fitted by thee to make a local hell,
For such must be the place where either of you dwell.

Thus, as I told you, I only moralize upon the subject; but as to the difficulty, I must leave it as I find it, unless, as I hinted at first, I could prevail with Satan to set pen to paper, and write this part of his own history: No question, but he could let us into the secret ; but to be plain, I doubt I shall tell so many plain truths of the Devil, in this history, and discover so many of his secrets, which it is not for his interest to have discovered, that, before I have done, the Devil and I may not be so good friends as you may suppose we are; at least, not friends enough to obtain such a favour of him, though it be for public good: so we must be content till we come on the other side the blue blanket, and then we shall know the whole story.

But now, though, as I said, I will not attempt to solve the difficulty, I may, I hope, venture to tell you, that there is not so much difficulty in it as at first sight appears; and especially not so much as some people would make us believe: let us see how others are mistaken in it; perhaps that may help us a little in the inquiry; for to know what it is not, is one help towards knowing what it is.

Mr. Milton has indeed told us a great many merry things of the Devil, in a most formal solemn manner; till, in short, he has made a good play of heaven and hell; and no doubt if he had lived in our times, he might have had it acted with our Pluto and Proserpine. He has made fine speeches both for God and the Devil, and a little addition might have turned it *a la modern* into a *harlequin dieu & diable.*

I confess I do not well know how far the dominion of poetry extends itself: it seems the buts and bounds of Parnassus are not yet ascertained; so that, for ought I know, by virtue of their ancient privileges called *Licentia Poetarum,* there can be no blasphemy in verse; as some of our divines say, there can be no treason in the pulpit. But they that will venture to write that way, ought to be better satisfied about that point than I am.

Upon this foot Mr. Milton, to grace his poem, and give room for his towering fancy, has gone a length beyond all that ever went before him, since Ovid in his Metamorphosis. He has indeed complimented God Almighty with a flux of lofty words, and great sounds; and has made a very fine story of the Devil; but he has made a meer *je ne scay quoi* of Jesus Christ. In one line he has him riding on a cherub, and in another sitting on a throne, both in the very same moment of action. In another place, he has brought him in making a speech to his saints, when it is evident he had none there ; for we all know man was not created till a long while after ; and no body can be so dull as to say the angels may be called saints, without the greatest absurdity in nature. Besides, he makes Christ himself distinguish them, as in two several bands, and of differing persons and species, as to be sure they are.

4.   L

Stand still in bright array, ye saints————
———————— ———— ————Here stand,
Ye angels.———— ————

Par. Lost, lib. vi. *fol.* 174.

So that Christ here is brought in drawing up his army
before the last battle, and making a speech to them, to
tell them they shall only stand by in warlike order, but
that they shall have no occasion to fight, for he alone
will engage the rebels. Then in embattling his legions,
he places the saints here, and the angels there; as if one
were the main battle of infantry, and the other the wings
of cavalry. But who are those saints? They are indeed all of Mr. Milton's own making: it is certain there
were no saints at all in heaven or earth at that time;
God and his angels filled up the place; and till some
of the angels fell, and men were created, had lived, and
were dead, there could have been no saints there. Saint
Abel was certainly the proto-saint of all that ever were
seen in heaven, as well as the proto-martyr of all that
have been upon earth.

Just such another mistake, not to call it a blunder, he
makes about hell; which he not only makes local, but
gives it a being before the fall of the angels; and brings
it in opening its mouth to receive them. This is so contrary to the nature of the thing, and so great an absurdity, that no poetic licence can account for it; for though
poesy may form stories, as idea and fancy may furnish
materials, yet poesy must not break in upon chronology,
and make things which in time were to exist, act before
they existed.

Thus a painter may make a fine piece of work, the

Satan's station in heaven before his fall.

fancy may be good, the strokes masterly, and the beauty of the workmanship inimitably curious and fine, and yet have some unpardonable improprieties which marr the whole work. So the famous painter of Toledo, painted the story of the three wise men of the East coming to worship, and bring their presents to our Lord upon his birth at Bethlehem, where he represents them as three Arabian or Indian kings: two of them are white, and one black. But unhappily, when he drew the latter part of them kneeling, which to be sure were done after their faces, their legs being necessarily a little intermixed, he made three black feet for the Negro king, and but three white feet for the two white kings; and yet never discovered the mistake till the piece was presented to the king, and hung up in the great church. As this is an unpardonable error in sculpture or limning, it must be much more so in poetry, where the images must have no improprieties, much less inconsistencies.

In a word, Mr. Milton has indeed made a fine poem, but it is the devil of a history. I can easily allow Mr. Milton to make hills and dales, flowery meadows and plains (and the like) in heaven; and places of retreat and contemplation in hell; though I must add, that it can be allowed to no poet on earth but Mr. Milton. Nay, I will allow Mr. Milton, if you please, to set the angels a dancing in heaven, lib. v. fol. 138, and the devils a singing in hell, lib. i. fol. 44, though they are in short, especially the last, most horrid absurdities. But I cannot allow him to make their music in hell to be harmonious and charming as he does; such images being incongruous, and indeed shocking to nature. Neither can I think we should allow things to be placed out of time in poetry, any more than in history: it is a confusion of images, which is allowed to be disallowed by all the critics, of what tribe or species soever in the world, and is indeed unpardonable. But we shall find so many more of these things in Mr. Milton, that really taking notice of them all, would carry me quite out of my way, I being at this time not writing the history of Mr. Milton, but of the Devil: besides, Mr. Milton is such a celebrated man, that who but he that can write the history of the Devil dare meddle with him?

But to come back to the business. As I had cautioned you against running to scripture for shelter in cases of difficulty, Scripture weighing very little among the people I am directing my speech to; so indeed Scripture gives but very little light into any thing of the Devil's story before his fall, and but to very little of it for some time after.

Nor has Mr. Milton said one word to solve the main difficulty (viz.) How the Devil came to fall, and how sin came into heaven? How the spotless seraphic nature could receive infection; whence the contagion proceeded, what noxious matter could emit corruption there, how and whence any vapour to poison the angelic frame could rise up, or how it increased and grew up to crime. But all this he passes over, and, hurrying up that part in two or three words, only tells us,

—————— his pride
Had cast him out of heaven with all his host
Of rebel angels, by whose aid aspiring
He trusted to have equal'd the Most High.

Lib. 1. *fol.* 3.

~~~~~~~~~~~~~~~~~~~~~~~~~~~~~~~~~~

Satan's station in heaven before his fall.

~~~~~~~~~~~~~~~~~~~~~~~~~~~~~~~~~~

His pride! but how came Satan, while an arch-angel, to be proud? How did it consist, that pride and perfect holiness should meet in the same person? Here we must bid Mr. Milton good night? for, in plain terms, he is in the dark about it, and so we are all; and the most that can be said, is, that we know the fact is so, but nothing of the nature or reason of it.

But to come to the history: The angels fell; they sinned (wonderful!) in heaven, and God cast them out: what their sin was is not explicit, but in general it is called a rebellion against God: all sin must be so.

Mr. Milton here takes upon him to give the history of it, as particularly as if he had been born there, and came down hither on purpose to give us an account of it; (I hope he is better informed by this time;) but this he does in such a manner, as jostles with religion, and shocks our faith in so many points, necessary to be believed, that we must forbear to give up to Mr. Milton, or must set aside part of the sacred text, in such a manner, as will assist some people to set it all aside.

I mean by this, his invented scheme of the Son's being declared in heaven to be begotten then, and then to be declared generalissimo of all the armies of heaven; and of the Father's summoning all the angels of the heavenly host to submit to him, and pay him homage. The words are quoted already, page 42.

I must own the invention, indeed, is very fine; the images exceeding magnificent, the thought rich and bright, and, in some respect, truly sublime: but the authorities fall most wretchedly, and the mis-timing of it is unsufferably gross, as is noted in the introduction to this work; for Christ is not declared the Son of God

but on earth : it is true, it is spoken from heaven, but
then it is spoken as perfected on earth ; if it was at all
to be assigned to heaven, it was from eternity, and there,
indeed, his eternal generation is allowed: but to take
upon us to say, that on a day, a certain day, for so our
poet assumes,

Lib. v. *fol*. 137.

――――― ' When on a day,
――――― ' On such a day,
' As heaven's great year brings forth, the empyreal host
' Of angels, by imperial summons call'd,
' Forthwith from all the ends of heaven, appear'd.'

This is, indeed, too gross : at this meeting he makes
God declare the Son to be that day begotten, as before:
had he made him not begotten that day, but declared
general that day, it would be reconcileable with Scripture and with sense ; for either the begetting is meant of
ordaining to an office, or else the eternal generation falls
to the ground; and if it was to the office (Mediator),
then Mr. Milton is out in ascribing another fixed day to
the work; see *lib*. x. *fol*. 194. But then the declaring
him that day, is wrong chronology too ; for Christ is
declared *the Son of God with power*, only *by the resurrection of the dead;* and this is both a declaration in
heaven and in earth. Rom. i. 4. And Milton can have
no authority to tell us, there was any declaration of it
in heaven before this, except it be that dull authority
called poetic license, which will not pass in so solemn
an affair as that.

But the thing was necessary to Milton, who wanted to

assign some cause or original of the Devil's rebellion; and so, as I said above, the design is well laid; it only wants two trifles, called truth and history : so I leave it to struggle for itself.

This ground-plot being laid, he has a fair field for the Devil to play the rebel in ; for he immediately brings him in, not satisfied with the exaltation of the Son of God. The case must be thus: Satan being an eminent arch-angel, and, perhaps, the highest of all the angelic train, hearing this sovereign declaration, that the Son of God was declared to be head or generalissimo of all the heavenly host, took it ill to see another put into the high station over his head, as the soldiers call it ; he, perhaps, thinking himself the senior officer, and disdaining to submit to any but to his former immediate sovereign : in short, he threw up his commission, and, in order not to be compelled to obey, revolted and broke out in open rebellion.

All this part is a decoration noble and great, nor is there any objection to be made against the invention, because a deduction of probable events; but the plot is wrong laid, as is observed above, because contradicted by the Scripture account, according to which Christ was declared in heaven, not then, but from eternity, and not declared with power, but on earth, (viz.) in his victory over sin and death, by the resurrection from the dead. So that Mr. Milton is not orthodox in this part, but lays an avowed foundation for the corrupt doctrine of Arius, which says, there was a time when Christ was not the Son of God.

But to leave Mr. Milton to his flights, I agree with him in this part, viz. that the wicked or sinning angels,

with the great arch-angel at the head of them, revolted
from their obedience, even in heaven itself; that Satan
began the wicked defection, and being a chief among
the heavenly host, consequently carried over a great
party with him, who all together rebelled against God;
that upon this rebellion they were sentenced by the
righteous judgment of God, to be expelled the holy
habitation: this, besides the authority of Scripture, we
have visible testimonies of, from the devils themselves;
their influences and operations among us every day, of
which mankind are witnesses; in all the merry things
they do in his name, and under his protection, in almost
every scene of life they pass through, whether we talk of
things done openly or in masquerade, things done in —
or out of it, things done in earnest or in jest.

But then, what comes of the long and bloody war
that Mr. Milton gives such a full and particular account
of, and the terrible battles in heaven between Michael
with the royal army of angels on one hand, and Satan
with his rebel host on the other; in which he supposes
the numbers and strength to be pretty near equal; but at
length brings in the Devil's army, upon doubling their
rage and bringing new engines of war into the field, putting Michael and all the faithful army to the worst;
and, in a word, defeats them? For though they were not
put to a plain flight, in which case he must, at least,
have given an account of two or three thousand millions
of angels cut in pieces and wounded, yet he allows them
to give over the fight, and make a kind of retreat; so
making way for the complete victory of the Son of
God. Now this is all invention, or at least a borrowed
thought from the old poets, and the fight of the giants

against Jupiter, so nobly designed by Ovid, almost two thousand years ago; and there it was well enough; but whether poetic fancy should be allowed to fable upon heaven, or no, and upon the King of heaven too, that I leave to the sages.

By this expulsion of the devils, it is allowed by most authors, they are, *ipso facto*, stript of the rectitude and holiness of their nature, which was their beauty and perfection; and being ingulphed in the abyss of irrecoverable ruin, it is no matter where, from that very time they lost their angelic beautiful form, commenced ugly frightful monsters and devils, and became evil doers, as well as evil spirits; filled with a horrid malignity and enmity against their Maker, and armed with a hellish resolution to shew and exert it on all occasions; retaining, however, their exalted spirituous nature, and having a vast extensive power of action, all which they can exert in nothing else but doing evil; for they are entirely divested of either power or will to do good: and even in doing evil, they are under restraints and limitations of a superior power, which it is their torment, and, perhaps, a great part of their hell that they cannot break through.

90　　　THE HISTORY

The Devil's condition from his expulsion until the creation.

CHAPTER VI.

What became of the Devil and his host of fallen spirits, after their being expelled from heaven, and his wandering condition till the creation; with some more of Mr. Milton's absurdities on that subject.

Having thus brought the Devil and his innumerable legions to the edge of the bottomless pit, it remains, before I bring them to action, that some inquiry should be made into the posture of their affairs immediately after their precipitate fall, and into the place of their immediate residence; for this will appear to be very necessary to Satan's history, and indeed, so as that without it, all the farther account we have to give of him will be inconsistent and imperfect.

And, first, I take upon me to lay down some fundamentals, which I believe I shall be able to make out historically, though, perhaps, not so geographically as some have pretended to do.

1. That Satan was not immediately, nor is yet, locked down in the abyss of a local hell, such as is supposed by some, and such as he shall be at last; or that,

2. If he was, he has certain liberties allowed him for excursions into the regions of this air, and certain spheres of action, in which he can and does move, to do, like a very devil as he is, all the mischief he can, and of which we see so many examples

both about us and in us; in the inquiry afte
which, I shall take occasion to examine whether the
Devil is not in most of us, sometimes, if not in all
of us one time or other.

3.   That Satan has no particular residence in this
globe on earth, where we live; that he rambles
about among us, and marches over and over our
whole country, he and his devils in *camps volant ;*
but that he pitches his grand army or chief encampment in our adjacencies or frontiers, which the
philosophers call atmosphere; and whence he is
called the Prince of the Power of that element or
part of the world we call Air; from whence he
sends out his spies, his agents, and emissaries, to get
intelligence, and to carry his commissions to his
trusty and well-beloved cousins and counsellers on
earth, by which his business is done, and his affairs carried on in the world.

Here, again, I meet Mr. Milton full in my face, who
will have it, that the Devil, immediately at his expulsion, rolled down directly into hell proper and local;
nay, he measures the very distance, at least, gives the
length of the journey by the time they were passing or
falling, which he says, was nine days; a good poetical
flight, but neither founded on Scripture or philosophy:
he might every jot as well have brought hell up to the
walls of heaven, advanced to receive them, or he ought
to have considered the space which is to be allowed to
any locality, let him take what part of infinite distance
between heaven and a created hell he pleases.

But let that be as Mr. Milton's extraordinary genius

92 THE HISTORY

The Devil's condition from his expulsion until the creation.

pleases to place it; the passage, it seems, is just nine days betwixt heaven and hell: well might Dives then see father Abraham, and talk to him too; but then the great gulph which Abraham tells him was fixed between them does not seem to be so large, as according to Sir Isaac Newton, Dr. Halley, Mr. Whiston, and the rest of our men of science, we take it to be.

But suppose the passage to be nine days, according to Mr. Milton, What followed? Why hell gaped wide, opened its frightful mouth, and received them all at once; millions and thousands of millions as they were, it received them all at a gulp, as we call it; they had no difficulty to go in, no, none at all.

> *Facilis desensus averni, sed revocare gradam*
> *Hoc opus hic labor est.——*
>
> VIRG.

All this, as poetical, we may receive, but not at all as historical; for then come difficulties insuperable in our way, some of which may be as follow: (1.) Hell is here supposed to be a place; nay, a place created for the punishment of angels and men, and likewise created long before those had fallen, or these had being: this makes me say, Mr. Milton was a good poet, but a bad historian. Tophet was prepared of old, indeed, but it was for the king, that is to say, it was prepared for those whose lot it should be to come there: but this does not at all suppose it was prepared before it was resolved whether there should be subjects for it, or no; else we must suppose both men and angels were made by the glorious and upright Maker of all things, on pur-

The Devil's condition from his expulsion until the creation.

pose for destruction, which would be incongruous and absurd.

But there is worse yet to come: in the next place he adds, that hell, having received them, closed upon them; that is to say, took them in, closed or shut its mouth: and, in a word, they were locked in, as it was said, in another place, they were locked in, and the key is carried up to heaven and kept there; for we know the angel came down from heaven, having the key of the bottomless pit; but first, see Mr. Milton.

'Nine days they fell, confounded chaos roar'd,
'And felt ten-fold confusion in their fall:
                           '————Hell at last
'Yawning receiv'd them all, and on them clos'd;
'Down from the verge of heaven, eternal wrath
'Burnt after them————
'Unquenchable.

This scheme is certainly deficient, if not absurd, and I think is more so than any other he has laid: 'tis evident, neither Satan or his host of devils are, no, not any of them, yet, even now, confined in the eternal prison, where the Scripture says, he shall be *reserved in chains of darkness.* They must have mean thoughts of hell, as a prison, a local confinement, that can suppose the Devil able to break gaol, knock off his fetters, and come abroad, if he had been once locked in there, as Mr. Milton says he was. Now we know that he is abroad again, he presented himself before God, among his neighbours, when Job's case came to be discoursed of;

and more than that, it's plain he was a prisoner at large, by his answer to God's question ; which was, *Whence comest thou?* to which he answered, *From going to and fro through the earth*, &c. This, I say, is plain, and if it be as certain that hell closed upon them, I demand then how got he out ? and why was there not a proclamation for apprehending him, as there usually is, after such rogues as break prison ?

In short, the true account of the Devil's circumstances, since his fall from heaven, is much more likely to be thus : That he is more of a vagrant than a prisoner, that he is a wanderer in the wild unbounded waste, where he and his legions, like the hoords of Tartary, who, in the wild countries of Karakathay, the deserts of Barkan, Kassan, and Astracan, live up and down where they find proper : so Satan and his innumerable legions rove about *hic & ubique,* pitching their camps (being beasts of prey) where they find the most spoil; watching over this world, (and all the other worlds for ought we know, and if there be any such,) I say watching, and seeking who they may devour, that is, who they may deceive and delude, and so destroy, for devour they cannot.

Satan being thus confined to a vagabond, wandering, unsettled condition, is without any certain abode; for though he has, in consequence of his angelic nature, a kind of empire in the liquid waste or air, yet, this is certainly part of his punishment, that he is continually hovering over this inhabited globe of earth ; swelling with the rage of envy, at the felicity of his rival, man ; and studying all the means possible to injure and ruin him ; but extremely limited in power, to his unspeakable mortification. This is his present state, without any fixed abode, place, or space, allowed him to rest the sole of his foot upon.

From his expulsion, I take his first view of horror to be that of looking back towards the heaven, which he had lost; there to see the chasm or opening made up, out at which, as at a breach in the wall of the holy place, he was thrust head-long by the power which expelled him; I say, to see the breach repaired, the mounds built up, the walls garrisoned with millions of angels, and armed with thunders; and, above all, made terrible by that glory from whose presence they were expelled, as is poetically hinted at before.

Upon this sight, it is no wonder (if there was such a place) that they fled till the darkness might cover them, and that they might be out of the view of so hated a sight.

Wherever they found it, you may be sure they pitched their first camp, and began, after many a sour reflection upon what was passed, to consider and think a little, upon what was to come.

If I had as much personal acquaintance with the Devil, as would admit it, and could depend upon the truth of what answer he would give me, the first question I would ask him; should be, what measures they resolved on at their first assembly? and the next should be, how they were employed in all that space of time, between their so flying the face of their almighty Conqueror, and the creation of man? as for the length of the time, which, according to the learned, was twenty thousand years, and according to the more learned, not half a quarter so much, I would not concern my curiosity much about

it ; it is most certain, there was a considerable time between, but of that immediately; first, let me enquire
what they were doing all that time.

The Devil and his host, being thus, I say, cast out
of heaven, and not yet confined strictly to hell, 'tis plain
they must be somewhere.   Satan and all his legions
did not lose their existence, no, nor the existence of
Devils, neither: God was so far from annihilating him,
that he still preserved his being ; and this not Mr. Milton
only, but God himself, has made known to us, having
left his history so far upon record; several expressions
in Scripture also make it evident, as particularly the
story of Job, mentioned before; the like in our Saviour's
time, and several others.

If hell did not immediately ingulph them, as Milton
suggests, it is certain, I say, that they fled somewhere,
from the anger of heaven, from the face of the avenger;
and his absence, and their own guilt, wonder not at
it, would make hell enough for them wherever they
went.

Nor need we fly to the dreams of our astronomers,
who take a great deal of pains to fill up the vast spaces of
the starry heavens with innumerable habitable worlds;
allowing as many solar systems as there are fixed stars,
and that not only in the known constellations, but even
in Gallaxie itself; who, to every such system, allow
a certain number of planets, and to every one of those
planets so many satellites or moons, and all these planets
and moons to be worlds ? solid, dark, opaque bodies,
habitable, and (as they would have us believe) inhabited by the like animals, and rational creatures as on
this earth ? so that they may, at this rate, find room

OF THE DEVIL. 97

The Devil's condition from his expulsion until the creation.

enough for the Devil and all his angels, without making a hell on purpose; nay, they may, for aught I know, find a world for every Devil, in all the Devil's host, and so every one may be a monarch or master-devil, separately in his own sphere or world, and play the devil there by himself.

And even if this were so, it cannot be denied but that one Devil in a place would be enough for a whole systemary world, and be able, if not restrained, to do mischief enough there too, and even to ruin and overthrow the whole body of people contained in it.

But, I say, we need not fly to these shifts, or consult the astronomers in the decision of this point; for wherever Satan and his defeated host went at their expulsion from heaven, we think we are certain none of all these beautiful worlds, or be they worlds or no, I mean the fixed stars, planets, &c. had then any existence; for the beginning, as the Scripture calls it, was not yet begun.

But to speak a little by the rules of philosophy, that is to say so as to be understood by others, even when we speak of things we cannot fully understand ourselves: Though in the beginning of time all this glorious creation was formed, the earth, the starry heavens, and all the furniture thereof, and there was a time when they were not; yet we cannot say so of the void or that nameless nowhere, as I called it before, which now appears to be a somewhere, in which these glorious bodies are placed. That immense space which those take up, and which they move in at this time, must be supposed, before they had being, to be placed there: as God himself was, and existed before all being, time, or place, so the

5　　　　　　　　　　N

98　　　THE HISTORY

The Devil's condition from his expulsion until the creation.

heaven of heavens, or the place where the thrones and dominions of his kingdom then existed, inconceivable and ineffable, had an existence before the glorious seraphs, the innumerable company of angels which attended about the throne of God existed; these all had a being long before, as the eternal creator of them all had before them.

Into this void or abyss of nothing, however unmeasurable, infinite, and even to those spirits themselves inconceivable, they certainly launched from the bright precipice which they fell from, and here they shifted as well as they could.

Here expanding those wings which fear, and horror at their defeat furnished them, as I hinted before, they hurried away to the utmost distance possible, from the face of God their conqueror, and then most dreaded enemy ; formerly their joy and glory.

Be this utmost removed distance, where it will, here, certainly, Satan and all his gang of devils, his numberless, though routed armies retired. Here Milton might with some good ground, have formed his pandemonium, and have brought them in, consulting what was next to be done, and whether there was any room left to renew the war, or to carry on the rebellion; but had they been cast immediately into hell, closed up there, the bottomless-pit locked upon them, and the key carried up to heaven to be kept there, as Mr. Milton himself in part confesses, and the Scripture affirms ; I say had this been so, the Devil himself could not have been so ignorant as to think of any future steps to be taken, to retreive his affairs, and therefore a pandemonium or divan in hell, to consult of it, was ridiculous.

All Mr. Milton's scheme of Satan's future conduct, and all the Scripture expressions about the Devil and his numerous attendants, and of his actings since that time, make it not reasonable to suggest that the devils were confined to their eternal prison, at their expulsion out of heaven; but that they were in a state of liberty to act, though limited in acting, of which I shall also speak in its place.

CHAPTER VII.

Of the number of Satan's host; how they came first to know of the new created worlds, now in being, and their measures with mankind upon the discovery.

SEVERAL things have been suggested to set us calculating the number of this frightful throng of devils, who with Satan the master-Devil, was thus cast out of heaven; I cannot say, I am so much master of political arithmetic as to cast up the number of the beast, no, nor the number of the beasts or devils, who make up this throng. St. Francis, they tell us, or some other saint, they do not say who, asked the Devil once how strong he was? for St. Francis you must know was very familiar with him: the Devil it seems did not tell him, but presently raised a great cloud of dust, by the help, I suppose, of a gust of wind, and bid that saint count it: he was, I suppose, a calculator, that would be called

grave, who dividing Satan's troops into three lines, cast
up the number of the devils of all sorts in each batta-
lia, at ten hundred times a hundred thousand millions
of the first line, fifty millions of times as many in the
second line, and three hundred thousand times as many as both in the third line.

The impertinence of this account would hardly have
given it a place here, only to hint that it has always
been the opinion that Satan's name may well be called
a noun of multitude, and that the Devil and his angels
are certainly no inconsiderable number. It was a smart
repartee that a Venetian nobleman made to a priest who
rallied him upon his refusing to give something to the
church, which the priest demanded for delivering him
from purgatory; when the priest asking him, If he knew
what an innumerable number of devils there were to
take him? He answered, Yes, he knew how many devils there were in all: How many? says the priest, his
curiosity, I suppose, being raised by the novelty of the
answer, Why ten millions five hundred and eleven
thousand, six hundred and seventy-five devils and an
half, says the nobleman : A half ! says the priest, pray
what kind of a devil is that ? Yourself, says the nobleman, for you are half a devil already (and will be a
whole one when you come there) for you are for deluding all you deal with, and bringing us soul and body
into your hands, that yon may be paid for letting us
go again. So much for their number.

Here also it would come in very aptly, to consider the
state of that long interval between the time of their expulsion from heaven, and the creation of the world,
and what the posture of the Devil's affairs might be

during that time. The horror of their condition can only be conceived of at a distance, and especially by us, who being embodied creatures, cannot fully judge of what is, or is not a punishment to seraphs and spirits; but 'tis just to suppose they suffered all that spirits of a seraphic nature were capable to sustain, consistent with their existence; notwithstanding which they retained still the hellishness of their rebellious principles; namely, their hatred and rage against God, and their envy at the felicity of his creatures.

As to how long their time might be, I shall leave that search; no lights being given me that are either probable or rational, and we have so little room to make a judgment of it, that we may as well believe father M-—-, who supposes it to be a hundred thousand years, as those who judge it one thousand years; 'tis enough that we are sure, it was before the creation, how long before is not material to the Devil's history, unless we had some records of what happened to him, or was done by him in the interval.

During the wandering condition the Devil was in at that time, we may suppose, he and his whole clan to be employed in exerting their hatred and rage at the Almighty, and at the happiness of the remaining faithful angels, by all the ways they had power to shew it.

From this determined stated enmity of Satan and his host against God, and at every thing that brought glory to his name, Mr. Milton brings in Satan (when first he saw Adam in paradise, and the felicity of his station there) swelling with rage and envy, and taking up a dreadful resolution to ruin Adam and all his posterity

merely to disappoint his maker of the glory of his creation ; I shall come to speak of that in its place.

How Satan, in his remote situation, got intelligence
of the place where to find Adam out, or that any such
thing as a man was created, is matter of just speculation, and there might be many rational schemes laid for
it : Mr. Milton does not undertake to tell us the particulars, nor indeed could he find room for it ; perhaps,
the Devil having, as I have said, a liberty to range
over the whole void or abyss, which we want as well a
name for, as indeed powers to conceive of; might have
discovered that the almighty Creator had formed a
new and glorious work, with infinite beauty and variety, filling the immense waste of space, in which he (the
Devil) and his angels, had roved for so long a time,
without finding any thing to work on, or to exert their
apostate rage in against their maker.

That at length they found the infinite untrodden
space, on a sudden spread full with glorious bodies,
shining in self-existing beauty, with a new, and to
them unknown lustre, called light : They found these
luminous bodies, though immense in bulk, and infinite
in number, yet fixed in their wonderous stations, regular and exact in their motions, confined in their proper orbits, tending to their particular centers, and enjoying every one their peculiar systems, within which
was contained innumerable planets with their satellites or moons, in which (again) a reciprocal influence,
motion and revolution conspired to form the most admirable uniformity of the whole.

Surprised, to be sure, with this sudden and yet glori-

ous work of the almighty ; for the creation was enough
with its lustre, even to surprise the devils ; they might
reasonably be supposed to start out of their dark retreat,
and with a curiosity not below the seraphic dignity; for
these are some of the things which the angels desire to
look into, to take a flight through all the amazing systems of the fixed suns or stars, which we see now but
at a distance, and only make astronomical guesses at.

Here the Devil found not subject of wonder only, but
matter to swell his revolted spirit with more rage, and
to revive the malignity of his mind against his maker,
especially against this new increase of glory, which to
his infinite regret was extended over the whole waste,
and which he looked upon as we say in human affairs,
as a *pays conquis*, or, if you will have it in the language of the Devil, as an invasion upon his kingdom.

Here it naturally occurred to them, in their state of
envy and rebellion, that though they could not assault
the impregnable walls of heaven, and could no more
pretend to raise war in the place of blessedness and
peace ; yet that perhaps they might find room in this
new, and however glorious, yet inferior kingdom or
creation, to work some despite to their great creator,
or to affront his majesty in the person of some of his
new-made creatures ; and upon this they may be justly supposed to double their vigilance, in the survey
they resolve to take of these new worlds, however
great, numberless and wonderful.

What discoveries they may have made in the other
and greater worlds than this earth, we have not yet had
an account ; possibly they are conversant with other
parts of God's creation, besides this little globe, which

is but as a point in comparison of the rest ; and with
other of God's creatures besides man, who may according to the opinion of our philosophers, inhabit those
worlds ; but as nobody knows that part but the Devil,
we shall not trouble ourselves with the enquiry.

But 'tis very reasonable, and indeed probable, that
the devils were more than ordinarily surprised at the
nature and reason of all this glorious creation, after they
had, with the utmost curiosity, viewed all the parts of
it ; the glories of the several systems ; the immense
spaces in which those glorious bodies that were created
and made part of it were allowed respectively to move,
the innumerable fixed stars as so many suns in the
center of so many distant solar systems ; the (likewise
innumerable) dark opaque bodies receiving light, and
depending upon those suns respectively for such light,
and then reflecting that light again upon and for the use
of one another : to see the beauty and splendour of
their forms, the regularity of their position, the order
and exactness, and yet inconceivable velocity of their
motions, the certainty of their revolutions, and the
variety and virtue of their influences ; and then, which
was even to the devils themselves most astonishing that
after all the rest of their observations they should find
this whole immense work was adapted for, and made
subservient to the use, delight and blessing only of one
poor species, in itself small, and in appearance contemptible ; the meanest of all the kinds supposed to
inhabit so many glorious worlds, as appeared now to
be formed ; I mean, that moon called the Earth, and
the creature called Man : that all was made for him,
upheld by the wise Creator, on his account only, and

would necessarily end and cease whenever that species should end and be determined.

That this creature was to be found no where but (as
above) in one little individual moon; a spot less than
almost any of the moons, which were in such great
numbers to be found attendant upon, and prescribed
within every system of the whole created heavens :
This was astonishing even to the Devil himself, nay the
whole clan of devils could scarce entertain any just ideas
of the thing; till at last Satan, indefatigable in his
search or enquiry into the nature and reason of this new
work, and particularly searching into the species of
man, whom he found God had thus placed in the little
globe, called Earth; he soon came to an eclaircissement,
or a clear understanding of the whole. For example,

1. He found this creature, called Man, was, however
   mean and small in his appearance, a kind of a
   seraphic species; that he was made in the very
   image of God, endowed with reasonable faculties
   to know good and evil, and possessed of a certain
   thing till then unknown and unheard of, even in
   hell itself; that is, in the habitation of devils, let
   that be where it would, viz.

2. That God had made him indeed of the lowest and
   coarsest materials, but that he had breathed into
   him the breath of life, and that he became a living
   thing called Soul, being a kind of an extraordinary
   heavenly and divine emanation; and consequently
   that man, however mean and terrestrial his body
   might be, was yet, heaven-born, in his spiritual
   part completely seraphic; and after a space of life

5   O

here, (determined to be a state of probation) he
should be translated through the regions of death
into a life purely and truly heavenly, and which
should remain so for ever ; being capable of knowing and enjoying God his maker, and standing in
his presence, as the glorified angels do.

3. That he had the most sublime faculties infused
into him ; was capable not only of knowing and
contemplating God, and which was still more, of
enjoying him, as above ; but (which the Devil now
was not) capable of honouring and glorifying his
maker ; who also had condescended to accept of
honour from him.

4. And which was still more, that being of an angelic
nature, though mixed with, and confined for the
present in a case of mortal flesh ; he was intended
to be removed from this earth after a certain time of
life here, to inhabit that heaven, and enjoy that
very glory and felicity, from which Satan and his
angels had been expelled.

When he found all this, it presently occurred to
him, that God had done it all as an act of triumph
over him (Satan) and that these creatures were only
created to people heaven, depopulated or stript of its
inhabitants by his expulsion, and that these were all
to be made angels in the Devil's stead.

If this thought increased his fury and envy, as far as
rage of devils can be capable of being made greater ;
it doubtless set him on work to give a vent to that rage
and envy, by searching into the nature and constitution of this creature called Man ; and to find out

whether he was invulnerable, and could by no means be hurt by the power of hell, or deluded by his subtilty ; or whether he might be beguiled and deluded, and so, instead of being preserved in holiness and purity, wherein he was certainly created, be brought to fall and rebel as he (Satan) had done before him ; by which, instead of being transplanted into a glorious state, after this life in heaven, as his maker had designed him to be, to fill up the angelic choir, and supply the place from whence he (Satan) had fallen, he might be made to fall also like him, and in a word be made a devil like himself.

This convinces us that the Devil has not lost his natural powers by his fall ; and our learned commentator Mr. Pool is of the same opinion ; though he grants t hat the Devil has lost his moral power, or his power of doing good, which he can never recover. Vide Mr. Pool upon Acts xix. 17. where we may particularly observe, when the man possessed with an evil spirit flew upon the seven sons of Scæva the Jew, who would have exorcised them in the name of Jesus, without the authority of Jesus, or without faith in him : He flew on them and mastered them, so that they fled out of the house from the Devil conquered, naked and wounded : But of the power of the Devil I shall speak by itself.

In a word, and to sum up all the Devil's story from his first expulsion, it stands thus : For so many years as were between his fall and the creation of man, though we have no memoirs of his particular affairs, we have reason to believe he was without any manner of employment : but a certain tormenting endeavour to be always expressing his rage and enmity against heaven ; I call it tormenting, because ever disappointed ; every thought

about it proving empty; every attempt towards it
abortive; leaving him only light enough to see still
more and more reason to despair of success; and that
this made his condition still more and more a hell than
it was before.

After a space of duration in this misery, which we
have no light given us to measure or judge of, he at
length discovered the new creation of man, as above,
upon which he soon found matter to set himself to
work upon, and has been busily employed ever since,

And now indeed there may be room to suggest a local hell, and the confinement of souls (made corrupt
and degenerate by him) to it, as a place; though he
himself, as is still apparent by his actings, is not yet
confined to it; of this hell, its locality, extent, dimen-
sions, continuance and nature, as it does not belong to
Satan's history, I have a good excuse for saying nothing, and so put of my meddling with that, which if I
would meddle with, I could not say nothing of to the
purpose.

CHAPTER VIII.

Of the power of the Devil at the time of the creation
of this world ; whether it has not been further strait-
ened and limited since that time, and what shifts
and stratagems he is obliged to make use of to com-
pass his designs upon mankind.

CUNNING men have fabled, and though it be without
either religion, authority or physical foundation, it may
be we may like it ne'er the worse for that ; that when
God made the stars and all the heavenly luminaries, the
Devil, to mimic his maker and insult his new creation,
made comets, in imitation of the fixed stars ; but that
the composition of them being combustible, when they
came to wander in the abyss, rolling by an irregular ill-
grounded motion, they took fire, in their approach to
some of those great bodies of flame, the fixed stars; and
being thus kindled (like a firework unskilfully let off)
they then took wild and eccentric, as also different
motions of their own, out of Satan's direction, and
beyond his power to regulate ever after.

Let this thought stand by itself, it matters not to
our purpose whether we believe any thing of it or no ;
'tis enough to our case, that if Satan had any such
power then, he has no such power now, and that leads
me to enquire into his more recent limitations.

I am to suppose, he and all his accomplices being
confounded at the discovery of the new creation, and
racking their wits to find out the meaning of it, had at

last (no matter how) discovered the whole system, and concluded as I have said, that the creature called man was to be their successor in the heavenly mansions ; upon which I suggest that the first motion of hell was to destroy this new work, and if possible to overwhelm it.

But when they came to make the attempt, they found their chains were not long enough, and that they could not reach to the extremes of the system : they had no power either to break the order, or stop the motion, dislocate the parts, or confound the situation of things ; they traversed, no doubt, the whole work, visited every star, landed upon every solid, and sailed upon every fluid upon the whole scheme, to see what mischief they could do.

Upon a long and full survey, they came to this point in their enquiry, that in short they could do nothing by force ; that they could not displace any part, annihilate any atom, or destroy any life in the whole creation, but that as omnipotence had created it so the same omnipotence had armed it at all points against the utmost power of hell, had made the smallest creature in it invulnerable as to Satan ; so that without the permission of the same power which had made heaven and conquered the Devil, he could do nothing at all, as to destroying any thing that God had made, no, not the little diminutive thing called Man, who Satan saw so much reason to hate, as being created to succeed him in happiness in heaven.

Satan found him placed out of his power to hurt, or out of his reach to touch ; and here, by the way, appears the second conquest of heaven over the Devil ; that having placed his rival, as it were, just before his face, and shewed the hateful sight to him, he saw written upon his image, Touch him if you dare.

It cannot be doubted, but, had it not been thus, man is so far from being a match for the Devil, that one of Satan's least imps or angels could destroy all the race of them in the world, ay, world and all in a moment.

As he is prince of the power of the air, taking the air for the elementary world, how easily could he, at one blast, sweep all the surface of the earth into the sea, or drive weighty immense surges of the ocean over the whole plain of the earth, and deluge the globe at once with a storm! or how easily could he, who by the situation of the empire must be supposed able to manage the clouds, draw them up in such a position as should naturally produce thunders and lightnings, cause those lightnings to blast the earth, dash in pieces all the buildings, burn all the populous towns and cities, and lay waste the world.

At the same time he might command suited quantities of sublimated air to burst out of the bowels of the earth, and overwhelm and swallow up, in the opening chasms, all the inhabitants of the globe!

In a word, Satan left to himself as a devil, and to the power which by virtue of his seraphic original he must be vested with, was able to have made devilish work in the world, if by a superior power he was not restrained.

But there is no doubt, at least to me, but that with his fall from heaven, as he lost the rectitude and glory of his angelic nature, I mean his innocency, so he lost the power too that he had before; and that when he first commenced Devil, he received the chains of restraint too, as the badge of his apostacy, viz. a general prohibition, to do anything to the prejudice of this creation, or to act any thing by force or violence without special permission.

This prohibition was not sent him by a messenger, or by an order in writing, or proclaimed from heaven by a law; but Satan by a strange invisible and unaccountable impression, felt the restraint within him; and at the same time that his moral capacity was not taken away, yet his power of exerting that capacity felt the restraint, and left him unable to do, even what he was able to do at the same time.

I make no question, but the Devil is sensible of this restraint, that is to say, not as it is a restraint only, or as an effect of his expulsion from heaven; but as it prevents his capital design against man, who, for the reason I have given already, he entertains a mortal hatred of, and would destroy with all his heart, if he might; and therefore, like a chained mastiff, we find him oftentimes making a horrid hellish clamour and noise, barking and howling, and frighting the people, letting them know, that if he was loose he would tear them in pieces; but at the same time his very fury shakes his chain, which lets them know, to their satisfaction, he can only bark, but cannot bite.

Some are of opinion that the devil is not restrained so much by the superior power of his sovereign and maker, but that all his milder measures with man are the effect of a political scheme, and done upon mature delibera. tion; that it was resolved to act thus in the great council or p——t of devils, called upon this very occasion, when the first were informed of the creation of man, and especially when they considered what kind of creature he was, and what might probably be the reason of making him, (viz.) to fill up the vacancies in heaven ; I say, that then the devils resolved, that it was not for their interest to fall upon him with fury and rage, and so destroy the species, for that this would be no benefit at all to them, and would only cause another original man to be created ; for that they knew God could, by the same omnipotence, form as many new species of creatures as he pleased ; and, if he thought fit, create them in heaven too, out of the reach of devils or evil spirits, and that therefore, to destroy man would no way answer their end.

On the other hand, examining strictly the mould of this new made creature, and of what materials he was formed, how mixt up of a nature convertible and pervertible, capable indeed of infinite excellence, and consequently of eternal felicity ; but subject likewise to corruption and degeneracy, and consequently to eternal misery : That instead of being fit to supply the places of Satan and his rejected tribe (the expelled angels) in heaven, and filling up the thrones or stalls in the celestial choir, they might, if they could but be brought into crime, become a race of rebels and traitors like the rest ; and so come at last to keep them company, as well in the place of eternal misery, as in the merit of it, and in a word, become devils instead of angels.

Upon this discovery, I say, they found it infinitely more for the interest of Satan's infernal kingdom, to go another way to work with mankind, and see if it were possible, by the strength of their infernal wit and counsels, to lay some snare for him, and by some stratagem to bring him to eternal ruin and misery.

5   P

Of the Devil's power at the time of the creation.

This being then approved as their only method, (and the Devil shewed he was no fool in the choice) he next resolved that there was no time to be lost; that it was to be set about immediately, before the race was multiplied, and by that means the work be not made greater only, but perhaps the more difficult too; accordingly the diligent Devil went instantly about it, agreeably to all the story of Eve and the Serpent, as before; the belief of which, whether historically or allegorically, is not at all obstructed by this hypothesis.

I do not affirm that this was the case at first, because being not present in that black divan, at least not that I know of, for who knows where he was or was not in his pre-existent state? I cannot be positive in the resolve that passed there: but except for some very little contradiction, which we find in the Sacred Writings, I should, I confess, incline to believe it historically: and I shall speak of those things which I call contradictions to it more largely hereafter.

In the mean time, be it one way or other, that is to say, either that Satan had no power to have proceeded with man by violence, and to have destroyed him as soon as he was made; or that he had the power, but chose rather to proceed by other methods to deceive and debauch him; I say, be it which you please, I am still of the opinion, that it really was not the Devil's business to destroy the species: that it would have been nothing to the purpose, and no advantage at all to him, if he had done it; for that, as above, God could immediately have created another species to the same end, whom he either could have made invulnerable, and not subject to the Devil's power, or removed him out of Satan's reach, placed him out of the Devil's ken, in heaven or some other place, where the Devil could not come to hurt him ; and that therefore it is infinitely his advantage, and more suited to his real design of defeating the end of man's creation, to debauch him and make a Devil of him, that he may be rejected like himself, and increase the infernal kingdom and company in the lake of misery in *æternum*.

It may be true, for aught I know, that Satan has not the power of destruction put into his hand, and that he cannot take away the life of a man : And it seems probable to be so, from the story of Satan and Job, when Satan appeared among the Sons of God, as the text says, Job i. 6. Now when God gave such a character of Job to him, and asked him, *if he had considered his servant Job*, ver. 8. Why did not the Devil go immediately and exert his malice against the good man at once, to let his maker see what would become of his servant Job in distress ? On the contrary, we see he only answers by shewing the reason of Job's good behaviour ; that it was but common gratitude for the blessing and protection he enjoyed, ver 10. and pleaded that if his estate was taken away, and he was exposed, as he (Satan) was, to be a beggar and a vagabond, going *to and fro in the earth, and walking up and down therein*, he should be a very devil too, like himself, and curse God to his face.

Upon this, the text says, that God answered, ver. 11. *Behold all that he hath is in thy power ;* now it is plain here, that God gave up Job's wealth and estate, nay his family, and the lives of his children and servants into the Devil's power ; and accordingly, like a true merci-

less Devil, as he is, he destroyed them all ; he moved
the Sabeans to fall upon the oxen and the asses, and
carry them off ; he moved the Chaldeans to fall upon
the camels and the servants, to carry off the first, and
murder the last; he made lightning flash upon the poor
sheep, and kill them all; and he blowed his house
down upon his poor children, and buried them all in
the ruins.

Now here is (1.) a specimen of Satan's good will to
mankind, and what havock the Devil would make in
the world, if he might; and here is a testimony too,
that he could not do this without leave ; so that I cannot but be of the opinon he has some limitations, some
bounds set to his natural fury : a certain number of
links in his chain, which he cannot exceed, or, in a
word, that he cannot go a foot beyond his tether.

The same kind of evidence we have in the gospel,
Matt. viii. 31. where Satan could not so much as possess the filthiest and meanest of all creatures, the
swine, till he had asked leave; and that still, to shew
his good will, as soon as he had gotten leave, he hurried them all into the sea, and choaked them; these, I
say, are some of the reasons why I am not willing to
say, the Devil is not restrained in power : But on the
other side, we are told of so many mischievous things
the Devil has done in the world, by virtue of his dominion over the elements, and by other testimonies of
his power, that I do not know what to think of it ;
though, upon the whole, the first is the safest opinion ;
for if we should believe the last, we might, for aught
I know, be brought like the American Indians, to
worship him at last, that he may do us no harm.

And now I have named these people in America, I
confess it would go a great way in favour of Satan's
generosity, as well as in testimony of his power, if we
might believe all the accounts which indeed authors
are pretty well agreed in the truth of, namely, of the
mischiefs the Devil does in those countries, where his
dominion seems to be established; how he uses them
when they deny him the homage he claims of them as
his due; what havock and combustion he makes among
them; and how beneficent he is (or at least negative
in his mischiefs) when they appease him by their hellish sacrifices.

Likewise we see a test of his wicked subtilty in his
management of those dark nations, when he was more
immediately worshipped by them; namely, the making
them believe that all their good weather, rains, dews,
and kind influences upon the earth, to make it fruitful,
was from him; whereas they really were the common
blessings of a higher hand, and came not from him, the
Devil, but from him that made the Devil, and made
him a Devil or a fallen angel by his curse.

But to go back to the method the Devil took with
the first of mankind; it is plain the policy of hell was
right, though the execution of the resolves they took
did not fully answer their ends neither: For Satan
fastening upon poor, proud, ridiculous mother Eve, as
I have said before, made presently a true judgment of
her capacities, and of her temper; took her by the
right handle, and soothing her vanity (which is to this
day the softest place in the head of all the sex) wheedled her out of her senses, by praising her beauty, and
promising to make her a goddess.

The foolish woman yielded presently; and that we
are told is the reason why the same method so strangely
takes with all her posterity, viz. that you are sure to prevail with them, if you can but once persuade them that
you believe they are witty and handsome; for the Devil,
you may observe, never quits any hold he gets, and having once found a way into the heart, always takes care
to keep the door open, that any of his agents may enter him without any more difficulty : Hence the same
argument, especially the last, has so bewitching an influence on the sex, that they rarely deny you any thing,
after they are but weak enough and vain enough to accept of the praises you offer them on that head ; on the
other hand, you are sure they never forgive you the unpardonable crime of saying they are ugly or disagreeable : It is suggested that the first method the Devil
took to insinuate all those things into Eve's giddy head
was by creeping close to her one night, when she was
asleep, and laying his mouth to her ear, whispering all
the fine things to her, which he knew would set her fancy a tip-toe, and so made her receive them involuntarily
into her mind ; knowing well enough that when she
had formed such ideas in her soul, however they came
there, she would never be quiet till she had worked
them up to some extraordinary thing or other.

It was evident what the Devil aimed at, namely, that
she should break in upon the command of God, and so
having corrupted herself, bring the curse upon herself
and all the race, as God had threatened.   But why the
pride of Eve should be so easily tickled by the mention
of her exquisite beauty, when there then was no prospect
of the use or want of those charms, that indeed makes a

kind of difficulty here, which the learned have not determined. For,

1. If she had been as ugly as the Devil, she had no body to rival her, so that she need not fear Adam should leave her and get another mistress.

2. If she had been bright and as beautiful as an angel, she had no other admirer but poor Adam, and he could have no room to be jealous of her, or afraid she should cuckold him ; so that in short, Eve had no such occasion for her beauty, nor could she make any use to a bad purpose or to a good ; and therefore I believe the Devil, who is too cunning to do any thing that signifies nothing, rather tempted her by the hope of encreasing her wit, than her beauty.

But to come back to the method of Satan's tempting her, viz. by whispering to her in her sleep, it was a cunning trick, that is the truth of it, and by that means he certainly set her head a madding after deism, and to be made a goddess, and than back'd it by the subtle talk he had with her afterward.

I am the more particular upon this part, because, however the Devil may have been the first that ever practised it, yet I can assure him the experiment has been tried upon many a woman since, to the wheedling her out of her modesty, as well as her simplicity ; and the cunning men tell us still, that if you can come at a woman when she is in a deep sleep, and whisper to her close to her ear, she will certainly dream of the thing you say to her ; and so will a man too.

Well, be this so to her race or not, it was it seems
so to her; for she waked with her head fill'd with plea-
sing ideas, and as some will have it, unlawful desires;
such, as to be sure she never had entertained before ;
These are supposed to be fatally infused in her dream,
and suggested to her waking soul, when the organ ear
which conveyed them was dozed and insensible ;
strange fate of sleeping in Paradise ! that whereas we
have notice but of two sleeps there, that in one a woman should go out of him, and in the other, the Devil should come into her.

Certainly, when Satan first made the attempt upon
Eve, he did not think he should have so easily conquered her, or have brought his business about so
soon; the Devil himself could not have imagined she
should have been so soon brought to forget the command given, or at least who gave it, and have ventured
to transgress against him, and made her forget that God
had told her, it should be death to her to touch it; and
above all, that she should aspire to be as wise as him,
who was so ignorant before, as to believe it was for
fear of her being like himself, that he had forbid it her.

Well might she be said to be the weaker vessel,
though Adam himself had little enough to say for his
being the stronger of the two, when he was over-per-
suaded (if it were done by persuasion) by his wife to
do the same thing.

And mark how wise they were after they had eaten,
and what fools they both acted like, even to one another ; nay, even all the knowledge they attained to, by
it, was, for ought I see, only to know that they were
fools, and to be sensible both of sin and shame; and see

how simply they acted, I say, upon their having committed the crime, and being detected in it.

> ' View them to day conversing with their God,
> ' His image both enjoy'd and understood,
> ' To morrow skulking with a sordid flight
> ' Among the bushes from the infinite,
> ' As if that power was blind which gave them sight ;
> ' With senseless labour tagging fig-leaf vests,
> ' To hide their bodies from the sight of beasts.
>   ' Hark ! how the fool pleads faint, for forfeit life,
> ' First he reproaches heaven, and then his wife :
> ' *The woman which thou gav'st*, as if the gift
> ' Could rob him of the little reason left ;
> ' A weak pretence to shift his early crime,
> ' As if accusing her would excuse him ;
> ' But thus encroaching crime dethrones the sense,
> ' And intercepts the heavenly influence,
> ' Debauches reason, makes the man a fool,
> ' And turns his active light to ridicule.'

It must be confessed that it was unaccountable degeneracy, even of their common reasoning, which Adam and Eve both fell into upon the first committing the offence of taking the forbidden fruit : If that was their being made as gods, it made but a poor appearance in its first coming, to hide their nakedness when there was no body to see them, and cover themselves among the bushes from their maker ; but thus it was, and this the Devil had brought them to ; and well might he, and all the clan of hell, as Mr. Milton brings them in, laugh and triumph over the man, after the blow was

given, as having so egregiously abused and deluded
them both.

But here, to be sure, began the Devil's new kingdom;
as he had now seduced the two first creatures, he was
pretty sure of success upon all the race, and therefore
prepared to attack them also, as soon as they came on ;
nor was their increasing multitude any discouragement
to his attempt, but just the contrary ; for he had agents
enough to employ, if every man and woman that should
be born was to want a Devil to wait upon them,
separately and singly to seduce them ; whereas some
whole nations have been such willing subjects to him,
that one of his seraphic imps may, for ought we know,
have been enough to guide a whole country ; the people
being entirely subjected to his government for many
ages ; as in America, for example, where some will have
it, that he conveyed the first inhabitants, at least if he
did not, we do not well know who did, or how they got
thither.

And how came all the communication to be so entirely cut off between the nations of Europe and Africa,
from whence America must certainly have been peopled,
or else the Devil must have done it indeed ? I say, how
came the communication to be so entirely cut off
between them, that except the time, whenever it was,
that people did at first reach from one to the other, none
ever came back to give their friends any account of their
success, or invite them to follow ? Nor did they hear
of one another afterwards, as we have reason to think.
Did Satan politically keep them thus asunder, lest news
from heaven should reach them, and so they should be
recovered out of his government ? We cannot tell how

to give any other rational account of it, that a nation, nay a quarter of the world, or as some will have it be, half the globe, should be peopled from Europe or Africa, or both, and no body ever go after them, or come back from them in above three thousand years after.

Nay, that those countries should be peopled when there was no navigation in use in these parts of the world, no ships made that could carry provisions enough to support the people that sailed in them, but that they must have been starved to death before they could reach the shore of America; the ferry from Europe or Africa, in any part (which we have known navigation to be practised in) being at least 1000 miles, and in most places much more.

But as to the Americans, let the Devil and they alone to account for their coming thither, this we are certain of, that we knew nothing of them for a many hundred years; and when we did, when the discovery was made, they that went from hence found Satan in a full and quiet possession of them, ruling them with an arbitrary government, particular to himself; he had led them into a blind subjection to himself, nay, I might call it devotion, (for it was all of religion that was to be found among them) worshipping horrible idols in his name, to whom he directed human sacrifices continually to be made, till he deluged the country with blood, and ripened them up for the destruction that followed, from the invasion of the Spaniards, who he knew would hurry them all out of the world as fast as he (the Devil) himself could desire of them.

But to go back a little to the original of things : It

is evident that Satan has made a much better market of mankind, by thus subtilly attacking them, and bringing them to break with their maker, as he had done before them, than he could have done by fulminating upon them at first, and sending them all out of the world at once ; for now he has peopled his own dominions with them ; and though a remnant are snatched as it were out of his clutches, by the agency of invincible grace, of which I am not to discourse in this place ; yet this may be said of the Devil, without offence, that he has in some sense carried his point, and as it were forced his maker to be satisfied with a part of mankind, and the least part too, instead of the great glory he would have brought to himself by keeping them all in his service.

Mr. Milton, as I have noted above, brings in the Devil and all hell with him, making a *feu de joye* for the victory Satan obtained over one silly woman ; indeed it was a piece of success greater in its consequence than in the immediate appearance ; nor was the conquest so complete as Satan himself imagined to make, since the promise of a redemption out of his hands, which was immediately made to the man, in behalf of himself and his believing posterity, was a great disappointment to Satan, and as it were snatched the best part of his victory out of his hands.

It is certain the devils knew what the meaning of that promise was, and who was to be the seed of the woman ; namely, the incarnate Son of God, and that it was a second blow to the whole infernal body ; but as if they had resolved to let that alone, Satan went on with his business ; and as he had introduced crime into the common parent of mankind, and thereby secured the contamination of blood, and the descent or propagation of the corrupt seed, he had nothing to do but to assist nature in time to come, to carry on its own rebellion, and act itself in the breasts of Eve's tainted posterity ; and that indeed has been the Devil's business ever since his first victory upon the kind, to this day.

His success in this part has been such, that we see upon innumerable occasions a general defection has followed ; a kind of a taint upon nature, call it what you will, a blast upon the race of mankind ; and were it not for one thing, he had ruined the whole family ; I say, were it not for one thing, namely, a selected company or number, which his maker had resolved he shall not be able to corrupt, or if he does, the sending the promised seed shall recover back again from him, by the power of irresistible grace; which number thus selected or elected, call it which we will, are still to supply the vacancies in heaven, which Satan's defection left open ; and what was before filled up with created seraphs, is now to be restored by recovered saints, by whom infinite glory is to accrue to the kingdom of the Redeemer.

This glorious establishment has robbed Satan of all the joy of his victory, and left him just where he was, defeated and disappointed ; nor does the possession of all the myriads of the sons of perdition, who yet, some are of the opinion, will be snatched from him too at last ; I say, the possession of all these makes no amends to him, for he is such a Devil in his nature, that the envy at those he cannot seduce, eats out all the satisfaction of the mischief he has done in seducing all the rest ; but I must not preach, so I return to things as much needful to know, though less solemn.

CHAPTER IX.

Of the progress of Satan in carrying on his con-
quest over mankind, from the fall of Eve to the
deluge.

Ⅱ DOUBT if the Devil was asked the question plainly,
he would confess that after he had conquered Eve by his
own wicked contrivance, and then by her assistance had
brought Adam too (like a fool as he was) into the same
gulph of misery, he thought he had done his work, com-
passed the whole race, that they were now his own, and
that he had put an end to the grand design of their
creation; namely, of peopling heaven with a new
angelic race of souls, who when glorified, should make
up the defection of the host of hell, that had been
expunged by their crime; in a word, that he had gotten
a better conquest than if he had destroyed them all.

But in the midst of his conquest, he found a check
put to the advantages he expected to reap from his
victory, by the immediate promise of grace to a part of
the posterity of Adam, who, notwithstanding the fall,
were to be purchased by the Messiah, and snatched out
of his (Satan's) hands, and over whom he could make
no final conquest; so that his power met with a new
limitation, and that such, as indeed fully disappointed
him in the main thing he aimed at, viz. preventing the
beatitudes of mankind, which were thus secured; (and
what if the numbers of mankind were upon this account
encreased in such a manner, that the selected number

should, by length of time, amount to just as many as the whole race, had they not fallen, would have amounted to in all ?) and thus, indeed, the world may be said to be upheld and continued for the sake of those few, since till their number can be completed, the creation cannot fall, any more than, that without them, or but for them it would not have stood.

But leaving this speculation, and not having enquired of Satan what he has to say on that subject, let us go back to the antediluvian world : The Devil, to be sure, gained his point upon Eve, and in her upon all her race : He drew her into sin ; got her turned out of paradise, and the man with her : The next thing was to go to work with her posterity, and particularly with her two sons Cain and Abel.

Adam having, notwithstanding his fall, repented very sincerely of his sin ; received the promise of redemption and pardon, with an humble but believing heart ; charity bids us suppose that he led a very religious and sober life ever after ; and especially in the first part of his time, that he brought up his children very soberly, and gave them all the necessary advantages of a religious education, and a good introduction into the world, that he was capable of ; and that Eve likewise assisted to both in her place and degree.

Their two eldest sons Cain and Abel ; the one heir apparent to the patriarchal empire, and the other heir presumptive, I suppose also, lived very sober and religious lives ; and as the principles of natural religion dictated a homage and subjection due to the almighty maker, as an acknowledgment of his mercies, and a recognition of their obedience ; so the received usage of

religion dictating at that time that this homage was to be
paid by a sacrifice, they either of them brought a free-
will offering to be dedicated to God respectively for
themselves and families.

How it was, and for what reason that God had respect
to the offering of Abel, which the learned say, was a
lamb of the firstlings of the flock, and did not give any
testimony of the like respect to Cain and his offering,
which was of the first fruits of the earth, the offerings
being equally suited to the respective employment of
the men, that is not my present business ; but this we
find made heart-burnings, and raised envy and jealousy
in the mind of Cain ; and at that door the Devil immediately entered ; for he, who from the beginning, was
very diligent in his way, never slipped any opportunity,
or missed any advantages that the circumstances of mankind offered him to do mischief.

What shape or appearance the Devil took up to enter
into a conversation with Cain upon the subject, that
authors do not take upon them to determine ; but it is
generally supposed he personated some of Cain's sons or
grandsons to begin the discourse, who attacked their
father, or perhaps grandfather, upon this occasion, in
the following manner, or to that purpose.

D. Sir, I perceive your majesty (for the first race
were certainly all monarchs as great as kings, to their
immediate posterity) to be greatly disturbed of late, your
countenance is changed, your noble chearfulness (the
glories of your face) are strangely sunk and gone, and
you are not the man you used to be ; please your majesty
to communicate your griefs to us your children, you may

be sure, that if it be possible, we would procure you relief, and restore your delights, the loss of which, if thus you go on to subject yourself to too much melancholy, will be very hurtful to you, and in the end destroy you.

Cain. It is very kind, my dear children, to shew your respect thus to your true progenitor, and to offer your assistance : I confess, as you say, my mind is oppressed and displeased ; but though 'tis very heavy, yet I know not which way to look for relief, for the distemper is above our reach, no cure can be found for it on earth.

D. Do not say so, sir ; there can be no disease sure on earth but may be cured on earth ; if it be a mental evil, we have heard that your great ancestor, the first father of us all, who lives still on the great western plains towards the sea, is the oracle to which all his children fly for direction in such cases as are out of the reach of the ordinary understanding of mankind ; please you to give leave, we will take a journey to him, and representing your case to him, we will hear his advice, and bring it to you with all speed, for the ease of your mind.

Cain. I know not whether he can reach my case or no.

D. Doubtless he may, and if not, the labour of our journey is nothing when placed in competition with the ease of your mind ; 'tis but a few days travel lost, and you will not be worse if we fail of the desired success.

Cain. The offer is filial, and I accept your affectionate concern for me, with a just sense of an obliged parent ; go then, and my blessing be upon you ; but alas ! why do I bless ? can he bless whom God has not blessed !

6   R

D. O ! sir, do not say so, has not God bless'd you ? are you not the second sovereign of the earth ? and does he not converse with you face to face ? are not you the oracle to all your growing posterity, and next after his sovereign imperial majesty lord Adam, patriarch of the world ?

Cain. But has not God rejected me, and refused to converse any more with me, while he daily favours and countenances my younger brother Abel, as if he resolved to set him up to rule over me ?

D. No, sir, that cannot be, you cannot be disturbed at such a thing ? is not the right of sovereignty yours by primogeniture ? can God himself take that away, when 'tis once given ? are you not lord Adam's eldest son ? are you not the first-born glory of the creation ? and does not the government descend to you by the divine right of birth and blood ?

Cain. But what does all that signify to me, while God appears to favour and caress my younger brother, and to shine upon him, while a black dejection and token of displeasure surrounds me every day, and he does not appear to me as he used to do ?

D. And what need your majesty be concern'd at that, if it be so ? if he does not appear pleased, you have the whole world to enjoy yourself in, and all your numerous and rising posterity adore and honour you ; what need those remote things be any disturbance to you ?

Cain. How ! my children, not the favour of God be valued ! Yes, yes, in his favour is life ; what can all the world avail without the smiles and countenance of him that made it ?

D. Doubtless, sir, he that made the world and placed you at the head of it all, to govern and direct it, has made it agreeable, and it is able to give you a full satisfaction and enjoyment, if you please to consider it well, though you were never to converse with him all the while you live in it.

Cain. You are quite wrong there, my children, quite wrong.

D. But do you not, great sir, see all your children as well as us, rejoicing in the plenty of all things, and are they not completely happy, and yet they know little of this great God? He seldom converses among us, we hear of him indeed by your sage advices, and we bring our offerings to you for him, as you direct, and when that is done, we enjoy whatever our hearts desire; and so doubtless may you in an abundant manner if you please.

Cain. But your felicity is wrong placed then, or you suppose that God is pleased and satisfied in that your offerings are brought to me; but what would you say, if you knew that God is displeased? that he does not accept your offerings? that when I sacrificed to him in behalf of you all, he rejected my offerings, though I brought a princely gift, being of the finest of the wheat, the choicest and earliest fruits, and the sweetest of the oil, an offering suited to the giver of them all?

D. But if you offered them, sir, how are you sure they were not accepted?

Cain. Yes, yes, I am sure; did not my brother Abel offer at the same time a lamb of his flock, for he, you know, delights in cattle, and covers the mountains with

his herds ? over him, all the while he was sacrificing, a
bright emanation shone chearing and enlivening ; a
pledge of favour, and light ambient flames played hovering in the lower air, as if attending his sacrifice ; and
when ready prepared, immediately descended and burnt
up the flesh, a sweet odoriferous savour ascending to
him, who thus testified his acceptance ; whereas, over
my head a black cloud, misty, and distilling vapour,
hung dripping upon the humble altar I had raised, and
wetting the finest and choicest things I had prepared,
spoiled and defaced them ; the wood unapt to burn by
the moisture which fell, scarce received the fire I
brought to kindle it, and even then, rather smothered
and choaked, than kindled into a flame ; in a word, it
went quite out, without consuming what was brought to
be offered up.

D. Let not our truly reverenced lord and father be
disquieted at all this ; if he accepts not what you bring,
you are discharged of the debt, and need bring no more ;
nor have the trouble of such laboured collections of rari-
ties any more ; when he thinks fit to require it again, you
will have notice, no question, and then it being called
for, will be accepted, or else why should it be required ?

Cain. That may indeed be the case, nor do I think of
attempting any more to bring an offering, for I rather
take it, that I am forbidden for the present ; but then
what is it that my younger brother triumphs in ? and
how am I insulted, in that he and his house are all joy
and triumph, as if they had some great advantage over
me, in that their offering was accepted when mine was
not ?

D. Does he triumph over your majesty, our lord and

sovereign ? give us but your order, and we will go and pull him and all his generation in pieces ; for to triumph over you who are his elder brother, is a horrid rebellion and treason, and he ought to be expelled the society of mankind.

Cain. I think so too, indeed ; however, my dear children and faithful subjects, though I accept your offer of duty and service, yet I will consider very well, before I take up arms against my brother ; besides, our sovereign father, and patriarchal lord, Adam, being yet alive, it is not in my right to act offensively without his command.

D. We are ready therefore to carry your petition to him, and doubt not to obtain his licence and commission too, to empower you to do yourself justice upon your younger brother ; who being your vassal, or at least inferior, as he is junior in birth, insults you upon the fancied opinion of having a larger share in the divine favour, and receiving a blessing on his sacrifices, on pretence of the same favour being denied you.

Cain. I am content, go then, and give a just account of the state of our affairs.

D. We shall soon return with the agreeable answer ; let not our lord and father continue sad and dejected, but depend upon a speedy relief, by the assistance of thy numerous issue, all devoted to thy interest and felicity.

Cain. My blessing be with you in your way, and give you a favourable reception at the venerable tent of our universal lord and father.

Note, here the cursed race being fully given up to the direction of the evil-spirit, which so early possess'd them, and swelling with rage at the innocent Abel and his whole family, they resolved upon forming a most wicked and detestable lie, to bring about the advice which they had already given their father Cain a touch of ; and to pretend that Adam being justly provok'd at the undutiful behaviour of Abel, had given Cain a commission to chastise him, and by force to cut him off and all his family, as guilty of rebellion and pride.

Fill'd with this mischievous and bloody resolution, they came back to their father Cain, after staying a few days, such as were sufficient to make Cain believe they had been at the spacious plains, were Adam dwelt ; the same which are now called the blessed valleys, or the plains of Mecca in Arabia Fælix, near the banks of the Red-sea.

Note here also, that Cain having received a wicked hint from these men, his children and subjects, as before, intimating that Abel had broken the laws of primogeniture in his behaviour towards him, (Cain) and that he might be justly punish'd for it ; Satan, that cunning manager of all our wayward passions, fann'd the fire of envy and jealousy with his utmost skill all the while his other agents were absent ; and by the time they came back had blown it up into such a heat of fury and rage, that it wanted nothing but air to make it burn out, as it soon afterwards did in a furious flame of wrath and revenge, even to blood and destruction.

Just in the very critical moment, while things stood thus with Cain, Satan brings in his wicked instruments, as if just arriv'd with the return of his message from Adam, at whose court they had been for orders ; and thus they, that is the Devil assuming to speak by them, approach their father with an air of solemn but chearful satisfaction at the success of their embassy.

D. Hail sovereign, reverend, patriarchal lord! we come with joy to render thee an account of the success of our message.

Cain. Have you then seen the venerable tents where dwell the heaven-born, the angelic pair, to whom all human reverence highly due, is and ought always to be humbly paid?

D. We have.

Cain. Did you, together with my grand request, a just, a humble homage for me pay, to the great sire and mother of mankind.

D. We did.

Cain. Did you in humble language represent the griefs and anguish which oppress my soul?

D. We did, and back their blessing to thee bring.

Cain. I hope with humblest signs of filial duty you took it for me on your bending knees?

D. We did, and had our share; the patriarch lifting his hands to heaven express'd his joy to see his spreading race, and bless'd us all.

Cain. Did you my solemn message to deliver, my injuries impartially lay down, and due assistance and direction crave?

D. We did.

Cain. What spoke the oracle? he's God to me; what just command d'ye bring, what's to be done? Am I to bear the insulting junior's rage? and meekly suffer what unjustly he, affronting primogeniture and laws of God and man, imposes by his pride unsufferable!

Am I to be crush'd, and be no more the first-born son on earth, but bow and kneel to him ?

D. Forbid it, heaven ! as Adam too forbids, who with a justice God-like and peculiar to injur'd parents, Abel's pride resents, and gives his high command to thee to punish.

Cain. To punish ? say you, did he use the word, the very word ? am I commissioned then to punish Abel ?

D. Not Abel only, but his rebel race, as they alike in crime alike are joined in punishment.

Cain. The race indeed have shared the merit with him ; how did they all insult, and with a shout of triumph mock my sorrow, when they saw me from my sacrifice dejected come, as if my disappointment was their joy ?

D. This too the venerable prince resents, and to preserve the race in bounds of laws subordinate and limited to duty, commands that this first breach be not passed by, lest the precedent upon record stand to future times to encourage like rebellion.

Cain. And is it then my sovereign parent's will ?

D. It is his will, that thou his eldest son, his image, his beloved, should be maintained in all the rights of sovereignty derived to thee from him : And not be left exposed to injury and power usurped, but should do thyself justice on the rebel race.

Cain. And so I will ; Abel shall quickly know what it is to trample on his elder brother ; shall know that he is thus sentenced by his father, and I am commissioned but to execute his high command, his sentence, which is God's, and that he falls by the hand of heavenly justice.

So now Satan had done his work, he had deluded the mother to a breach against the first and only command, he had drawn Adam to the same snare, and now he brings in Cain prompted by his own rage, and deluded by his (Satan's) craft, to commit murder, nay a fratricide, an aggravated murder.

Upon this he sends out Cain, while the bloody rage was in its ferment, and wickedly at the same time bringing Abel, innocent and fearing no ill, just in his way, he suggests to his thoughts such words as these :

Look you, Cain, see how divine justice concurs with your father's righteous sentence, see there's thy brother Abel directed by heaven to fall into thy hands unarmed, unguarded, that thou mayest do thyself justice upon him without fear ; see thou mayest kill him, and if thou hast a mind to conceal it, no eyes can see, or will the world ever know it, so that no resentment or revenge upon thee, or thy posterity, can be apprehended, but it may be said some wild beast had rent him ; nor will any one suggest that thou, his brother, and superior, could possibly be the person.

Cain prepared for the fact, by his former avowed rage and resolution of revenge, was so much the less prepared to avoid the snare thus artfully contrived by the master of all subtilty, the Devil ; so he immediately runs upon his brother Abel, and after a little unarmed resistance, the innocent poor man expecting no such mischief, was conquered and murdered ; after which, as is to be supposed, the exasperated crew of Cain's outrageous race, over-run all his family and household, killing man, woman and child.

It is objected here that we have no authority in Scrip-

6   S

ture to prove this part of the story; but I answer, 'tis not likely but that Abel, as well as Cain, being at man's estate long before this, had several children by their own sisters, for they were the only men in the world who were allowed the marrying their own sisters, there being no other women then in the world; and as we never read of any of Abel's posterity, 'tis likewise as probable they were all murdered, as that they should kill Abel only, whose sons might immediately fall upon Cain for the blood of their father, and so the world have been involved in a civil war as soon as there were two families in it.

But be it so or not, 'tis not doubted the Devil wrought with Cain in the horrid murder, or he had never done it; whether it was directly or by agents is not material, nor is the latter unlikely; and if the latter, then there is no improbability in the story, for why might not he that made use of the serpent to tempt Eve, be as well supposed to make a tool of some of Cain's sons or grandsons to prompt him in the wicked attempt of murdering his brother? and why must we be obliged to bring in a miracle or an apparition into the story, to make it probable that the Devil had any hand in it, when it was so natural to a degenerate race to act in such a manner?

However it was, and by whatever tool the Devil wrought, it is certain that this was the consequence, poor Abel was butchered, and thus the Devil made a second conquest in God's creation; for Adam was now, as may be said, really childless, for his two sons were thus far lost, Abel was killed, and Cain was curst and driven out from the presence of the Lord, and his race blasted with him.

It would be a useful enquiry here, and worthy our giving an account of, could we come to a certainty in it, namely, what was the mark that God set upon Cain, by which he was kept from being fallen upon by Abel's friends or relations? but as this does not belong to the Devil's history, and it was God's mark, not the Devil's, I have nothing to do with it here.

The Devil had now gained his point, the kingdom of grace, so newly erected, had been as it were extinct without a new creation, had not Adam and Eve been alive, and had not Eve, though now 130 years of age, been a breeding young lady, for we must suppose the women in that state of longevity, bare children till they were seven or eight hundred years old : This teeming of Eve peopled not the world so much as it restored the blessed race ; for though Abel was killed, Cain had a numerous offspring presently, which had Seth, (Adam's third son) never been born, would soon have replenished the world with people, such as they were ; the seed of a murderer, cursed of God, branded with a mark of infamy, and who afterwards fell all together in the universal ruin of the race by the deluge.

But after the murder of Abel, Adam had another son born, namely, Seth, the father of Enos, and indeed the father of the holy race ; for during his time and his son Enos, the text says that men began to call on the name of the Lord ; that is to say, they began to look back upon Cain and his wicked race, and being convinced of the wickedness they had committed, and led their whole posterity into, they began to sue to heaven for pardon of what was past, and to lead a new sort of life.

But the Devil had met with too much success in his

first attempts, not to go on with his general resolution of debauching the minds of men, and bringing them off from God ; and therefore as he kept his hold upon Cain's cursed race, embroiled already in blood and murder ; so he proceeded with his degenerate offspring, till in a word he brought both the holy seed and the degenerate race to join in one universal consent of crime, and to go on in it with such aggravating circumstances, as that it repented the Lord that he had made man, and he resolved to overwhelm them again with a general destruction, and clear the world of them.

The succession of blood in the royal original line of Adam, is preserved in the sacred histories, and brought down as low as Noah and his three sons, for a continued series of 1450 years, say some, 1640 say others ; in which time sin spread itself so generally through the whole race, and the sons of God, for so the Scripture calls the men of the righteous seed, the progeny of Seth, came in unto the daughters of men, that is, joined themselves to the cursed race of Cain, and married promiscuously with them, according to their fancies, the women it seems being beautiful and tempting ; and though the Devil could not make the women handsome or ugly in one or other families, yet he might work up the gust of wicked inclination on either side, so as to make both the men and women tempting and agreeable to one another, where they ought not to have been so ; and perhaps, as it is often seen to this day, the more tempting for being under legal restraint.

It is objected here, that we do not find in the Scripture that the men and women of either race were at that time forbidden intermarrying with one another ; and it is true, that literally it is not forbid ; but if we did not search rather to make doubts than to explain them, we might suppose it was forbidden by some particular command at that time ; seeing we may reasonably allow every thing to be forbidden, which they are taxed with a crime in committing ; and as the sons of God taking them wives as they thought fit to choose, though from among the daughters of the cursed race, is there charged upon them as a general depravation, and a great crime ; and for which, it is said, God even repented that he had made them, we need go no farther to satisfy ourselves that it was certainly forbidden.

Satan no doubt too had a hand in this wickedness ; for as it was his business to prompt men to do every thing which God had prohibited, so the reason given why the men of those days did this thing was, they saw the daughters of men, that is, of the wicked race or forbidden sort, were fair, he tempted them by the lust of the eye ; in a word, the ladies were beautiful and agreeable, and the Devil knew how to make use of the allurement ; the men liked and took them by the meer direction of their fancy and appetite ; without regarding the supreme prohibition ; They took them wives of all which they chose, or such as they liked to choose.

But the text adds, that this promiscuous generation went farther than the meer outward crime of it, for it shewed that the wickedness of the heart of man was great before God, and that he resented it : In short, God perceived a degeneracy or defect of virtue had seized upon the whole race, that there was a general corruption of manners, a depravity of nature upon them, that even the holy seed was tainted with it, that the

Devil had broken in upon them, and prevailed to a great degree ; that not only the practice of the age was corrupt, for that God could easily have restrained, but that the very heart of man was debauched, his desires wholly viciated, and his senses engaged in it ; so that in a word, it became necessary to shew the divine displeasure, not in the ordinary manner, by judgment and reproofs of such kind as usually reclaim men, but by a general destruction to sweep them away, clear the earth of them, and put an end to the wickedness at once, removing the offence and the offenders all together ; this is signified at large, Gen. vi. 5. *God saw that the wickedness of man was great in the earth, and that every imagination of the thoughts of his heart was only evil continually.* And again, ver. 11. 12. *The earth also was corrupt before God ; and the earth was filled with violence. And God looked upon the earth, and behold it was corrupt ; for all flesh had corrupted his way upon the earth.*

It must be confessed it was a strange conquest the Devil had made in the antediluvian world, that he had, as I may say, brought the whole race of mankind into a general revolt from God ; Noah was indeed a preacher of righteousness, and he had preached about 500 years to as little purpose as most of the good ministers ever did ; for we do not read there was one man converted by him, or at least not one of them left, for that at the deluge there was either none of them alive, or none spared but Noah and his three sons, and their wives ; and even they are (it is evident) recorded, not so much to be saved for their own goodness, but because they were his sons : Nay, without breach of charity we may conclude, that at least one went to the Devil even of those three, namely, Ham or Cham, for triumphing in a brutal manner over his father's drunkenness ; for we find the special curse reached to him and his posterity for many ages ; and whether it went no farther than the present state of life with them, we cannot tell.

We will suppose now, that through this whole 1500 years the Devil having so effectually debauched mankind, had advanced his infernal kingdom to a prodigious height ; for the text says, *the whole earth was filled with violence ;* in a word, blood, murder, rape, robbery, oppression, and injustice, prevailed every where ; and men, like the wild bear in the forest, lived by prey, biting and devouring one another.

At this time Noah begins to preach a new doctrine to them, for as he had before been a preacher of righteousness, now he becomes a preacher of vengeance ; first he tells them they shall be all overwhelmed with a deluge, that for their sins God repented they were made, and that he would destroy them all ; adding, that to prevent the ruin of himself and family, he resolved to build him a ship to have recourse to when the water should come over the rest of the world.

What jesting, what scorn, what contempt did this work expose the good old man to for above 100 years ? for so long the work was building, as ancient authors say : Let us represent to ourselves in the most lively manner how the witty world at that time behaved to poor old Noah ; how they took their evening walks to see what he was doing, and passed their judgment upon it, and upon the progress of it ; I say, to represent this to ourselves, we need go no further than to our own witti-

cisms upon religion, and upon the most solemn mysteries
of divine worship ; how we damn the serious for enthusiasts, think the grave mad, and the sober melancholy ;
call religion itself flatus and hyppo ; make the devout
ignorant, the divine mercenary, and the whole scheme
of divinity a frame of priestcraft ; and thus, no doubt,
the building an ark or boat, or whatever they called it,
to float over the mountains, and dance over the plains,
what could it be but a religious frenzy, and the man that
so busied himself, a lunatic ? And all this in an age when
divine things came by immediate revelation into the
minds of men ! The Devil must therefore have made a
strange conquest upon mankind, to obliterate all the reverence which but a little before was so strongly impressed
upon them concerning their maker.

This was certainly the height of the Devil's kingdom,
and we shall never find him arrive to such a pitch
again ; he was then truly and literally the universal
monarch, nay the god of this world ; and as all tyrants
do, he governs them with an arbitrary absolute sway ;
and had not God thought fit to give him a writ of eject-
ment, and afterwards drown him out of possession, I
know not what would have been the case, he might
have kept his hold for ought I know, till the seed of the
woman came to bruise his head, that is to say, cripple
his government, dethrone him, and depose his power, as
has been fulfilled in the Messiah.

But as he was, I say, drowned out of the world, his
kingdom for the present was at an end ; at least, if he had
a dominion he had no subjects, and as the creation was in
a manner renewed, so the Devil had all his work to do
over again : Unhappy man ! how has he, by his weak

resistance, made the Devil recovering his hold too easy to him, and given him all the advantages, except as before excepted, which he had before? Now whether he retired in the mean time, and how he got footing again after Noah and his family were landed upon the new surface, that we come next to enquire.

CHAPTER X.

Of the Devil's second kingdom, and how he got footing in the renewed world by his victory over Noah and his race.

THE story of Noah, his building the ark, his embarking himself and all nature's stock for a new world on board it; the long voyage they took, and the bad weather they met with, though it would embellish this work very well, and come in very much to the purpose in this place, yet as it does not belong to the Devil's story, for I cannot suggest (viz.) that he was in the ark among the rest, I say for that reason I must omit it.

And now having mentioned Satan's being in the ark; as I say, I cannot prove it, so there are, I think, some good reasons to believe he was not there: First, I know no business he had there; secondly, we read of no mischief done there, and these joined together make me conclude he was absent; the last I chiefly insist upon, that we read of no mischief done there, which if he had

T

been in the ark, would certainly have happened ; and therefore I suppose rather, that when he saw his kingdom dissolved, his subjects all ingulphed in an inevitable ruin and desolation, a sight suitable enough to him, except as it might unking him for a time : I say, when he saw this, he took care to speed himself away as well as he could, and make his retreat to a place of safety ; where that was, is no more difficult to us, than it was to him.

It is suggested that as he is prince of the power of the air, he retired only into that region. It is most rational to suppose he went no farther on many ac- counts, of which I shall speak by and by : Here he stayed hovering in the earth's atmosphere, as he has often done since, and perhaps now does ; or if the at- mosphere of this globe was affected by the indraft of the absorption, as some think, then he kept himself up- on the watch to see what the event of the new phæno- menon would be ; and this watch, wherever it was, I doubt not, was as near the earth as he could place him- self, perhaps in the atmosphere of the moon, or, in a word, the next place of retreat he could find.

From hence I took upon me to insist, that Satan has not a more certain knowledge of events than we; I say, he has not a more certain knowledge ; that he may be able to make stronger conjectures and more rational conclusions from what he sees, I will not deny ; and that which he most outdoes us in is, that he sees more to conclude from than we can ; but I am satisfied he knows nothing of futurity more than we can see by observa- tion and inference; nor, for example, did he know whe- ther God would re-people the world any more or no.

Of the Devil's second kingdom, and his victory over Noah.

I must therefore allow that he only waited to see what
would be the event of this strange eruption of water,
and what God proposed to do with the ark, and all
that was in it

Some philosophers tell us, besides what I hinted
above, that the Devil could have no retreat in the
earth's atmosphere, for that the air being wholly con-
densed into water, and having continually poured
down its streams to deluge the earth, that body was become so small, and had suffered such convulsions, that
there was but just enough air left to surround the water, or as might serve by its pressure to preserve the
natural position of things, and supply the creatures in
the ark with a part to breathe in.

The atmosphere indeed might suffer some strange
and unnatural motions at that time, but not, I believe,
to that degree ; however I will not affirm that there
could be room in it, or is now for the Devil, much less
for all the numberless legions of Satan's host ; but there
was, and now certainly is, sufficient space to receive
him, and a sufficient body of his troops for the business
he had for them at that time, and that is enough to the
purpose ; or if the earth's atmosphere did suffer any
particular convulsion on that occasion, he might make
his retreat to the atmosphere of the moon, or of Mars,
or of Venus, or of any of the other planets ; or to any
o ther place, for he that is prince of the air could not
want retreats in such a case, from whence he might
watch for the issue of things ; certainly he did not go
far, because his business lay here, and he never goes
out of his way of doing mischief.

In particular, his more than ordinary concern was, to

see what would become of the ark ; he was wise enough,
doubtless, to see that God, who had directed its making,
nay even the very structure of it, would certainly take
care of it, preserve it upon the water, and bring it to
some place of safety or other, though where it should be,
the Devil, with all his cunning, could not resolve whether on the same surface the waters drawing off, or in
any other created or to be created place; and this state
of uncertainty, being evidently his case, and which
proves his ignorance of futurity, it was his business, I
say, to watch with the utmost vigilance for the event.

If the ark was, as Mr. Burnet thinks, guided by two
angels, they not only held it from foundering or being
swallowed up in the water, but certainly kept the waters calm about it, especially when the Lord brought a
strong wind to blow over the whole globe, which by the
way was the first, and, I suppose, the only universal
storm that ever blew, for to be sure it blew over the
whole surface at once; I say, if it was then guided, to
be sure the Devil saw it, and that with envy and regret
that he could do it no injury, for doubtless had it been
in the Devil's power, as God had drowned the whole
race of man, except of what was in the ark, he would
have taken care to have dispatched them too, and so
made an end of the creation at once; but either he was
not empowered to go to the ark, or it was well guard-
ed by angels, that when he came near it he could do it
no harm : So it rested at length, the waters abating,
on the mountains of Arrarat in Armenia, or some
where else that way, and where they say a piece of
the keel is remaining to this day; of which, however,
with Dr. — I say, I believe not one word.

The ark being safe landed, it is reasonable to believe Noah prepared to go on shore, as the seamen call it, as soon as the dry land began to appear ; and here you must allow me to suppose Satan though himself clothed with a cloud, so as not to be seen, came immediately, and perching on the roof, saw all the heaven-kept houshold safely landed, and all the host of living creatures dispersing themselves down the sides of the mountain, as the search of their food or other proper occasions directed them.

This sight was enough ; Satan was at no loss to conclude from hence that the design of God was to repeople the world by the way of ordinary generation, from the posterity of these eight persons, without creating any new species.

Very well, says the Devil, then my advantage over them, by the snare I laid for poor Eve, is good still ; and I am now just where I was after Adam's expulsion from the garden, and when I had Cain and his race to go to work with ; for here is the old expunged corrupted race still, as Cain was the object then, so Noah is my man now ; and if I do not master him one way or another, I am mistaken in my mark. Pardon me for making a speech for the Devil.

Noah, big with a sense of his late condition, and while the wonders of the deluge were fresh in the mind, spent his first days in the extasies of his soul, giving thanks, and praising the power that had been his protection in and through the flood of waters, and which had in so miraculous a manner safely landed him on the surface of the newly discovered land ; and the text tells us, as one of the first things he was employed in, *He built*

*an altar unto the Lord, and offered burnt-offerings upon
the altar.* Gen. viii. 20.

While Noah was thus employed he was safe, the
Devil himself could no where break in upon him; and
we may suppose very reasonably, as he found the old
father invulnerable, he left him for some years, watching notwithstanding all possible advantages against
his sons and their children; for now the family began
to encrease, and Noah's sons had several children;
whether himself had any more children after the flood,
or not, that we are not arrived to any certainty about.

Among his sons the Devil found Japhet and Shem,
good, pious, religious, and very devout persons; serving God daily, after the example of their good old father Noah, and he could make nothing of them, or of
any of their posterity; but Ham the second, or according to some, the younger son of Noah, had a son who
was named Canaan, a loose young profligate fellow,
his education was probably but cursory and superficial,
his father Ham not being near so religious and serious
a man as his brothers Shem and Japhet were; and
as Canaan's education was defective, so he proved, as
untaught youth generally do, a wild, and in short, a
very wicked fellow, and consequently a fit tool for the
Devil to go work with.

Noah, a diligent industrious man, being with all his
family thus planted in the rich fruitful plains of Armenia
or wherever you please, let it be near the mountains of
Caucasus or Ararat; went immediately to work, cul-
tivating and improving the soil, encreasing his cattle and
pastures, sowing corn, and among other things planted
trees for food, and among the fruit-trees he planted

vines, of the grapes thereof he made no doubt, as they still in the same country do make, most excellent wine, rich, luscious, strong, and pleasant.

I cannot come into the notion of our critics, who to excuse Noah from the guilt of what followed, or at least from the censure, tell us, he knew not the strength or the nature of wine, but that gathering the heavy clusters of the grapes, and their own weight crushing out their balmy juices into his hand, he tasted the tempting liquor, and that the Devil assisting he was charmed with the delicious fragrance, and tasted again and again, pressing it out in a bowl or dish, that he might take a larger quantity; till at length the heady froth ascended and seized his brain, he became intoxicate and drunk, not in the least imagining there was any such strength in the juice of that excellent fruit.

But to make out this story, which is indeed very favourable for Noah, but in itself extremely ridiculous, you must necessarily fall into some absurdities, and beg the question most egregiously in some particular cases, which way of arguing will by no means suppose what is suggested; at first you must suppose there was no such thing as wine made before the deluge, and that no body had ever been made drunk with the juice of the grape before Noah, which, I say, is begging the question in the grossest manner.

If the contrary is true, as I see no reason to question, if, I say, it was true that there was wine drank, and that men were or had been drunk with it before, they cannot then but suppose that Noah, who was a wise, a great and a good man, and a preacher of righteousness, both knew of it, and without doubt had in his preaching against their crimes, preached against this among the rest, upbraided them with it, reproved them for it, and exhorted them against it.

Again, it is highly probable they had grapes growing, and consequently wines made for them, in the antediluvian world, how else did Noah come by the vines which he planted? For we are to suppose, he could plant no trees or shrubs, but such as he found the roots of in the earth, and which no doubt had been there before in their highest perfection, and had consequently grown up and brought forth the same luscious fruit before

Besides as he found the roots of the vines, so he understood what they were, and what fruit they bore, or else it may be supposed also he would not have planted them; for he planted them for their fruit, as he did it in the provision of his family; and if he did not know what they were, he would not have set them, for he was not planting for diversion but for profit.

Upon the whole itseems plain to me he knew what he did, as well when he planted the vines as when he pressed out the grapes ; and also when he drank the juice, that he knew it was wine, was strong and would make him drunk if he took enough of it : He knew that other men had been druuk with such liquor before the flood, and that he had reprehended them for it; and therefore it was not his ignorance, but the Devil took him at some advantage when his appetite was eager, or he thirsty, and the liquor cooling and pleasant; and in short, as Eve said, the Serpent beguiled her, and she did eat, so the Devil beguiled Noah, and he did drink; the temptation was too strong for Noah, not the wine;

he knew well enough what he did, but as the drunk-
ards say to this day, it was so good he could not forbear it, and so he got drunk before he was aware; or
as our ordinary speech expresses it, he was overtaken
with drink; and Mr. Pool and other expositors are
partly of the same mind.

No sooner was the poor old man conquered, and the
wine had lightened his head, but it may be supposed he
falls off from the chair or bench where he sat, and
tumbling backward, his clothes, which in those hot
countries were only loose open robes, like the vests
which the Armenians wear to this day, flying abroad, or
the Devil so assisting on purpose to expose him, he lay
there in a naked indecent posture not fit to be seen.

In this juncture who should come by but young Canaan, say some; or as others think, this young fellow
first attacked him by way of kindness and pretended
affection; prompted his grandfather to drink, on pretence of the wine being good for him, and proper for the
support of his old age, and subtilly set upon him, drinking also with him, and so, his head being too strong
for the old man's, drank him down, and then, Devil like,
triumphed over him: boasted of his conquest, insulted
the body as it were dead, and uncovered him on purpose to expose him, and leaving him in that indecent
posture, went and made sport with it to his father Ham,
who in that part, wicked like himself, did the same to
his brethren Japhet and Shem; but they like modes
and good men, far from carrying on the wicked insult
on their parent, went and covered him, as the scripture expresses it, and as may be supposed informed
him how he had been abused, and by whom.

7 U

Why else should Noah, when he came to himself, shew his resentment so much against Canaan his grandson, rather than against Ham his father, and who it is supposed in the story the guilt chiefly lay upon? we see the curse is, as it were, laid wholly upon Canaan the grandson, and not a word of the father is mentioned, Gen. ix. 25, 26, 27. *Cursed be Canaan, a servant of servants shall he be,* &c.

That Ham was guilty, that is certain from the history of fact, but I cannot suppose his grandson was the occasion of it; and in this case the Devil seems to have made Canaan the instrument or tool to delude Noah, and draw him into drunkenness, as he made the serpent the tool to beguile Eve, and draw her into obedience.

Possibly Canaan might do it without deisgn at first, but might be brought into ridicule and make a jest of the old patriarch afterward, as is too frequent since in the praetice of our days; but I rather believe he did it really with a wicked design, and on purpose to expose and insult his reverend old parent; and this seems more likely too, because of the great bitterness with which Noah resented it, after he came to be informed of it.

But be that as it will, the Devil certainly made a great conquest here, and as to outward appearance no less than that which he gained before over Adam; nor did the Devil's victory consist barely in his having drawn in the only righteous man of the whole antediluvian world, and so beginning or initiating the new young progeny with a crime; but here was the great oracle silenced at once; the preacher of righteousness, for such no doubt he would have been to the new world, as he was to the old, I say, the preacher was turned out of office, or his

mouth stopt, which was worse ; nay, it was a stopping
of his mouth in the worst kind, far worse than stopping
his breath, for had he died, the office had descended to
his sons Shem and Japhet, but he was dead to the office
of an instructor, though alive as to his being; for of
what force could his preachings be, who had thus fallen
himself into the most shameful and beastly excess ?

Besides some are of the opinion, though I hope without ground, that Noah was not only overtaken once in
his drink, but that being fallen into that sin it became
habitual, and he continned in it a great while, and that
it was this which was the meaning of his being uncovered in his tent, and that his son saw his nakedness; that
is, he continually exposed himself for a long time, a
hundred years, say they, and that his son Ham, and his
grandson Canaan having drawn him into it, kept him
in it, encouraged and prompted it, and all the while
Satan still prompting them, joined their scoffs and con_
tempt of him, with their wicked endeavours to promote
the wickedness ; and both with as much success as the
Devil himself could wish for.

Then as for his two sons modestly and decently covering their father, they tell us, that represents Shem
and Japhet applying themselves in an humble and du-
tiful manner to their father, to entreat and beseech him
to consider the antient glory, his own pious exhorta-
tions to the late drowned world, and to consider the
offence which he gave by his evil courses of God, and
the scandal to his whole family, and also that they are
brought in effectually prevailing upon him ; and that
then Noah cursed the wickedness of Ham's degenerate
race, in testimony of his sincere repentance after the fact.

The story is not so very likely as it is cert ain that it is not to be proved, and therefore we had better tak^e it as we find it, viz, for one single act; but suppose it was so, it is still certain that Noah's preaching was sadly interrupted, the energy of his words flatted, and the force of his persuasions enervated and abated, by this shame. ful fall; that he was effectually silenced for an in-structor ever after, and this was as much as the Devil had occasion for; and therefore indeed we read little more of him, except that he lived three hundred and fifty years after the flood; nay, we do not so much as read that he had any more children, but the contrary; nor in-deed could Noah have any more children, except by his old and perhaps super-annuated wife, who it was very likely he had had four or five hundred years, unless you will suppose he was allowed to marry some of his own progeny, daughters or grand-daughters which we do not suppose was allowed, no not to Adam himself.

This was certainly a master-piece of the Devil's po-licy, and a fatal instance of his unhappy diligence, viz. that the door of the ark was no sooner open, and the face of the world hardly dry from the universal destruction of mankind but he was at work among them; and that not only to form a general defection among the race, upon the foot of the original taint of nature, but like a bold Devil he strikes at the very root, and flies at the next general representative of mankind, attacks the head of the family, that in his miscarriage the rise and progress of a reformation of the new world should receive an early check, and should be at once prevented; I say like a bold Devil, he strikes at the root, but alas! poor un-happy Noah, he proved too weak for him, Satan prevailed in his very first attempt, and got the victory over him at once.

Noah thus overcome at Satan's conquest carried on to the utmost of his own wishes, the Devil had little more to do in the world for some ages, than to carry on an universal degeneracy among mankind, and to finish it by a like diligent application, in deluding the generality of the race, and them as they came on gradually into life; this he found the less difficult, because of the first defection which spread like a contagion upon the earth immediately after.

The first evidence we have of his success in this mischievous design, was in the building that great stupendous staircase, for such it seems it was intended, called Babel, which, if the whole world had not been drunk or otherwise infatuated, they would never have undertaken; even Satan himself could never have prevailed with them to undertake such a preposterous piece of work, for it had neither end nor means, possibility or probability in it.

I must confess I am sometimes apt to vindicate our old ancestors, in my thoughts, from the charge itself, as we generally understand it, namely that they really designed to build a tower which should reach up to heaven, or that it should secure them in case of another flood; and father Casaubon is of my opinion, whether I am of his or no, is a question by itself; his opinion is that the confusion was nothing but a breach among the undertakers and directors of the work, and that the buiding was designed chiefly for a store-house for provisions, in case of a second deluge; as to their notion of its reaching up to heaven, he takes the expression to be allegorical

rather than literal, and only to mean that it should be
exceeding high; perhaps they might not be astronomers
enough to measure the distance of space between the
earth and heaven, as we pretend to do now; but as Noah
was then alive, and as we believe all his three sons were
so too, they were able to have informed them how absurd
it was to suppose either the one or the other, viz.(1.)
that they could build up to heaven, or (2.) that they
could build firm enough to resist, or high enough to
overtop the waters, supposing such another flood should
happen; I would rather think it was only that they intended to build a most glorious and magnificent city,
where they might all inhabit together; and that this
tower was to be built for ornament and also for strength,
or as above, and for a store-house to lay up vast maga-
zines of provisions, in case of extraordinary floods or
other events, the city being built in a great plain, namely, the plains of Shimar, near the river Euphrates.

But the story, as it is recorded, suits better with
Satan's measures at that time; and as he was from the
beginning prompting them to every thing that was contrary to the happiness of man, so the more preposterous
it was, and the more inconsistent with common sense,
the more to his purpose; and it shewed the more what
a complete conquest he had gained over the reason as
well as the religion of mankind at that time.

Again, it is evident in this case, they were not only
acting contrary to the nature of things, but contrary to
the design and to the command of heaven ; for God's
command was that they should replenish the earth, that
is, that they should spread their habitations over it, and
people the whole globe; whereas they were pitching in

one place, as if they were not to multiply sufficient to take up any more.

But what cared the Devil for that, or to put it a little handsomer, that was what Satan aimed at; for it was enough for him, to bring mankind to act just contrary to what heaven had directed or commanded them in any thing, and if possible in every thing.

But God himself put a stop to this foolish piece of work, and it was time indeed to do so, for a madder thing the Devil himself never proposed to them; I say, God himself put a stop to this new undertaking, and disappointed the Devil; and how was it done? not in judgement and anger, as perhaps the Devil expected and hoped for, but as pitying the simplicity of that dreaming creature man, he confused their speech, or as some say, divided and confused their councils, so that they could not agree with one another, whtch would be the same thing as not to understand one another; or the put a new shibboleth upon their tongues, thereby separating them into tribes or families, for by this every family found themselves under a necessity of keeping together, and this naturally increased that differing jargons of language, for at first it might be no more.

What a confusion this was to them we all know, by their being obliged to leave off their building, and immediately separating one from another; but what a surprise it was to the old Serpent, that remains to be considered of, for indeed it belongs to his history.

Satan had never met with any disappointment in all his wicked attempts till now; for first, he succeeded even to triumph upon Eve, he did the like upon Cain, and in short upon the whole world, one man (Noah) excepted ; when he blended the sons of God, and the daughters of hell, for so the word is understood, together, in promiscuous voluptuous living as well as generation.

As to the deluge, authors are not agreed whether it was a disappointment to the Devil or no, it might be indeed a surprize to him, for though Noah had preached of it for a hundred years together, yet as he (Satan) daily prompted the people not to heed or believe what that old fellow Noah said to them, and to ridicule his whimsical building a monstrous tub to swim or float in, when the said deluge should come ; so I am of the opinion he did not believe it himself, and am positive he could not foresee it, by any insight into futurity that he was master of.

'Tis true the astronomers tell us, there was a very terrible comet seen in the air, that it appeared for 180 days before the flood continually ; and that as it approached nearer and nearer every day all the while, so that at last it burst and fell down in a continual spout or stream of water, being of a watery substance, and the quantity so great, that it was forty days a falling ; so that this comet not only foretold the deluge or drowning of the earth, but actually performed it, and drowned it from himself.

But to leave this tale to them that told it, let us consider the Devil, surprised, and a little amazed at the absorption or inundation, or whatever we are to call it, of the earth, in the deluge, not, I say, that he was much concerned at it, perhaps just the contrary ; and if God would drown it again, and as often as he thought fit, I do not see by any thing I meet with in Satan's history,

or in the nature of him, that he would be at all disturbed at it : all that I can see in it, that could give Satan
any concern, would be that all his favourites were gone,
and he had his work to do over again, to lay a foundation for a new conquest in the generation that was
to come; but in this his prospect was fair enough, for
why should he be discouraged, when he had now eight
people to work upon, who met with such success when
he had but two ? and why should he question breaking
in now where nature was already vitiated and corrupted, when he had before conquered the same nature,
when in its primitive rectitude and purity, just come
out of the hands of its maker, and fortified with the awe
of its high and solemn command just given them, and
the threatening of death also annexed to it, if broken?

But I go back to the affair of Babel : This confusion
of language or of councils, take it which way you will,
is the first disappointment that I find the Devil met
with, in all his attempts and practices upon mankind,
or upon the new creature, which I mentioned above :
For now he foresaw what would follow ; namely, that
the people would separate and spread themselves over
the whole surface of the earth, and a thousand new
scenes of actions would appear, in which he therefore
prepares himself to behave as he should see occasion.

How the Devil learned to speak all the languages that
were now to be used, and how many languages they were
the several ancient writers of the devil's story have not
yet determined ; some tell us they were divided only into fifteen, some into seventy-two, others into one hundred
and eighty, and others again into several thousands.

It also remains a doubt with me, and, I suppose, will

7   X

be so with others also, whether Satan has yet found out
a method to converse with mankind, without the help of
language and words, or not; seeing man has no other
medium of conversing, no not with himself: This I
have not time to enter upon here; however this seems
plain to me, viz. that the Devil soon learned to make
mankind understand him, whatever language he spoke,
and no doubt but he found ways and means to understand them, whatever language they spoke.

After the confusion of languages, the people necessarily sorted themselves into families and tribes, every
family understanding their own particular speech, and
that only; and these families multiplying, grew into
nations, and those nations wanting room, and seeking
out habitations wandering some this way, some that,
till they found out countries respectively proper for
their settling, and there they became a kingdom,
spreading and possessing still more and more land as
their people encreased, till at last the whole earth was
scarce big enough for them: This presented Satan with
an opportunity to break in upon their morals at another
door, viz. their pride; for men being naturally proud
and envious, nations and tribes began to jostle with one
another for room; either one nation enjoyed better ac-
commodations, or had a better soil or a more favorable
climate than another; and these being numerous and
strong thrust the other out, and encroached upon their
land; the other liking their situation, prepare for
their defence, and so began oppression, invasion, war,
battle, and blood, Satan all the while beating the
drums, and his attendants clapping their hands as
men do when they set dogs on upon one another.

The bringing mankind thus to war and confusion, as
it was the first game the Devil played after the con-
founding of languages and divisions at Babel, so it was
a conquest upon mankind, purely devilish, born from
hell and so exactly tinctured with Satan's original sin
ambition, that it really transformed men into mere
devils; for when is man transformed into the very
image of Satan himself, when is he turned into a mere
Devil, if it is not when he is fighting with his fellow
creatures and dipping his hands in the blood of his
own kind? Let his picture be considered, the fire of
hell flames or sparkles in his eyes, a voracious grin sits
upon his countenance; rage and fury distort the mus-
cles of his face; his passions agitate his whole body,
and he is metamorphosed from a comely beauteous angelic creature, into a future, a satyr, a terrible and
frightful monster, nay, into a Devil; for Satan himself is described by the same word which on his very
account is changed into a substantive, and the devils
are called Furies.

This sowing the seeds of strife in the world, and
bringing nations to fight and make war upon one another, would take up a great part of the Devil's history,
and abundance of extraordinary things would occur in
relating the particulars; for there have been very great
conflagrations kindled in the world, by the artifice of
hell, under this head, viz. of making war; in which it
has been the Devil's master-piece, and he has indeed
shewn himself a workman in it, that he has wheedled
mankind into strange unnatural notions of things, in
order to propagate and support the fighting principle in
the world; such as laws of war, fair fighting, behaving

like men of honour, fighting at the last drop, and the like, by which killing and murdering is understood to be justifiable. Virtue and a true greatness in spirit is rated now by rules which God never appointed, and the standard of honour is quite different from that of reason and of nature : Bravery is denominated not from a fearless undaunted spirit in the just defence of life and liberty, but from a daring defiance of God and man, fighting, killing and treading under foot his fellow creatures, at the ordinary command of the officer, whether it be right or wrong, and whether it be in a just defence of life, and our country's life, that is liberty, or whether it be for the support of injury and oppression.

A prudent avoiding causeless quarrels is called cowardice, and to take an affront, baseness and meanness of spirit ; to refuse fighting, and putting life at a cast on the point of a sword, a practice forbid by the laws of God and of all good government, is yet called cowardice ; and a man is bound to die duelling, or live and be laughed at.

This trumping up these imaginary things called bravery and gallantry, naming them virtue and honour, is all from the devil's new management, and his subtle influencing the minds of men to fly in the face of God and nature, and to act against their senses; nor but for his artifice in the management, could it be possible that such inconsistencies could go down with mankind, or they could pass such absurd things among them, for reasoning ; for example, A is found in bed with B's wife, B is the person injured, and therefore offended, and coming into the chamber with his sword in his hand, A exclaims loudly, Why sir, you won't murder me will you ? as you are a man of honour let me rise and take my sword.

A very good story indeed! fit for no body but the Devil to put into any man's head ; but so it is, B being put in mind, forsooth, thst he is a man of honour, starts back and must act the honourable part ; so he lets A get up, put on his clothes, and take his sword ; then they fight, and B is killed for his honour ; whereas had the laws of God, of nature and of reason taken place, the adulterer and the adulteress should have been taken prisoners and carried before the judge, and being taken in the fact, should have been immediately sentenced, he to the block, and she to the stake, and the innocent abused husband had no reason to have run any risk of his life for being made a cuckold.

But thus has Satan abused the reason of man ; and if a man does me the greatest injury in the world, I must do myself justice upon him, by venturing my life upon an even lay with him, and must fight him upon equal hazard, in which the injured person is as often killed as the person offering the injury : Suppose now it be in the same case as above, a man abuses my wife, and then to give me satisfaction, tells me, he will fight me, which the French call doing me reason ; No, sir, say I, let me lie with your wife too, and then if you desire it, I may fight you ; then I am upon even terms with you ; but this indeed is the reasoning which the Devil has brought mankind to at this day : But to go back to the subject, viz. the Devil bringing the nations to fall out, and to quarrel for room in the world, and so to fight in order to dispossess one another of their settlements : This began at a time when certainly there were places enough in the

world to choose in, and therefore the Devil, not the
want of elbow room, must be the occasion of it; and
it is carried on ever since, as apparently from the
same interest, and by the same original.

But we shall meet with this part again very often
in the Devil's story, and as we bring him farther on
in the management of mankind; I therefore lay it by
for the present, and come to the next steps the Devil
took with mankind after the confusion of languges,
and this was in the affair of worship: It does not appear yet, that ever the Devil was so bold, as either,

1. To set himself up to be worshipped as a god, or
   which was still worse,
2. To persuade man to believe there was no God at
   all to worship.

Both these are introduced since the deluge, one indeed by the Devil, who soon found means to set himself up for a god in many parts of the world, and holds
it to this day; but the last is brought in by the invention of man, in which it must be confessed man has
out-sinned the Devil; for to do Satan justice, he never
thought it could ever pass upon mankind, or that any
thing so gross would go down with them; so that, in
short, these modern casuists, in the reach of our days,
have, I say, out-sinned the Devil.

As then both these are modern inventions, Satan went
on gradually, and being to work upon human nature by
stratagem, not by force, it would have been too gross
to have set himself up as an object of worship, at first,
it was to be done step by step; for example.

Of the Devil's second kingdom, and his victory over Noah.

1. It was sufficient to bring mankind to a neglect
of God, to worship him by halves, and give little
or no regard to his laws, and so grow loose and
immoral, in direct contradiction to his commands;
this would not go down with them at first, so the
Devil went on gradually.

2. From a negligence in worshipping the true God,
he by degrees introduced the worship of false gods;
and to introduce this he began with the sun, moon,
and stars, called in the holy text, The host of heaven; these had greater majesty upon them, and
seemed fitter to command the homage of mankind;
so it was not the hardest thing in the world to bring
men, when they had once forgotten the true God,
to embrace the worship of such gods as those.

3. Having thus debauched their principles in worship
and led them from the true and only object of worship to a false, it was the easier to carry them on;
so in a few gradations more he brought them to
downright idolatry, and even in that idolatry he proceeded gradually too; for he began with awful
names, such as were venerable in the thoughts of
men, as Baal or Bell, which, in Chaldaic and He-
brew, signifies lord or sovereign, or mighty and
magnificent, and this was therefore a name ascrib-
ed at first to the true God; but afterwards they descended to make images and figures to represent him
and then they were called by the same name, as
Baal, Baalim, and afterwards Bell; from which, by
a hellish degeneracy, Satan brought mankind to

adore every block of their own hewing, and to
worshipping stocks, stones, monsters, hobgoblins,
and every sordid frightful thing, and at last the
Devil himself.

What notions some people may entertain of the for-
wardness of the first ages of the world, to run into idolatry, I do not enquire here; I know they tell us strange
things of its being the product of mere nature, one
remove from its primitive state; but I, who pretend to
have so critically enquired into Satan's history, can
assure you, and that from very good authority, that
the Devil did not find it so easy a task to obliterate
the knowledge of the true God, in the minds and consciences of men, as those people suggest.

It is true he carried things a great length under the
patriarchal government of the first ages, but still he was
sixteen hundred years bringing it to pass; and though
we have reason to believe the old world, before the
flood, was arrived to a very great height of wickedness,
and Ovid very nobly describes it by the war of the Ti-
tians against Jupiter, yet we do not read that ever Satan was come to such a length as to bring them to idolatry: indeed, we do read of wars carried on among
them, whether it was one nation against another, or only
personal, we cannot tell; but the world seemed to be
swallowed up in a life of wickedness, that is to say, of
luxury and lewdness, rapine and violence, and there
were giants among them, and men of renown, that is to
say, men famed for their mighty valour, great actions of
war we may suppose, and their strength, who personally
opposed others. We read of no considerable wars in-

deed, but it is not to be doubted but there was such wars, or else it is to be understood that they lived (in common) a life somewhat like the brutes, the strong devouring the weak ; for the text says, *the whole earth was filled with violence,* hunting and tearing one another in pieces, either for dominion or for wealth, either for ambition or for avarice, we know not well which.

Thus far the old antediluvian world went, and very wicked they were, there is no doubt of that ; but we have reason to believe that was no idolatry, the Devil had not brought them to that length yet ; perhaps it would soon have followed, but the deluge intervened.

After the deluge, as I have said, he had all his work to do over again, and he went on by the same steps ; first he brought them to violence and war, then to oppression and tyranny, then to neglect of true worship, then to false worship, and then idolatry by the meer natural consequence of the thing : Who were the first nation or people that fell from the worship of the true God, is something hard to determine ; the Devil, who certainly of all God's creatures is best able to inform us, having left us nothing upon record upon that subject, but we have reason to believe it was thus introduced.

Nimrod was the grandson of Ham, Noah's second son, the same who was cursed by his father for exposing him in his drunkenness : This Nimrod was the first who it seems Satan picked out for a hero : Here he inspired him with ambitious thoughts, dreams of empire, and having the government of all the rest, that is to say, universal monarchy ; the very same bait with which he has played upon the frailty of princes, and ensnared the greatest of them ever since, even from his most august

8   Y

imperial majesty king Nimrod the first, to his most christian majesty Louis XIV. and many a mighty monarch between.

When these mighty monarchs and men of fame went off the stage, the world had their memories in esteem many ages after ; and as their great actions were no otherwise recorded than by oral tradition, and the tongues and memories of fallible men, time and the custom of magnifying the past actions of kings, men soon fabled up their histories, Satan assisting, into miracle and wonder : Hence their names were had in veneration more and more ; statues and bustoes representing their persons and great actions were set up in public places, till from heroes and champions, they made gods of them ; and thus (Satan prompting) the world was quickly filled with idols.

This Nimrod is he, who according to the received opinion, though I do not find Satan's history exactly concurring with it, was first called Belus, then Baal, and worshipped in most of the Eastern countries under those names ; sometimes with additions of sir-names, according to the several countries, or people, or towns where he was particularly set up, as Baal Peor, Baal Zephon, Baal Phegor, and in other places plain Baal, as Jupiter in after times had the like additions ; as Jupiter Ammon, Jupiter Capitolinus, Jupiter Pistor, Jupiter Feretrius, and about ten or twelve Jupiters more.

I must acknowledge, that I think it was a masterpiece of hell to bring the world to idolatry so soon after they had had such an eminent example of the infinite power of the true God, as was seen in the deluge, and particularly in the escape of Noah in the ark, to bring them (even before Noah or his sons were dead) to forget whose hand it was, and give the homage of the world to a name, and that a name of a mortal man dead and rotten, who was famous for nothing when he was alive but blood and war; I say, to bring the world to set up this nothing, this meer name, nay the very image and picture of him, for a god, it was first a mark of most prodigious stupidity in the whole race of men, a monstrous degeneracy from nature, and even from common sense; and in the next place it was a token of an inexpressible craft and subtilty in the Devil, who had now gotten the people into so full and complete a management, that in short, he could have brought them, by the same rule, to have worshipped any thing; and in a little while more, did bring many of them to worship himself, plain Devil as he was, and knowing him to be such.

As to the antiquities of this horrible defection of mankind, though we do not find the beginning of it particularly recorded, yet we are certain it was not long after the confusion of Babel; for Nimrod, as is said, was no more than Noah's great-grandson, and Noah himself, I suppose, might be alive some years after Nimrod was born; and as Nimrod was not long dead, before they forgot that he was a tyrant and a murderer, and made a Baal, that is a lord or idol of him, I say, he was not long dead, for Nimrod was born in the year of the world 1847, and built Babylon in the year 1879; and we find Terah, the father of Abraham, who lived from the year 1879, was an idolator, as was, doubtless, Bethuel, who was Terah's grandson; for we find Laban, who was Bethuel's son, was so, and all this was during the life of the first post-diluvian family, for Terah was

born within one hundred ninety-three years after the
flood, and one hundred fifty-seven years before Noah
was dead; and even Abraham himself was eight and
fifty years old before Noah died; and yet idolatry had
been then, in all probability, above an hundred years
practised in the world.

> **N. B.** It is worth remark here, what a terrible ad-
> vantage the Devil gained by the debauching poor
> Noah, and drawing him into the sin of drunken-
> ness; for by this, as I said, he silenced and stopped
> the mouth of the great preacher of righteousness,
> that father and patriarch of the whole world, who
> not being able, for the shame of his own foul mis-
> carriage, to pretend to instruct or reprove the world
> any more, the Devil took hold of them immediate-
> ly, and for want of a prophet to warn and admonish,
> run that little of religion which there might be left
> in Shem and Japhet, quite out of the world, and
> deluged them all in idolatry.

How long the whole world may be said to be thus
overwhelmed in ignorance and idolatry, we may make
some tolerable guess at by the history of Abraham; for
it was not till God called him from his father's house,
that any such thing as a church was established in the
world; nor even then, except in his own family and
successors, for almost four hundred years after that call;
and till God brought the Israelites back out of Egypt,
the whole world may be said to be involved in idolatry
and devil worship.

So absolute a conquest had the Devil made over man-

kind, immediately after the flood, and all taking its rise
and beginning at the fatal defeat of Noah, who had he
lived untainted and invulnerable, as he had done for six
hundred years before, would have gone a great way to
have stemed the torrent of wickedness which broke in
upon mankind ; and therefore the Devil, I say, was
very cunning and very much in the right of it, take him
as he is a meer Devil, to attack Noah personally, and
give him a blow so soon.

It is true, the Devil did not immediately raze out the
notion of religion and of a God from the minds of men,
nor could he easily suppress the principle of worship
and homage to be paid to a sovereign being, the author
of nature and guide of the world ; the Devil saw this
clearly in the first ages of the new world, and therefore,
as I have said, he proceeded politically and by degrees :
That it was so, is evident from the story of Job and his
three friends, who, if we may take it for a history, not
a fable, and may judge of the time of it by the length
of Job's life, and by the family of Eliphaz the Te-
manite, who it is manifest was at least grandson or
great-grandson to Esau, Isaac's eldest son, and by the
language of Abimilech, king of Gerar, to Abraham, and
of Laban to Jacob, both the latter being at the same
time idolaters ; I say, if we may judge of it by all these,
there were still very sound notions of religion in the
minds of men ; nor could Satan, with all his cunning
and policy, deface those ideas, and root them out of the
minds of the people.

And this put him upon taking new measures to keep
up his interest, and preserve the hold he got upon mankind ; and his method was like himself, subtle and
politic to the last degree, as his whole history makes ap-

pear ; for seeing he found they could not but believe the
being of a God, and that they would needs worship
something, it is evident, he had no game left him to play
but this, namely, to set up wrong notions of worship,
and bring them to a false worship instead of a true, supposing the object worshipped to be still the same.

To finish this stratagem, he first insinuates that the
true God was a terrible, a dreadful, unapproachable
being ; that to see him was so frightful, that it would be
present death ; that to worship him immediately, was a
presumption that would provoke his wrath ; and that as
he was a consuming fire in himself, so he would burn up
those in his anger that dared to offer up any sacrifice to
him, but by the interposition of some medium which
might receive their adorations in his name.

Hence it occurred presently, that subordinate gods
were to be found out and set up, to whom the people
might pay the homage due to the supreme God, and
who they might worship in his name.   This I take from
the most ancient account of idolatry in the world ; nor
indeed could the Devil himself find out any other reason
why men should canonize or rather deify their princes
and men of fame, and worship them after they were
dead, as if they could save them from death and calamity, who were not able to save themselves when they
were alive ; much less could Satan bring men to swallow
so gross, so absurd a thing as the bowing the knee to a
stock, or a stone, a calf, an ox, a lion, nay the image or
figure of a calf, such as the Israelites made at mount
Sinai, and say, *These be thy gods, O Israel, who
brought thee out of the land of Egypt.*

Having thus, I say, brought them to satisfy themselves that they worshipped the true God and no other,

under the figures and appearances which they made to represent him, it was easy, after that, to worship any thing for the true God : and thus in a few ages they worshipped nothing but idols, even throughout the whole world ; nor has the Devil lost his hold in some parts of the world, nay not in most parts of the world to this day. He holds still all the eastern parts of Asia, and the southern parts of Africa, and the northern parts of Europe, and in them the vast countries of China and Tartary, Persia and India, Guinea, Ethiopia, Zanquebar, Congo, Angola, Monomotapa, &c. in which, except Ethiopia, we find no vestiges of any other worship but that of idols, monsters, and even the Devil himself ; till after the very coming of our Saviour, and even then, if it be true that the gospel was preached in the Indies and China by St. Thomas, and in other remote countries by other of the apostles ; we see that whatever ground Satan lost, he seems to have recovered it again ; and all Asia and Africa are at present over-run with Paganism or Mahometanism, which I think of the two is rather the worst ; besides all America, a part of the world, as some say, equal in bigness to all the other, in which the Devil's kingdom was never interrupted from it first being inhabited, whenever it was, to the first discovery of it by the European nations in the sixteenth century.

In a word, the Devil got what we may call an entire victory over mankind, and drove the worship of the true God, in a manner quite out of the world, forcing, as it were, his maker in a new kind of creation, the old one proving thus ineffectual, to recover a certain number by force and meer omnipotence to return to their duty, serve him and worship him ; but of that hereafter.

CHAPTER XI.

Of God's calling a church out of the midst of a degenerate world, and of Satan's new measures upon that incident: How he attacked them immediately, and his success in those attacks.

SATAN having, as I have said in the preceding chapter, made, as it were, a full conquest of mankind, debauched them all to idolatry, and brought them at least to worshipping the true God by the wretched medium of corrupt and idolatrous representations; God seemed to have no true servants or worshippers left in the world, but, if I may be allowed to speak so, was obliged, in order to restore the world to their senses again, to call a select number out from among the rest, who he himself undertook should own his godhead or supreme authority, and worship him as he required to be worshipped; this, I say, God was oblidged to do, because it is evident it has not been done so much by the choice and council of men, for Satan would have overruled that part, as by the power and energy of some irresistible and invincible operation, and this our divines give high names to ; but be it what they will, it is the second defeat or disappointment that the Devil has met with in his progress in the world; the first I have spoken of already.

It is true, Satan very well understood what was threatened to him in the original promise to the woman, immediately after the fall, namely, *thou shalt bruise his head*, &c. but he did not expect it so suddenly, but thought himself sure of mankind, till the fullness of time when the Messiah should come ; and therefore it was a great surprize to him, to see that Abraham being called was so immediately received and established, though he did not so immediately follow the voice that directed him, yet in him, in his loins, was all God's church at that time contained.

In the calling of Abraham, it is easy to see that there was no other way for God to form a church, that is to say, to single out a people to himself, as the world was then stated, but by immediate revelation and a voice from heaven : All mankind were gone over to the enemy, overwhelmed in idolatry, in a word, were engaged to the Devil ; God almighty, or as the Scripture distinguishes him, the Lord, the true God, was out of the question ; mankind knew little or nothing of him, much less did they know any thing of his worship, or that there was such a being in the world.

Well might it said, the Lord appeared to Abraham, Gen. xii. 7. for if God had not appeared himself, he must have sent a messenger from heaven, and perhaps it was so too, for he had not one true servant or worshipper that we know of then on earth, to send on that errand ; no prophet, no preacher of righteousness ; Noah was dead, and had been so above seventeen years ; and if he had not, his preaching, as I observed, after his great miscarriage, had but little effect. We are indeed told, that Noah left behind him certain rules and orders for the true worship of God, which were called the precepts of Noah, and remained in the world for a long time ; though how written, when neither any letters, much less

8   Z

writing, were known in the world, is a difficulty which
remains to be solved ; and this makes me look upon
those laws, called the precepts of Noah, to be a modern
invention, as I do also the *alphabetum Noachi*, which
Bochart pretends to give an account of.

But to leave that fiction, and come back to Abraham ;
God called him ; whether at first by voice, without any
vision, whether in a dream or night vision, which was
very significant in those days, or whether by some awful
appearance, we know not ; the second time, it is indeed
said expressly, God appeared to him : Be it which way
it will, God himself called him, shewed him the land of
Canaan, gave him the promise of it for his posterity,
and withal gave him such a faith, that the Devil soon
found there was no room for him to meddle with Abraham.   This is certain, we do not read that the Devil
ever so much as attempted Abraham at all ; some will
suggest that the command to Abraham to go and offer
up his son Isaac, was a temptation of the Devil, if possible to defeat the glorious work of God's calling a holy
seed into the world ; for the first, if Abraham had dis-
obeyed that call, the new favourite had been overcome
and made a rebel of ; or, secondly, if he had obeyed,
then the promised seed had been cut off, and Abraham
defeated ; but as the text is express that God himself
proposed it to Abraham, I shall not start the suggestions
of the critics, in bar of the sacred oracle.

Be it one way or the other, Abraham shewed a hero-
like faith and courage, and if the Devil had been the
author of it, he had seen himself disappointed in both his
views ; (1.) by Abraham's ready and bold compliance,
as believing it to be God's command ; and (2.) by the

divine countermand of the execution, just as the fatal knife was lifted up.

But if the Devil left Abraham, and made no attack upon him, seeing him invulnerable, he made himself amends upon the other branch of his family, his poor nephew Lot; who, notwithstanding he was so immediately under the particular care of heaven, as that the angel who was sent to destroy Sodom, could do nothing till he was out of it; and who, though after he had left Zoar, and was retired into a cave to dwell, yet the subtle Devil found him out, deluded his two daughters, took an advantage of the fright they had been in about Sodom and Gomorrah, made them believe the whole world was burnt too, as well as those cities, and that in short, they could never have any husbands, &c. and so in their abundant concern to repeople the world, and that the race of mankind might not be destroyed, they go and lie with their own father; the Devil telling them, doubtless, how to do it, by intoxicating his head with wine; in all which story, whether they were not as drunk as their father, seems to be a question, or else they could not have supposed all the men in the earth were consumed, when they knew that the little city Zoar had been preserved for their sakes.

This now was the third conquest Satan obtained by the gust of human appetite; that is to say, once by eating, and twice by drinking, or drunkenness, and still the last was the worst and most shameful; for Lot, however his daughters managed him, could not pretend he did not understand what the strength of wine was; and one would have thought after so terrible a judgment as that of Sodom was, which was, as we may say, executed before his face, his thoughts should have been too solemnly engaged in praising God for sparing his life, to be made drunk, and that two nights together.

But the Devil played his game sure, he set his two daughters to work, and as the Devil's instruments seldom fail, so he secured his by that hellish stratagem of deluding the daughters, to think all the world was consumed but they two and their father : To be sure the old man could not suspect that his daughter's design was so wicked as indeed it was, or that they intended to debauch him with wine, and make him drink till he knew not what he did.

Now the Devil having carried his game here, gained a great point, for as there were but two religious families in the world before, from whence a twofold generation might be supposed to rise religious and righteous like their parents, (viz.) that of Abraham, and this of Lot ; this crime ruined the hopes of one of them ; it could no more be said that just Lot was in being, who vexed his righteous soul from day to day with the wicked behaviour of the people of Sodom ; righteous Lot was degenerated into drunken incestuous Lot, Lot fallen from what he was, to be a wicked and unrighteous man ; no pattern of virtue, no reprover of the age, but a poor fallen degenerate patriarch, who could now no more reprove or exhort, but look down and be ashamed, and nothing to do but to repent ; and see the poor mean excuses of all the three.

Eve says, *The serpent beguiled me, and I did eat.*

Noah says,——*My grandson beguiled me, or the wine beguiled me and I did drink.*

Lot says, *My daughters beguiled me, and I also did drink.*

It is observable, that as I said above, Noah was silenced, and his preaching at an end, after that one action, so the like may be said of Lot; and in short, you never hear one word more of either of them after it; as for mankind, both were useless to them, and as to themselves, we never read of any of their repentance, nor have we much reason to believe they did repent.

From this attack of the Devil upon Lot, we hear no more of the Devil being so busily employed as he had been before in the world; he had indeed but little to do for all the rest of the world was his own, lull'd asleep under the witchcraft of idolatry, and are so still.

But it could not be long that the Devil lay idle; as soon as God called himself a people, the Devil could not be at rest till he attacked them.

' Wherever God sets up a house of prayer,
' The Devil always builds a chapel there.'

Abraham indeed went off the stage free, and so did Isaac too, they were a kind of first-rate saints; we do not so much as read of any failing they had, or of any thing the Devil had ever the face to offer to them; no, or with Jacob either, if you will excuse him for beguiling his brother Esau, of both his birthright and his blessing, but he was busy enough with all his children; for example,

He sent Judah to his sheep-shearing, and placed a whore (Tamar) in his way, in the posture of temptation, so made him commit incest and whoredom both together.

He sent incestuous Reuben to lie with his father's con-
cubine Bilhah.

He sent Dinah to the ball, to dance with the Shechemite
ladies, and play the whore with their master.

He enraged Simeon and Levi, at the supposed injury,
and then prompted them to revenge, for which their
father heartily cursed them.

He set them all together to fall upon poor Joseph, first
to murder him intentionally, and then actually sell
him to the Midianites.

He made them shew the party-coloured coat, and tell
a lie to their father, to make the poor old man
believe Joseph was killed by a lion, &c.

He sent Potiphar's wife to attack Joseph's chastity,
and filled her with rage at the disappointment.

He taught Joseph to swear by the life of Pharoah.

In a word, he debauched the whole race, except Benjamin ; and never man had such a set of sons, so wicked
and so notorious, after so good an introduction into the
world as they all of them had, to be sure : for Jacob, no
doubt, gave them as good instruction as the circumstances of his wandering condition would allow him to do.

We must now consider the Devil and his affairs in a
quite differing situation : When the world first appeared
peopled by the creating power of God, he had only
Adam and Eve to take care of, and I think he ply'd his
time with them to purpose enough : After the deluge he
had Noah only to pitch upon, and he quickly conquered
him by the instigation of his grandson.

At the building of Babel, he gained them by their
acting all in a body as one man ; so that in short he

managed them with ease, taking them as a body politic ; and we find they came into his snare as one man ; but now, the children of Israel multiplying in the land of their bondage, and God seeming to shew a particular concern for them, the Devil was obliged to new measures, stand at a distance, and look on for some time.

The Egyptians were plagued even without his help, nor though the cunning artist, as I said, stood and looked on, yet he durst not meddle ; nor could he make a few lice, the least and meanest of the armies of insects raised to afflict the Egyptians.

However, when he perceived that God resolved to bring the Israelites out, he prepared to attend them, to watch them, and be at hand upon all the wicked occasions that might offer ; as if he had been fully satisfied such occasions would offer, and that he should not fail to have an opportunity to draw them into some snare or another, and that therefore it was his business not to be out of the way, but to be ready (as we say) to make his market of them in the best manner he could : How many ways he attempted them, nay, how many times he conquered them in their journey, we shall see presently.

First he put them in a fright at Baal Zephon, where he thought he had drawn them into a noose, and where he sent Pharoah and his army to block them up between the mountains of Piahiroth and the Red-Sea ; but there indeed Satan was outwitted by Moses ; so far as it appeared to be a human action, for he little thought of their going dry footed through the sea, but depended upon having them all cut in pieces the next morning by the Egyptians ; an eminent proof, by the way, that the

Devil has no knowledge of events, or any insight into futurity ; nay that he has not so much as a second sight,
or knows to-day, what his maker intends to do to-mor-
row ; for had Satan known that God intended to ford
them over the sea, if he had not been able to have prevented the miracle, he would certainly have prevented
the escape, by sending out Pharoah and his army time
enough to have taken the strand before them, and so
have driven them to the necessity of travelling on foot
round the north point of that sea, by the wilderness of
Etan, where he would have pursued and harrassed them
with his cavalry, and in all probability have destroyed
them : But the blind short-sighted Devil, perfectly in
the dark, and unacquainted with futurity, knew nothing
of the matter, was as much deceived as Pharoah himself,
stood still flattering himself with the hopes of his booty,
and the revenge he should take upon them the next
morning ; till he saw the frighted waves in an uproar,
and to his utter astonishment and confusion saw the passage laid open, and Moses leading his vast army in full
march over the dry space ; nay even then it is very probable Satan did not know that if the Egyptians followed
them, the sea would return upon and overwhelm them ;
for I can hardly think so hard of the Devil himself,
that if he had, he would have suffered, much less
prompted Pharoah to follow the chase at such an ex-
pense ; so that either he must be an ignorant unforeseeing
Devil, or a very ungrateful false Devil to his friends the
Egyptians.

I am inclined also to the more charitable opinion of
Satan too, because the escape of the Israelites was really
a triumph over himself ; for the war was certainly his,

or at least he was auxiliary to Pharaoh, it was a victory over hell and Egypt together, and he would never have suffered the disgrace, if he had known it beforehand ; that is to say, though he could not have prevented the escape of Israel, or the dividing the water, yet he might have warned the Egyptians, and cautioned them not to venture in after them.

But we shall see a great many weak steps taken by the Devil in the affair of this very people, and their forty years wandering in the wilderness ; and though he was in some things successful, and wheedled them into many foolish and miserable murmurings and wranglings against God, and mutinies against poor Moses, yet the Devil was oftentimes baulked and disappointed ; and it is for this reason that I choose to finish the first part of his history with the particular relation of his behaviour among the Jews, because also, we do not find any extraordinary things happening any were else in the world for above one thousand five hundred years, no variety, no revolutions ; all the rest of mankind lay still under his yoke, quietly submitted to his government, did just as he bade them, worshipped every idol he set up, and in a word, he had no difficulty with any body but the Jews, and for this reason, I say, this part of his story will be the more useful and instructing.

To return therefore to Moses and his dividing the Red Sea ; that the people went over or through it, that we have the sacred history for ; but how the Devil behaved, that you must come to me for, or I know not where you will find a true account of it, at least not in print.

1. It was in the night they marched through, whether the Devil saw it in the dark or no, that is not my business.

But when he had day-light for it, and viewed the next day's work, I make no question but all hell felt the surprise, the prey being thus snatched out of their hands unexpectedly. It is true the Egyptians host was sent to him in their room, but that was not what he aimed at ; for he was sure enough of them his own way, and if it was not just at that time, yet he knew what and who they were ; but as he had devoured the whole Israelitish host in his imagination, to the tune of at least a million and a half of souls, men, women and children ; it was, no doubt, a great disappointment to the Devil to miss of his prey, and to see them all triumphing on the other side in safety.

It is true, Satan's annals do not mention this defeat, for historians are generally backward to register their own misfortunes ; but as we have an account of the fact from other hands, so as we cannot question the truth of it ; the nature of the thing will tell us it was a disappointment to the Devil, and a very great one too.

I cannot but observe here, that I think this part of the Devil's story very entertaining, because of the great variety of incidents which appear in every part of it ; sometimes he is like a hunted fox, curvetting and counter-running to avoid his being pursued and found out, while at the same time he is carrying on his secret designs to draw the people he pretends to manage, into some snare or other to their hurt ; at another time, though the comparison is a little too low for his dignity, like a monkey that has done mischief, and who making his own escape sits and chatters at a distance, as if he had triumphed in what he had done ; so Satan, when he had drawn them in to worship a calf, to offer strange fire, to

set up a schism, and the like ; and so to bring the divine
vengeance upon themselves, leaving them in their distress, kept at a distance, as if he looked on with satisfaction to see them burnt, swallowed up, swept away, and
the like ; as the several stories relate.

His indefatigable vigilance is, on the other hand, a
useful caveat, as well as an improving view to us ; no
sooner is he routed and exposed, defeated and disappointed in one enterprize, but he begins another, and,
like a cunning gladiator, warily defends himself, and
boldly attacks his enemy at the same time. Thus we see
him up and down, conquering and conquered, through
this whole part of his story, till at last he receives a total
defeat ; of which you shall hear in its place : In the
mean time, let us take up his story again at the Red Sea,
where he received a great blow, instead of which he expected a complete victory ; for doubtless the Devil and
the king of Egypt too, thought of nothing but conquest
at Piahiroth.

However, though the triumph of the Israelites over
the Egyptians must needs be a great mortification to the
Devil, and exasperated him very much, yet the consequence was only this, viz. that Satan, like an enemy who
is baulked and defeated, but not overcome, redoubles
his rage, and reinforces his army, and what the Egyptians could not do for him, he resolves to do for himself :
In order then to take his opportunity for what mischief
might offer, being defeated, and provoked, I say, at the
slur that was put upon him, he resolves to follow them
into the wilderness, and many a vile prank he played
them there ; as first, he straitens them for water, and
makes them murmur against God, and against Moses,

within a very few days, nay, hours, of their great deliverance of all.

Nor was this all, but in less than one year more we
find them (at his instigation too) setting up a golden
calf, and making all the people dance about it at mount
Sinai; even when God himself had but just before appeared to them in the terrors of a burning fire upon
the top of the mountain. And what was the pretence ?
Truly, nothing but that they had lost Moses, who used
to be their guide, and he had hid himself in the mount,
and had not been seen in forty days, so that they could
not tell what was become of him. This put them all
into confusion ; a poor pretence indeed, to turn them all
back to idolatry ! but the watchful Devil took the hint,
pushed the advantage, and insinuated that they should
never see Moses again, that he was certainly devoured
by venturing too near the flashes of fire in the mount,
and presuming upon the liberty he had taken before ; in
a word, that God had destroyed Moses, or he was starved to death for want of food, having been forty days
and forty nights absent.

All these were, it is true, in themselves most foolish
suggestions, considering Moses was admitted to the
vision of God, and that God had been pleased to appear
to him in the most intimate manner ; that as they might
depend God would not destroy his faithful servant, so
they might have concluded he was able to support his
being without food as long as he thought fit ; but to a
people so easy to believe any thing, what could be too
gross for the Devil to persuade them to ?

A people who could dance round a calf, and call it
their god, might do any thing ; that could say to one

another, that this was the great Jehovah, *that brought them out of the land of Egypt ;* and that within so few days after God's miraculous appearance to them, and for them ; I say, such a people were really fitted to be imposed upon, nothing could be too gross for them.

This was indeed his first considerable experiment upon them as a people, or as a body ; and the truth is, his affairs required it, for Satan, who had been a successful Devil in most of his attempts upon mankind, could hardly doubt of success in any thing after he had carried his point at mount Sinai : To bring them to idolatry in the very face of their deliverer, and just after the deliverance ! It was more astonishing in the main than even their passing the Red Sea : In a word, the Devil's whole history doth not furnish us with a story equally surprising.

And how was poor Aaron bewildered in it too ! He that was Moses's partner in all the great things that Moses did in Pharoah's sight, and that was appointed to be his assistant and oracle, or orator rather, upon all public occasions ; that he, above all the rest, should come into this absurd and ridiculous proposal, he that was singled out for the sacred priesthood, for him to defile his holy hands with a polluted abominable sacrifice, and with making the idol for them too (for it is plain that he made it,) how monstrous it was !

And see what an answer he gives to his brother Moses, how weak ! how simple ! *I did so and so, indeed, I bad them bring the ear-rings, &c. and I cast the gold into the fire, and it came out this calf.* Ridiculous ! as if the calf came out by mere fortuitous adventure, without a mould to cast it in ; which could not be supposed :

Of God's calling a church, and Satan's new measures.

And if it had not come out so without a mould, Moses would certainly have known of it : Had Aaron been innocent, he would have answered after quite another manner, and told Moses honestly that the whole body of the people came to him in a fright, and they forced him to make them an idol ; which he did, by taking first a proper mould to cast it in, and then taking the proper metal to cast it from : That indeed he had sinned in so doing, but that he was mobbed into it, and the people terrified him, perhaps they threatened to kill him ; and if he had added, that the Devil prompting his fear beguiled him, he had said nothing but what was certainly true ; for if it was in Satan's power to make the people insolent and outrageous enough to threaten and bully the old venerable prophet (for he was not yet a priest) who was the brother of their oracle Moses, and had been partner with him in so many of his commissions ; I say, if he could bring up the passions of the people to a height to be rude and unmannerly to him (Aaron) and perhaps to threaten and insult him, he may be easily supposed to be able to intimidate Aaron, and terrify him into a compliance.

See this cunning agent, when he has man's destruction in his view, how securely he acts ! he never wants a handle ; the best of men have one weak place or other, and he always finds it out, takes the advantage of it, and conquers them by one artifice or another ; only take it with you as you go, it is always by stratagem, never by force ; a proof that he is not empowered to use violence : He may tempt, and he does prevail ; but it is all legerdemain, it is all craft and artifice, he is still *Diabolè*, the calumniator and deceiver, that is, the misrepresenter ;

he misrepresents man to God, and misrepresents God to man ; also he misrepresents things, he puts false colours, and then manages the eye to see them with an imperfect view, raising clouds and fogs to intercept our sight ; in short, he deceives all our senses, and imposes upon us in things which otherwise would be the easiest to discern and judge of.

This indeed is in part the benefit of the Devil's history, to let us see that he has used the same method all along ; and that ever since he has had any thing to do with mankind, he has practised upon them with stratagem and cunning ; also it is observable that he has carried his point better that way than he would have done by fury and violence, if he had been allowed to make use of it ; for by his power indeed he might have laid the world desolate, and made a heap of rubbish of it long ago ; but, as I have observed before, that would not have answered his ends half so well, for by destroying men he would have made martyrs, and sent abundance of good men to heaven, would much rather have died, than yielded to serve him, and as he aimed to have it, to fall down and worship him ; I say, he would have made martyrs, and that not a few : But this was none of Satan's business ; his design lies quite another way ; his business is to make men sin, not to make them suffer ; to make devils of them, not saints ; to delude them, and draw them away from their maker, not send them away to him ; and therefore he works by stratagem, not by force.

We are now come to his story, as it relates to the Jewish church in the wilderness, and to the children of Israel in their travelling circumstances ; and this was the first scene of public management that the Devil had upon his hands in the world ; for, as I have said, till now, he dealt with mankind either in their separate condition, one by one, or else carried all before him, engrossing whole nations in his systems of idolatry, and overwhelming them in an ignorant destruction.

But having now a whole people as it were snatched away from him, taken out of his government, and, which was still worse, having a view of a kingdom being set up independent of him, and superior to his authority, it is not to be wondered at if he endeavoured to overthrow them in the infancy of their constitution, and tried all possible arts to bring them back into his own hands again.

He found them not only carried away from the country where they were even in his clutches, surrounded with idols, and where we have reason to believe the greatest part of them were polluted with idolatry of the Egyptians ; for we do not read of any stated worship which they had of their own, or if they did worship the true God, we scarce know in what manner they did it ; they had no law given them, nothing but the covenant of circumcision, and even Moses himself had not strictly observed that, till he was frighted into it ; we read of no sacrifices among them, no feasts were ordained, no solemn worship appointed, and how, or in what manner they performed their homage, we know not ; the passover was not ordained till just at their coming away ; so that there was not much religion among them, at least that we have any account of ; and we may suppose the Devil was pretty easy with them all the while they were in the house of their bondage.

But now, to have a million of people fetched out of his hands, as it were all at once, and to have the immediate power of heaven engaged in it, and that Satan saw evidently God had singled them out in a miraculous manner to favour them, and call them his own ; this alarmed him at once, and therefore he resolves to follow them, lay close siege to them, and take all the measures possible to bring them to rebel against, and disobey God, that he might be provoked to destroy them ; and how near he went to bring it to pass, we shall see presently.

This making a calf, and paying an idolatrous worship to it (for they acted the heathens and idolaters, not in the setting up the calf only, but in the manner of their worshipping, viz. dancing and music, things they had not been acquainted with in the worship of the true God) I mention here, to observe how the Devil not only imposed upon their principles, but upon their senses too, as if the awful majesty of heaven, whose glory they had seen in mount Sinai, where they stood, and whose pillar of cloud and fire was their guide and protection, would be worshipped by dancing round a calf ! and that not a living creature, or a real calf, but the mere image of a calf cast in gold, or, as some think, in brass gilded over.

But this was the Devil's way with mankind, namely, to impose upon their senses, and bring them into the grossest follies and absurdities ; and then, having first made them fools, it was much the easier to make them offenders.

In this very manner he acted with them through all the course of their wilderness travels ; for as they were led by the hand like children, defended by omnipotence, fed by miracles, instructed immediately from heaven,

and in all things had Moses for their guide; they had
no room to miscarry, but by acting the greatest absurdities, and committing the greatest follies in nature; and
even these, the Devil brought them to be guilty of, in a
surprising manner : 1. As God himself relieved them in
every exigence, and supplied them in every want,
one would think it was impossible they should be ever
brought to question either his willingness or his ability,
and yet they really objected against both; which was
indeed very provoking, and I doubt not, that when the
Devil had brought them to act in such a preposterous
manner, he really hoped and believed God would be
provoked effectually : The testimonies of his care of
them, and ability to supply them, were miraculous and
undeniable; he gave them water from the rock, bread
from the air, sent the fowls to feed them with flesh, and
supported them all the way by miracles; their health
was preserved, none were sick among them, their clothes
did not wear out, nor their shoes grow old upon their
feet; could any thing be more absurd, than to doubt
whether he could provide for them who had never let
them want for so many years ?

But the Devil managed them in spite of miracles;
nor did he ever give them over till he had brought six
hundred thousand of them to provoke God so highly
that he would not suffer above two of them to go into the
Land of Promise; so that in short, Satan gained his
point as to that generation, for all their carcasses fell in
the wilderness. Let us take but a short view to what a
height he brought them, and in what a rude, absurd
manner, they acted; how he set them upon murmuring
upon every occasion, now for water, then for bread;

nay, they murmured at their bread when they had it;
Our souls loathe this light bread.

He sowed the seeds of church-rebellion in the sons of
Aaron, and made Nadab and Abibu offer strange fire till
they were strangely consumed by fire for the doing it.

He set them a complaining at Taberah, and a lusting
for flesh at the first three days' journey from mount
Sinai.

He planted envy in the hearts of Miriam and Aaron,
against the authority of Moses, to pretend God had
spoke by them as well as by him, till he humbled the
father, and made a leper of the daughter.

He debauched ten of the spies, frighted them with
sham appearances of things, when they went out to
search the land ; and made them fright the whole people out of their understanding as well as duty, for which
six hundred thousand of their carcasses fell in the
wilderness.

He raised the rebellion of Korah, and the two hundred and fifty princes, till he brought them to be swallowed up alive.

He put Moses into a passion at Meribah, and ruffled
the temper of the meekest man upon earth, by which he
made both him and Aaron forfeit their share of the promise, and be shut out from the Holy Land.

He raised a mutiny among them when they travelled
from mount Hor, till they brought fiery serpents among
them to destroy them.

He tried to make Baalim the prophet curse them, but
there the Devil was disappointed : However, he brought
the Midianites to debauch them with women, as in the
case of Zimri and Cozbi.

He tempted Achan with the wedge of gold, and the
Babylonish garment, that he might take off the accursed
thing, and be destroyed.

He tempted the whole people, not effectually to drive
out the cursed inhabitants of the Land of Promise, that
they might remain, and be goads in their sides, till at
last they often oppressed them for their idolatry; and,
which was worse, debauched them to idolatry.

He prompted the Benjamites to refuse satisfaction to
the people, in the case of the wickedness of the men of
Gibeah, to the destruction of the whole tribe, four hundred men excepted, in the rock Rimmon.

At last he tempted them to reject the theocracy of their
maker, and call upon Samuel to make them a king;
and most of those kings he made plagues and sorrows to
them in their time, as you shall hear in their order.

Thus he plagued the whole body of the people continually, making them sin against God, and bring
judgments upon themselves, to the consuming some
millions of them, first and last, by the vengeance of their
maker.

As he did with the whole congregation, so he did with
their rulers, and several of the judges, who were made
instruments to deliver the people, yet were drawn into
snares by this subtle serpent, to ruin themselves or the
people they had delivered.

He tempted Gideon to make an ephod, contrary to
the law of the tabernacle, and made the children of
Israel go a whoring (that is, a worshipping) after it.

He tempted Sampson to debauch himself with a har-
lot, and betray his own happy secret to a whore, at the
expence of both his eyes, and at last of his life.

He tempted Eli's sons to lie with the women, in the very doors of the tabernacle, when they came to bring their offerings to the priest ; and he tempted poor Eli to connive at them, or not sufficiently reprove them.

He tempted the people to carry the ark of God into the camp, that it might fall into the hands of the Philistines. And

He tempted Uzzah to reach out his hand to hold it up ; as if he that preserved it in the house of Dagon the idol of the Philistines, could not keep it from falling out of the cart.

When the people had gotten a king, he immediately set to work in divers ways to bring that king to load them with plagues and calamities not a few.

He tempted Saul to spare the king of Amalek, contrary to God's express command.

He not tempted Saul only, but possessed him with an evil spirit, by which he was left to wayward dispositions, and was forced to have it fiddled out of him with a minstrel.

He tempted Saul with a spirit of discontent, and with a spirit of envy at poor David, to hunt him like a partridge upon the mountains.

He tempted Saul with a spirit of divination, and sent him to a witch to enquire of Samuel for him ; as if God would help him when he was dead, that had forsaken him when he was alive.

After that, he tempted him to kill himself, on a pretence that he might not fall into the hands of the uncircumcised ; as if self-murder was not half so bad, either for sin against God, or disgrace among men, as being taken prisoner by a Philistine ! A piece of madness none but the Devil could have brought mankind to submit to, though some ages after that he made it a fashion among the Romans.

After Saul was dead, and David came to the throne, by how much he was a man chosen and particularly favoured by heaven, the Devil fell upon him with the more vigour, attacked him so many ways, and conquered him so very often, that as no man was so good a king, so hardly any good king was ever a worse man; in many cases one would have almost thought the Devil had made sport with David, to shew how easily he could overthrow the best man God could chose of the whole congregation.

He made him distrust his benefactor so much as to feign himself mad before the king of Gath, when he had fled to him for shelter.

He made him march with his four hundred cut-throats, to cut off poor Nabal, and all his houshold, only because he would not send him the good chear he had provided for his honest sheep-shearers.

He made him, for his word's sake, give Ziba half his master's estate for his treachery, after he knew he had been the traitor, and betrayed poor Mephibosheth for the sake of it ; in which

> ‘ The good old king, it seems, was very loth
> ‘ To break his word, and therefore broke his oath.

Then he tempted him to the ridiculous project of numbering the people, though against God's express command ; a thing Joab himself was not wicked enough to do, till David and the Devil forced him to it.

And to make him completely wicked, he carried him to the top of his house, and shewed him a naked lady bathing herself in her garden, in which it appeared that the Devil knew David too well, and what was the particular sin of his inclination ; and so took him by the right handle ; drawing him at once into the sins of murder and adultery.

Then, that he might not quite give him over, (though David's repentance for the last sin kept the Devil off for a while) when he could attack him no farther personally, he fell upon him in his family, and made him as miserable as he could desire him to be, in his children, three of whom he brought to destruction before his face, and another after his death.

First, he tempted Amnon to ravish his sister Tamar ; so there was an end of her (poor girl !) as to this world, for we never hear any more of her.

Then he tempted Absalom to murder his brother Amnon, in revenge for Tamar's maidenhead.

Then he made Joab run Absalom through the body, contrary to David's command.

And after David's death he brought Adonijah (weak man !) to the block, for usurping king Solomon's throne.

As to Absalom, he tempted him to rebellion, and raising war against his own father, to the turning him shamefully out of Jerusalem, and almost out of the kingdom.

He tempted him, for David's farther mortification, to lie with his father's wives, in the face of the whole city ; and had Ahithophel's honest council been followed, he had certainly sent him to sleep with his fathers long

before his time.—But there Satan and Ahithophel were
both outwitted together.

Through all the reigns of the several successors of
David, the Devil took care to carry on his own game, to
the continual insulting the measures which God himself
had taken for the establishing his people in the world,
and especially as a church ; till at last he so effectually
debauched them to idolatry ; that crime which of all
others was most provoking to God, as it was carrying
the people away from their allegiance, and transposing
the homage they owed God their maker, to a contemptible block of wood, or an image of a brute beast ;
and this how sordid and brutish soever it was in itself,
yet so did his artifice prevail among them, that, first or
last, he brought them all into it, the ten tribes as well as
the two tribes ; till at last God himself was provoked
to unchurch them, gave them up to their enemies, and
the few that were left of them, after incredible slaughters
and desolation, were hurried away, some into Tartary,
and others into Babylon, from whence very few, of that
few that were carried away, ever found their way home
again ; and some, when they might have come, would
not accept of it, but continued there to the very coming
of the Messiah. See epistles of St. James and of St. Peter,
at the beginning.

But to look a little back upon this part (for it cannot
be omitted, it makes so considerable a part of the Devil's
history) I mean his drawing God's people, kings and
all, into all the sins and mischiefs which gradually con-
tributed to their destruction.

First, (for he began immediately with the very best
and wisest of the race) he drew in king Solomon, in the

midst of all his zeal for the building God's house, and for the making the most glorious and magnificent appearance for God's worship that ever the world saw; I say, in the middle of all this, he drew him into such immoderate and insatiable an appetite for women, as to set up the first, and perhaps the greatest seraglio of whores that ever any prince in the world had, or pretended to before; nay, and to bring whoring so much into reputation, that, as the text says, seven hundred of them were princesses; that is to say, ladies of quality : Not as the grand Seigniors, and great Moguls, (other princes of the eastern world) have since practised, namely, to pick up their most beautiful slaves; but these, it seems, were women of rank, king's daughters, as Pharaoh's daughter, and the daughters of the princes and prime men among the Moabites, Ammonites, Zidonians, Hittites, &c. 1 Kings xi. 1.

Nor was this all; but as he drew him into the love of these forbidden women (for such they were, as to their nation, as well as number) so he insnared him by those women to a familiarity with their worship; and by degrees brought that famous prince (famous for his wisdom) to be the greatest and most-imposed-upon old fool in the world; bowing down to those idols by the inticing of his whores, whom he had abhorred and detested in his youth, as dishonouring that God for whom, and for whose worship he had finished and dedicated the most magnificent building and temple in the world. Nothing but the invincible subtlety of this arch-Devil could ever have brought such a man as Solomon to such a degeneracy of manners, and to such meannesses; no, not

9   2 C

this Devil himself, without the assistance of his whores, nor the whores themselves, without the Devil to help them.

As to Solomon, Satan had made conquest enough there, we need hear no more of him ; the next advance he made, was in the person of his son Rehoboam ; had not the Devil prompted his pride and tyrannical hu-mour, he would never have given the people such an answer as he did ; and when he saw a fellow at the head of them too whom he knew wanted and waited for an occasion to raise a rebellion, and had ripened up the people's humour to the occasion : Well might the text call it, listening to the council of the young heads ; that it was indeed with a vengeance ! but those young heads too were acted by an old Devil, who for his craft is call-ed, as I have observed, the Old Serpent.

Having thus paved the way, Jeroboam revolts. So far God had directed him ; for the text says expressly, speaking in the first person of God himself, *This thing is of me.*

But though God might appoint Jeroboam to be king, (that is to say, of ten tribes) yet God did not appoint him to set up the two calves in the two extreme parts of the land, viz. in Dan, and in Bethel ; that was Jeroboam's own doing, and done on purpose to keep the people from falling back to Rehoboam, by being obliged to go to Jerusalem to the public worship : And the text adds, *Jeroboam made Israel to sin.* This was indeed a master-piece of the Devil's policy, and it was effectual to answer the end ; nothing could have been more to the purpose ; what reason he had to expect the people

would so universally come into it, and be so well satisfied with a couple of calves, instead of the true worship
of God at Jerusalem ; or what arts and management he
(Satan) made use of afterwards, to bring the people in,
to join with such a delusion, that we find but little of in
all the annals of Satan ; nor is it much to the case : It
is certain the Devil found a strange kind of propensity to
worshipping idols rooted in the temper of that whole
people, even from their first breaking away from the
Egyptian bondage ; so that he had nothing to do but to
work upon the old stock, and propagate the crime that
he found was so natural to them. And this is Satan's
general way of working, not with them only, but with
us also, and with all the world, even then, and ever
since.

When he had thus secured Jeroboam's revolt, we
need not trace him among his successors ; for the same
reason of state that held for the setting up the calves at
Bethel and Dan, held good for the keeping them up, to
all Jeroboam's posterity ; nor had they one good king
ever after ; even Jehu, who called his friends to come
and see his zeal for the Lord, and who fulfilled the
threatenings of God upon Ahab and his family, and
upon queen Jezebel and her offspring, and knew all the
while that he was executing the judgment of the true
God upon an idolatrous race ; yet he would not part
with his calves, but would have thought it have been
parting with his kingdom, and that as the people would
have gone up to Jerusalem to worship, so they would at
the same time have transferred their civil obedience to
the king of Judah, (whose right it really was, as far as

they could claim by birth and right line); so that by the way, Satan, any more than other politicians, is not for the *jus divinum* of lineal succession, or what we call hereditary right, any farther than serves for his purpose.

Thus Satan ridded his hands of ten of the twelve tribes; let us now see how he went on with the rest, for his work was now brought into a narrower compass; the church of God was now reduced to two tribes, except a few religious people, who separated from the schism of Jeroboam, and came and planted themselves among the tribes of Judah and Benjamin: The first thing the Devil did after this, was to foment a war between the two kings, while Judah was governed by a boy or youth, Abija by name, and he none of the best neither; but God's time was not come, and the Devil received a great disappointment; when Jeroboam was so entirely overthrown, that if the records of those ages do not mistake, no less than 500,000 men of Israel were killed; such a slaughter, that one would think the army of Judah, had they known how to improve, as well as gain a victory, might have brought all the rest back again, and have intirely reduced the house of Jeroboam, and the ten tribes that followed him, to their obedience; nay, they did take a great deal of the country from them, and among the rest Bethel itself; and yet so cunningly did Satan manage, that the king of Judah, who was himself a wicked king, and perhaps an idolater in his heart, did not take down the golden calf that Jeroboam had there, no nor destroy the idolatry itself, so that in short his victory signified nothing.

Of God's calling a church, and Satan's new measures.

From hence to the captivity, we find the Devil busy
with the kings of Judah, especially the best of them ; as
for such as Manasseh, and those who transgressed by
the general tenor of their lives, those he had no great
trouble with.

But such as Asa, Jehoshaphat, Hezekiah, and Josiah,
he hung about them and their courts, till he brought
every one of them into some mischief or another.

As first, good king Asa, of whom the scripture says,
his heart was perfect all his days, yet this subtle spirit,
that could break in upon him no where else, tempted
him when the king of Israel came out against him, to
send to hire Benhadad, the king of Syria, to help him ;
as if God, who had before enabled him to conquer the
Ethiopians, with an army of ten hundred thousand
men, could not have saved him from the king of the ten
tribes.

In the same manner he tempted Jehoshaphat to join
with that wicked king Ahab against the king of Syria,
and also to marry his son to Ahab's daughter, which was
fatal to Jehoshaphat and to his posterity.

Again, he tempted Hezekiah to shew all his riches to
the king of Babylon's messengers ; and who can doubt
but that he (Satan) is to be understood by the wicked
spirit which stood before the Lord, 2 Chron. xviii. 20.
and offered his service to entice Ahab the king of Israel
to come out to battle to his ruin, by being a lying spirit
in the mouths of all his prophets ; and who for that
time had a special commission, as he had another time
in the case of Job ? and indeed it was a commission
fit for nobody but the Devil : *Thou shalt entice him,*

and thou shalt also prevail: Go out and do even so,
verse 21.

Even good Josiah himself, of whom it is recorded,
that *like him there was no king before him, neither
after him arose there any like him,* 2 Kings xxiii. 26.
yet the Devil never left him with his machinations,
till finding he could not tempt him to any thing wicked
in his government, he tempted or moved him to a needless war with the king of Egypt, in which he lost his life.

From the death of this good king, the Devil prevailed
so with the whole nation of the Jews, and brought them
to such an incorrigible pitch of wickedness, that God
gave them up, forsook his habitation of glory, the temple, which he suffered to be spoiled first, then burnt and
demolished; destroying the whole nation of the Jews,
except a small number that were left, and those the
enemy carried away into captivity.

Nor was he satisfied with this general destruction of
the whole people of Israel, for the ten tribes were gone
before; but he followed them even into their captivity;
those that fled away to Egypt, which they tell us was
seventy thousand, he first corrupted, and then they were
destroyed there upon the overthrow of Egypt, by the
same king of Babylon.

Also he went very near to have them rooted out,
young and old, man, woman, and child, who were in
captivity in Babylon, by the ministry of that true agent
of hell, Haman the Agagite; but there Satan met with
a disappointment too, as in the story of Esther, which
was but the fourth that he had met with, in all his
management since the creation; I say, there he was

disappointed, and his prime minister, Haman, was exalted, as he deserved.

Having thus far traced the government and dominion of the Devil, from the creation of man to the captivity; I think I may call upon him to set up his standard of universal empire, at that period; it seemed just then as if God had really forsaken the earth, and given the entire dominion of mankind up to his outrageous enemy the Devil, for excepting the few Israelites which were left in the territories of the king of Babylon, and they were but a few; I say, except among them, there was not one corner of the world left where the true God was called upon, or his dominion so much as acknowledged; all the world was buried in idolatry, and that of so many horrid kinds, that one would think, the light of reason should have convinced mankind, that he who exacted such bloody sacrifices as that of Molech, and such a bloody cutting themselves with knives, as the priests of Baal did, could not be a God, a good and beneficent being, but must be a cruel, voracious, and devouring Devil, whose end was not the good, but the destruction of his creatures: But to such a height was the blind dementated world arrived to at that time, that in these sordid and corrupt ways, they went on worshipping dumb idols, and offering human sacrifices to them, and in a word, committing all the most horrid and absurd abominations that they were capable of, or that the Devil could prompt them to, till heaven was again put, as it were, to the necessity of bringing about a revolution, in favour of his own forsaken people, by miracle and surprize, as he had done before.

We come therefore to the restoration or return of the captivity : Had Satan been able to have acted any thing by force, as I have observed before, all the princes and powers of the world, having been, as they really were, at his devotion, he might easily have made use of them, armed all the world against the Jews, and prevented the rebuilding the temple, and even the return of the captivity.

But now the Devil's power manifestly received a check, and the hand of God appeared in it, and that he was resolved to re-establish his people the Jews, and to have a second temple built : The Devil, who knew the extent of his own power too well, and what limitations were laid upon him, stood still as it were looking on, and not daring to oppose the return of the captivity, which he very well knew had been prophesied, and would come to pass.

He did indeed make some little opposition to the building, and to the fortifying the city, but as it was to no purpose, so he was soon obliged to give it over ; and thus the captivity being returned, and the temple rebuilt, the people of the Jews encreased and multiplied to an infinite number and strength ; and from this time we may say, the power of the Devil rather declined and decreased, than went on with success, as it had done before : It is true, the Jews fell into sects and errors, and divisions of many kinds, after the return from the captivity ; and no doubt the Devil had a great hand in those divisions ; but he could never bring them back to idolatry, and his not being able to do that, made him turn his hand so many ways to plague and oppress them ; as particularly by Antiochus the Great, who brought the abomination of desolation into the holy place ; and there the Devil triumphed over them for some time ; but they were delivered many ways, till at last they came peaceably under the protection rather than the dominion of the Roman empire : When Herod the Great governed them as a king, and re-edified, nay almost rebuilt their temple, with so great an expence and magnificence, that he made it, as some say, greater and more glorious than that of Solomon's, though that I take to be a great —— fable, to say no worse of it.

In this condition the Jewish church stood, when the fullness of time, as it is called in Scripture, was come ; and the Devil was kept at bay, though he had made some encroachments upon them as above ; for there was a glorious remnant of saints among them, such as old Zacharias, the father of John the Baptist, and old Simeon, who waited for the salvation of Israel ; I say, in this condition the Jewish church stood when the Messiah came into the world, which was such another mortal stab to the thrones and principalities infernal, as that of which I have spoken already in chap. III. at the creation of man ; and therefore with this I break off the antiquities of the Devil's history, or the antient part of his kingdom : For from hence downward we shall find his empire has declined gradually ; and though by his wonderful address, his prodigious application, and the vigilance and fidelity of his instruments, as well human as infernal and diabolical, and of the human as well the ecclesiastic as the secular ; he has many times retrieved what he has lost, and sometimes bid fair for recovering the universal empire he once possessed over mankind; yet he has been still defeated again, repulsed and beaten back, and his kingdom has greatly declined in many parts of the world; and especially in the Northern parts, except Great Britain; and how he has politically maintained his interest, and encreased his dominion among the wise and righteous generation that we cohabit with and among, will be the subject of the modern part of Satan's history, and of which we are next to give an account.

POLITICAL HISTORY

DEVIL.

Part the Second.

CHAPTER I.

I HAVE examined the antiquities of Satan's history in the former part of this work, and brought his affairs down from the creation, as far as to our blessed christian times; especially to the coming of the Messiah, when one would think the Devil could have nothing to do among us. I have indeed but touched at some things which might have admitted of a farther description of Satan's affairs, and the particulars of which we may all come to a farther knowledge of hereafter; yet I think I have spoken to the material part of his conduct, as it relates to his empire in this world : What has happened to his more sublimated government, and his angelic capacities, I shall have an occasion to touch at in several solid particulars as we go along.

The Messiah was now born, *the fullness of time was come*, that the Old Serpent was to have his head broken, that is to say, his empire or dominion over man, which he gained by the fall of our first father and mother in Paradise, received a downfal or overthrow.

It is worth observing, in order to confirm what I have already mentioned of the limitation of Satan's power, that not only his angelic strength seems to have received a farther blow upon the coming of the Son of God into the world, but he seems to have had a blow upon his intellects; his serpentine craft and devil-like subtlety seems to have been circumscribed and cut short; and instead of his being so cunning a fellow as before, when, as I said, it is evident he outwitted all mankind, not only Eve, Cain, Noah, Lot, and all the patriarchs, but even nations of men, and that in their public capacity; and thereby led them into absurd and ridiculous things, such as the building of Babel, and deifying and worshipping their kings, when dead and rotten; idolizing beasts, stocks, stones, anything, and even nothing; and in a word, when he managed mankind just as he pleased.

Now, and from this time forward, he appeared a weak, foolish, ignorant Devil, compared to what he was before. He was, upon almost every occasion, resisted, disappointed, baulked and defeated, especially in all his attempts to thwart or cross the mission and ministry of the Messiah, while he was upon earth, and sometimes upon other and very mean occasions too.

And first, how foolish a project was it, and how below Satan's celebrated artifice in like cases, to put Herod upon sending to kill the poor innocent children in Bethlehem, in hopes to destroy the infant? for I take it for granted, it was the Devil put into Herod's thoughts that execution, how simple and foolish soever; now we must allow him to be very ignorant of the nativity himself, or else he might easily have guided his friend Herod to the place where the infant was.

This shews that either the Devil is in general ignorant as we are, of what is to come in the world, before it is really come to pass ; and consequently can foretel nothing, no not so much as our famous old Merlin or mother Shipton did, or else that great event was hid from him by an immediate power superior to his, which I cannot think neither, considering how much he was concerned in it, and how certainly he knew that it was once to come to pass.

But be that as it will, it is certain the Devil knew nothing where Christ was born, or when ; nor was he able to direct Herod to find him out, and therefore put him upon that foolish, as well as cruel order, to kill all the children, that he might be sure to destroy the Messiah among the rest.

The next simple step that the Devil took, and indeed the most foolish one that he could ever be charged with, unworthy the very dignity of a Devil, and below the understanding that he always was allowed to act with, was that of coming to tempt the Messiah in the wilderness. It is certain, and he owned it himself afterwards, upon many occasions, that the Devil knew our Saviour to be the Son of God ; and it is as certain that he knew, that as such he could have no power or advantage over him ; how foolish then was it in him to attack him in that manner, *If thou be the Son of God ?* why he knew him to be the Son of God well enough ; he said so afterwards, *I know thee who thou art, the Holy One of God ;* how then could he be so weak a Devil as to say, If thou art, then do so and so ?

The case is plain, the Devil, though he knew him to be the Son of God, did not fully know the mystery of the incarnation ; nor did he know how far the inanition of Christ extended, and whether, as man, he was not subject to fall as Adam was, though his reserved godhead might be still immaculate and pure ; and upon this foot, as he would leave no method untried, he attempted him three times, one immediately after another ; but then, finding himself disappointed, he fled.

This evidently proves that the Devil was ignorant of the great mystery of godliness, as the texts calls it, *God manifest in the flesh,* and therefore made that foolish attempt upon Christ, thinking to have conquered his human nature as capable of sin, which it was not ; and at this repulse hell groaned, the whole army of regimental devils received a wound, and felt the shock of it ; it was a second overthrow to them, they had had a long chain of success, carried a devilish conquest over the greatest part of the creation of God ; but now they were cut short, the Seed of the Woman was now come to break the Serpent's head, that is, to cut short his power, to contract the limits of his kingdom, and in a word, to dethrone him in the world : No doubt the Devil received a shock, for you find him always afterward, crying out in a horrible manner, whenever Christ met with him, or else very humble and submissive, as when he begged leave to go into the herd of swine, a thing he has often done since.

Defeated here, the first stratagem I find him concerned in after it, was his entering into Judas, and putting him upon betraying Christ to the chief priest ; but here again he was entirely mistaken, for he did not see, as much a devil as he was, what the event would be ; but when he came to know, that if Christ was put to death, he would become a propitiatory and be the great sacrifice of mankind, so to rescue the fallen race from that death they had incurred the penalty of, by the fall, that this was the fulfilling of all scripture prophecy, and that thus it was that Christ was to be the end of the law ; I say, as soon as he perceived this, he strove all he could to prevent it, and disturbed Pilate's wife in her sleep, in order to set her upon her husband to hinder his delivering him up to the Jews ; for then, and not till then, he knew how Christ was to vanquish hell by the power of his cross.

Thus the Devil was disappointed and exposed in every step he took, and as he now plainly saw his king-dom declining, and even the temporal kingdom of Christ, rising up upon the ruins of his (Satan's) power ; he seem-ed to retreat into his own region the air, and to consult there with his fellow Devils, what measures he should take next to preserve his dominion among men : Here it was that he resolved upon that truly hellish thing called Persecution, by which, though he proved a foolish Devil in that too, he flattered himself he should be able to destroy God's church, and root out its professors from the earth, even almost as soon as it was established ; whereas on the contrary, heaven counter-acted him there too, and though he armed the whole Roman em-pire against the christians, that is to say, the whole world, and they were fallen upon every where, with all the fury and rage of some of the most flaming tyrants that the world ever saw, of whom Nero was the first ; yet in spite of hell, God made all the blood, which the

Devil caused to be spilt, to be *semen ecclesiœ*, and the Devil had the mortification to see, that the number of christians encreased even under the very means he made use of to root them out and destroy them: This was the case through the reign of all the Roman emperors, for the first three hundred years after Christ.

Having thus tried all the methods that best suited his inclination, I mean those of blood and death, complicated with tortures, and all kinds of cruelty, and that for so long a stage a time as above; the Devil all on a sudden, as if glutted with blood, and satiated with destruction, sits still and becomes a peaceable spectator for a good while; as if he either found himself unable, or had no disposition to hinder the progress of christianity in the first ages of its settlement in the world: In this interval the christian church was established under Constantine, religion flourished in peace, and under the most perfect tranquility: The Devil seemed to be at a loss what he should do next, and things began to look as if Satan's kingdom was at an end, but he soon let them see that he was the same indefatigable Devil that ever he was, and the prosperity of the church gave him a large field of action; for knowing the disposition of mankind to quarrel and dispute, the universal passion rooted in nature, especially among the church-men, for precedency and dominion, he fell to work with them immediately; so that turning the tables, and re-assuming the subtlety and craft, which, I say, he seemed to have lost in the former four hundred years, he gained more ground in the next ages of the church, and went farther towards restoring his power and empire in the world, and towards overthrowing that very church which was so lately established, than all he had done by fire and blood before.

His policy now seemed to be edged with resentment for the mistakes he had made ; as if the Devil looking back with anger at himself, to see what a fool he had been to expect to crush religion by persecution, rejoiced for having discovered that liberty and dominion was the only way to ruin the church, not fire and faggot ; and that he had nothing to do but to give the zealous people their utmost liberty in religion, only sowing error and variety of opinion among them, and they would bring fire and faggot in fast enough among themselves.

It must be confessed these were devilish politics ; and so sure was the aim, and so certain was the Devil to hit his mark by them, that we find he not only did not fail then, but the same hellish methods have prevailed still, and will do so to the end of the world. Nor had the Devil ever a better game to play than this, for the ruin of religion, as we shall have room to shew in many examples, besides that of the dissenters in England, who are evidently weakened by the late toleration : Whether the Devil had any hand in baiting his hook with an A—— of Parliament or no, history is silent, but it is too evident he has catched the flesh by it ; and if the honest Church of England does not in pity and christian charity to the dissenters, straighten her hand a little, I cannot but fear the Devil will gain his point, and the dissenter will be undone by it.

Upon this new foot of politics the Devil began with the emperors themselves : Arius, the father of the heretics

10   2 E

of that age, having broached his opinions, and Athanasius, the orthodox bishop of the East, opposing him, the
Devil no sooner saw the door open to strife and imposi-
tion, but he thrust himself in, and raising the quarrel up
to a suited degree of rage and spleen, he involved the
good emperor himself in it first, and Athanasius was
banished and recalled, and banished and recalled again,
several times, as error ran high, and as the Devil either
got or lost ground : After Constantine, the next emperor
was a child of his own (Arian) and then the court came
all into the quarrel, as courts often do, and then the
Arians and the Orthodox persecuted one another, as
furiously as the Pagans persecuted them all before. To
such a height the Devil brought his conquest in the
very infancy of the question, and so much did he prevail over the true christianity of the primitive church,
even before they had enjoyed the liberty of the pure
worship twenty years.

Flushed with this success, the Devil made one push
for the restoring Paganism, and bringing on the old worship of the heathen idols and temples ; but like our king
James II. he drove too hard, and Julian had so provoked the whole Roman empire, which was generally at
that time become christian, that had the apostate lived,
he would not have been able to have held the throne ;
and as he was cut off in his beginning, Paganism expired
with him, and the Devil himself might have cried out as
Julian did, and with much more propriety, *Vicisti Ga-
lileane*.

Jovian, the next emperor, being a glorious christian,
and a very good and great man, the Devil abdicated for

a while, and left the christian armies to re-establish the orthodox faith ; nor could he bring the christians to a breach again among themselves a great while after.

However, time and a diligent Devil did the work at last, and when the emperors concerning themselves one way or other, did not appear sufficient to answer his end, he changed hands again, and went to work with the clergy : To set the doctors effectually together by the ears, he threw in the new notion of primacy among them, for a bone of contention ; the bait took, the priests swallowed it eagerly down, and the Devil, a cunninger fisherman than ever St. Peter was, struck them (as the anglers call it) with a quick hand, and hung them fast upon the hook.

Having them thus in his clutches, and they being now, as we may say, his own, they took their measures afterwards from him, and most obediently followed his directions ; nay, I will not say but he may have had pretty much the management of the whole society ever since, of what profession or party soever they may have been, with exception only to the reverend and right reverend among ourselves.

The sacred, as above, being thus hooked in, and the Devil being at the head of their affairs, matters went on most gloriously his own way ; first, the bishops fell to bandying and party-making for the superiority, as heartily as ever temporal tyrants did for dominion, and took as black and devilish methods to carry it on, as the worst of those tyrants ever had done before them.

At last Satan declared for the Roman pontif, and that upon excellent conditions, in the reign of the emperor Mauritius ; for Boniface, who had long contended for the title of supreme, fell into a treaty with Phocas, captain of the emperor's guards; whether the bargain from hell or not, let any one judge, the conditions absolutely entitle the Devil to the honour of making the contract, viz. That Phocas first murdering his master (the emperor) and his sons, Boniface should countenance the treason, and declare him emperor; and in return, Phocas should acknowledge the primacy of the church of Rome, and declare Boniface universal bishop. A blessed compact! which at once set the Devil at the head of affairs in the christian world, as well spiritual as temporal, ecclesiastic and civil. Since the conquest over Eve in Paradise, by which Death and the Devil, hand in hand, established their first empire upon earth, the Devil never gained a more important point than he gained at this time.

He had indeed prospered in his affairs tolerably well for some time before this, and his interest among the clergy had got ground for some ages; but that was indeed a secret management, was carried on privately, and with difficulty; as in sowing discord and faction among the people, perplexing the councils of their princes, and secretly wheedling in with the dignified clergy.

Also he had raised abundance of little church-rebellions, by setting up heretics of several kinds, and raising them favourers among the clergy, such as Ebion, Cerinthius, Pelagius, and others.

He had drawn in the bishops of Rome to set up the ridiculous pageantry of the key; and while he, the Devil, set open the gates of hell to them all, set them upon locking up the gates of heaven, and giving the bishop the key ; a cheat which, as gross as it was, the Devil so gilded over, or so blinded the age to receive it, that like Gideon's ephod, all the catholic world went a whoring after the idol ; and the bishop of Rome sent more fools to the Devil by it than ever he pretended to let into heaven, though he opened the door as wide as his key was able to do.

The story of this key being given to the bishop of Rome by St. Peter (who by the way, never had it himself) and of its being lost by somebody or other, (the Devil it seems did not tell them who) and its being found again by the Lombard soldier in the army of king Antharis, who attempting to cut it with his knife, was miraculously forced to direct the wound to himself, and cut his own throat ; that king Antharis and his nobles happened to see the fellow do it, and were converted to christianity by it, and that the king sent the key with another made like it, to pope Pelagius, then bishop of Rome, who thereupon assumed the power of opening and shutting heaven's gates ; and he afterwards setting a price or toll upon the entrance, as we do here at passing a turn-pike ; these fine things, I say, were successfully managed for some years before this I am now speaking of, and the Devil got a great deal of ground by it too ; but now he triumphed openly and having set up a murderer upon the temporal throne, and a church emperor upon the ecclesiastic throne, and both of his own chosing, the Devil may be said to begin his new kingdom from this epocha, and call it the Restoration.

Since this time indeed the Devil's affairs went very merrily on, and the clergy brought so many gewgaws into their worship, and such devilish principles were

mixed with that which we called the christian faith, that
in a word, from this time, the bishop of Rome commenced whore of Babylon, in all the most express terms that
could be imagined : Tyranny of the worst sort crept
into the pontificate, errors of all sorts into the profession,
and they proceeded from one thing to another, till the
very popes, for so the bishop of Rome was now called,
by way of distinction ; I say, the popes themselves,
their spiritual guides, professed openly to confederate
with the Devil, and to carry on a personal and private
correspondence with him at the same time, taking upon
them the title of Christ's vicar, and the infallible guide
of the consciences of christians.

This we have sundry instances of in some merry
popes, who, if fame lies not, were sorcerers, magicians,
had familiar spirits, and immediate conversation with
the Devil, as well visibly as invisibly, and by this means
became what we call devils incarnate : Upon this account
it is that I have left the conversation that passes between
devils and men to this place, as well because I believe it
differs much now in his modern state, from what it was
in its ancient state, and therefore that which most concerns us belongs rather to this part of his history ; as also
because, as I am now writing to the present age, I
choose to bring the most significant parts of his history,
especially as they relate to ourselves, into that part of
time that we are most concerned in.

The Devil had once, as I observed before, the universal monarchy or government of mankind in himself,
and I doubt not but in that flourishing state of his
affairs, he governed them like what he is, viz. an absolute tyrant ; during this theocracy of his, for Satan is

called *the god of this world*, he did not familiarise himself to mankind so much, as he finds occasion to do now, there was not then so much need of it; he governed then with an absolute sway; he had his oracles, where he gave audience to his votaries like a deity, and he had his sub-gods, who under his several dispositions received the homage of mankind in their names; such were all the rabble of the heathen deities, from Jupiter the supreme, to the lares or household gods of every family; these, I say, like residents, received the prostrations, but the homage was all Satan's; the Devil had the substance of it all, which was the idolatry.

During this administration of hell, there was less witchcraft, less true literal magic than there has been since; there was indeed no need of it, the Devil did not stoop to the mechanism of his more modern operations, but ruled as a deity, and received the vows and the bows of his subjects in more state, and with more solemnity; whereas since that, he is content to employ more agents and take more pains himself too; now he runs up and down hackney in the world, more like a drudge than a prince, and much more than he did then.

Hence all those things we call apparitions and visions of ghosts, familiar spirits and dealings with the Devil, of which there is so great a variety in the world at this time, were not so much known among the people, in those first ages of the Devil's kingdom; in a word, the Devil seems to be put to his shifts, and to fly to art and stratagem for the carrying on his affairs, much more now than he did then.

One reason for this may be, that he has been more discovered and exposed in these ages, than he was before;

then he could appear in the world in his own proper
shapes, and yet not be known ; when the sons of God
appeared at the divine summons, Satan came along with
them ; but now he has played so many scurvy tricks
upon men, and they know him so well, that he is
obliged to play quite out of sight and act in disguise ;
mankind will allow nothing of his doing, and hear
nothing of his saying, in his own name ; and if you propose any thing to be done, and it be but said the Devil
is to help in the doing it, or if you say of any man he
deals with the Devil, or the Devil has a hand in it,
every body flies him and shuns him, as the most frightful thing in the world.

Nay, if any thing strange and improbable be done or
related to be done, we presently say the Devil was at the
doing it : Thus the great ditch at Newmarket Heath, is
called the Devil's ditch ; so the Devil built Crowland
Abbey, and the whispering-place in Gloucester Cathe-
dral ; nay, the cave at Castleton, only because there's
no getting to the farther end of it, is called the Devil's
A——— and the like : The poor people of Wiltshire,
when you ask them how the great stones at Stonehenge
were brought thither ? they'll all tell you the Devil
brought them ; if any mischief extraordinary befalls us,
we presently say the Devil was in it, and the Devil
would have it so ; in a word, the Devil has got an ill
name among us, and so he is fain to act more *in tenebris*,
more *incog.* than he used to do, play out of sight himself, and work by the sap, as the engineers call it, and
not openly and avowedly in his own name and person,
as formerly, though perhaps not with less success than
he did before ; and this leads me to enquire more nar-

rowly into the manner of the Devil's management of his affairs since the christian religion began to spread in the world, which manifestly differs from his conduct in more antient times ; in which if we discover some of the most consummate fool's policy, the most profound simple craft, and the most subtle shallow management of things that can by our weak understandings be conceived, we must only resolve it into this, that in short it is the Devil.

CHAPTER II.

Of hell as it is represented to us, and how the Devil is to be understood, as being personally in hell, when at the same time we find him at liberty ranging over the world.

IT is true, as that learned and pleasant author the inimitable Dr. Brown says, the Devil is his own hell ; one of the most constituting parts of his infelicity is, that he cannot act upon mankind *brevi manu*, by his own inherent power, as well as rage ; that he cannot unhinge this creation, which, as I have observed in its place, he had the utmost aversion to from its beginning, as it was a stated design in the creator to supply his place in heaven, with a new species of beings called Man, and fill the vacancies occasioned by his degeneracy and rebellion.

This filled him with rage inexpressible, and horrible resolutions of revenge, and the impossibility of executing those resolutions torments him with despair; this added to what he was before, makes him a complete Devil, with a hell in his own breast, and a fire unquenchable burning about his heart.

I might enlarge here, and very much to the purpose, in describing spherically and mathematically that exquisite quality called a devilish spirit, in which it would naturally occur to give you a whole chapter upon the glorious articles of malice and envy, and especially upon that luscious, delightful, triumphant passion called Revenge; how natural to man, nay even to both sexes; how pleasant in the very contemplation, though there be not just at that time a power of execution; how palatable it is in itself, and how well it relishes when it is dished up with its proper sauces, such as plot, contrivance, scheme and confederacy, all leading on to execution: How it possesses a human soul in all the most sensible parts; how it empowers mankind to sin in imagination, as effectually to all future intents and purposes (damnation) as if he had sinned actually: How safe a practice it is too, as to punishment in this life, namely, that it empowers us to cut throats clear of the gallows, to slander virtue, reproach innocence, wound honour and stab reputation; and in a word, to do all the wicked things in the world, out of the reach of the law.

It would also require some few words to describe the secret operations of those nice qualities when they reach the human soul; how effectually they form a hell within us, and how imperceptibly they assimilate and transform

us into devils, meer human devils, as really devils as
Satan himself, or any of his angels ; and that therefore it
is not so much out of the way, as some imagine, to say,
such a man is an incarnate devil ; for as crime made
Satan a devil, who was before a bright immortal seraph,
or angel of light ; how much more easily may the same
crime make the same devil, though every way meaner
and more contemptible, of a man or a woman either ?
But this is too grave a subject for me at this time.

The Devil being thus, I say, fired with rage and envy,
in consequence of his jealousy upon the creation of man,
his torment is encreased to the highest by the limitation
of his power, and being forbid to act against mankind
by force of arms ; this is, I say, part of his hell, which,
as above, is within him, and which he carries with him
wherever he goes ; nor is it so difficult to conceive of
hell, or of the Devil, either under this just description, as
it is by all the usual notions that we are taught to entertain of them by (the old women) our instructors ; for
every man may, by taking but a common view of himself, and making a just scrutiny into his own passions,
on some of their particular excursions, see a hell within
himself, and himself a meer devil as long as the inflam-
mation lasts ; and that as really, and to all intents and
purposes, as if he had the angel (Satan) before his face,
in his locality and personality ; that is to say, all devil
and monster in his person, and an immaterial but intense
fire flaming about and from within him, at all the pores
of his body.

The notions we receive of the Devil, as a person being
in hell as a place, are infinitely absurd and ridiculous ;
the first we are certain is not true in fact, because he has

a certain liberty, (however limited that is not to the purpose) is daily visible, and to be traced in his several attacks upon mankind, and has been so ever since his first appearance in Paradise; as to his corporal visibility, that is not the present question neither; it is enough that we can hunt him by the foot, that we can follow him as hounds do a fox upon a hot scent: We can see him as plainly by the effect, by the mischief he does, and more by the mischief he puts us upon doing, I say, as plainly, as if we saw him by the eye.

It is not to be doubted but the Devil can see us when and where we cannot see him: And as he has a personality, though it be spirituous, he and his angels too may be reasonably supposed to inhabit the world of spirits, and to have free access from thence to the regions of life, and to pass and repass in the air, as really, though not perceptible to us, as the spirits of men do after their release from the body, pass to the place (wherever that is) which is appointed for them.

If the Devil was confined to a place (hell) as a prison, he could then have no business here; and if we pretend to describe hell, as not a prison, but that the Devil has liberty to be there, or not be there as he pleased, then he would certainly never be there, or hell is not such a place as we are taught to understand it to be.

Indeed according to some, hell should be a place of fire and torment to the souls that are cast into it, but not to the devils themselves; who we make little more or less than keepers and turnkeys to hell, as a gaol; that they are sent about to bring souls thither, lock them in when they come, and then away upon the scent to fetch more: That one sort of devils are made to live in the

world among men, and to be busy continually debauching and deluding mankind, bringing them as it were to
the gates of hell ; and then another sort are porters and
carriers to fetch them in.

This is, in short, little more or less than the old story
of Pluto, of Cerberus, and of Charon ; only that our tale
is not half so well told, nor the parts of the fable so well
laid together.

In all these notions of hell and Devil, the torments of
the first, and the agency of the last tormenting, we meet
with not one word of the main and perhaps only accent
of horror, which belongs to us to judge of about hell, I
mean the absence of heaven ; expulsion, and exclusion
from the presence and face of the chief ultimate, the
only eternal and sufficient good ; and this loss sustained
by a sordid neglect of our concern in that excellent part,
in exchange for the most contemptible and justly condemned trifles, and all this eternal and irrecoverable :
These people tell us nothing of the eternal reproaches of
conscience, the horror of desparation, and the anguish of
a mind hopeless of ever seeing the glory, which alone
constitutes heaven, and which makes all other places
dreadful, and even darkness itself.

And this brings me directly to the point in hand,
(viz.) the state of that hell we ought to have in view
when we speak of the Devil as in hell : This is the very
hell, which is the torment of the Devil ; in short, the
Devil is in hell, and hell is in the Devil ; he is filled
with this unquenchable fire, he is expelled the place of
glory, banished from the regions of light, absence from
the life of all beatitude is his curse, despair is the reigning passion in his mind, and all the little constituent

parts of his torment, such as rage, envy, malice, and
jealousy are consolidated in this, to make his misery
complete (viz.) the duration of it all, the eternity of his
condition ; that he is without hope, without redemption,
without recovery.

If any thing can inflame this hell, and make it hotter,
it is this only, and this does add an inexpressible horror
to the Devil himself; namely, the seeing man (the only
creature he hates) placed in a state of recovery, a glorious establishment of redemption formed for him in heaven, and the scheme of it perfected on earth ; by which
this man, though even the Devil by his art may have
deluded him, and drawn him into crime, is yet in a state
of recovery, which the Devil is not ; and that it is not in
his (Satan's) power to prevent it : Now take the Devil
as he is in his own nature angelic, a bright immortal
seraph, heaven-born, and having tasted the eternal beatitude, which these are appointed to enjoy ; the loss of
that state to himself, the possession of it granted to his
rival though wicked like and as himself : I say, take the
Devil as he is, having a quick sense of his own perdition,
and a stinging spirit of his rival's felicity, it is hell
enough, and more than enough, even for an angel to
support ; nothing we can conceive can be worse.

As to any other fire than this, such and so immaterially
intense as to torment a spirit, which is itself fire also ;
I will not say it cannot be, because to infinite every
thing is possible, but I must say, I cannot conceive
rightly of it.

I will not enter here into the wisdom or reasonableness
of representing the torments of hell to be fire, and that
fire to be a commixture of flame and sulphur ; it has

pleased God to let the horror of those eternal agonies about a lost heaven, be laid before us by those similitudes or allegories, which are most moving to our senses and to our understandings ; nor will I dispute the possibility ; much less will I doubt but that there is to be a consummation of misery to all the objects of misery, when the Devil's kingdom in this world, ending with the world itself, that liberty he has now may be farther abridged ; when he may be returned to the same state he was in between the time of his fall and the creation of the world ; with perhaps some additional vengeance on him, such as at present we cannot describe, for all that treason, and those high crimes and misdemeanours which he has been guilty of here, in his conversation with mankind.

As his infelicity will be then consummated and completed, so the infelicity of that part of mankind, who are condemned with him, may receive a considerable addition from those words in their sentence, to be tormented with the Devil and his angels ; for as the absence of the supreme good is a complete hell, so the hated company of the deceiver, who was the great cause of his ruin, must be a subject of additional horror, and he will be always saying, as a Scots gentleman, who died of his excesses, said to the famous Dr. P———, who came to see him on his death-bed, but had been too much his companion in his life,

O tu fundamenta jecisti———

I would not treat the very subject itself with any indecency, nor do I think my opinion of that hell, which

I say consists in the absence of him, in whom is heaven,
one jot less solemn than theirs who believe it all fire and
brimstone ; but I must own, that to me nothing can be
more ridiculous than the notion that we entertain and fill
our heads with about hell, and about the Devil's being
there tormenting of souls, broiling them upon gridirons,
hanging them up upon hooks, carrying them upon their
backs, and the like, with the several pictures of hell, represented by a great mouth with horrible teeth, gaping
like a cave on the side of a mountain ; suppose that
appropriated to Satan in the Peak, which indeed is not
much unlike it, with a stream of fire coming out of it, as
there is of water, and smaller devils going and coming
continually in and out, to fetch and carry souls the
Lord knows whither, and for the Lord knows what.

These things, however intended for terror, are indeed
so ridiculous, that the Devil himself to be sure, mocks at
them, and a man of sense can hardly refrain doing the
like, only I avoid it, because I would not give offence to
weaker heads.

However I must not compliment the brains of other
men, at the expence of my own, or talk nonsense because
they can understand no other ; I think all these notions
and representations of hell and of the Devil, to be as
prophane as they are ridiculous, and I ought no more to
talk prophanely than merrily of them.

Let us learn to talk of these things then, as we should
do ; and as we really cannot describe them to our reason
and understanding, why should we describe them to our
senses ; we had, I think, much better not describe them
at all, that is to say, not attempt it : The blessed apostle
St. Paul was, as he said himself, carried up, or caught

up into the third heaven, yet when he came down again, he could neither tell what he heard or describe what he saw ; all he could say of it was, that what he heard was unutterable, and what he saw was inconceivable.

It is the same thing as to the state of the Devil in those regions which he now possesses, and where he now more particularly inhabits ; my present business then is not to enter into those grave things, so as to make them ridiculous, as I think most people do that talk of them ; but as the Devil, let his residence be where it will, has evidently free leave to come and go, not into this world only, (I mean, the region of our atmosphere) but for ought we know, to all the other inhabited worlds which God has made, wherever they are, and by whatsoever names they are or may be known or distinguished ; for if he is not confined in one place, we have no reason to believe he is excluded from any place, heaven only excepted, from whence he was expelled for his treason and rebellion.

His liberty then being thus ascertained, three things seem to be material for us to give an account of, in order to form this part of his history.

1. What his business is on this globe of earth which we vulgarly call the World, how he acts among us, what affairs mankind and he have together, and how far his conduct here relates to us, and ours is, or may be influenced by him.

2. Where his principal residence is, and whether he has not a particular empire of his own, to which he retreats upon proper occasions ; where he entertains his friends when they come under his particular

administration ; and where, when he gets any victory over his enemies, he carries his prisoners of
war.

3. What may probably be the great business this
   black emperor has at present upon his hands, either
   in this world or out of it, and by what agents he
   works.

As these things may perhaps run promiscuously
through the course of this whole work, and frequently
be touched at under other branches of the Devil's history, so I do not propose them as heads of chapters or
particular sections, for the order of discourse to be handled apart ; for (by the way) as Satan's actings have not
been the most regular things in the world, so in our discourse about him, it must not be expected that we can
always tie ourselves down to order and regularity, either
as to time, or place, or persons ; for Satan being *hic &
ubique*, a loose ungoverned fellow, we must be content
to trace him where we can find him.

It is true, in the foregoing chapter, I shewed you the
Devil entered into the herd ecclesiastic, and gave you
some account of the first successful step he took with
mankind since the christian epocha ; how having secretly managed both temporal and spiritual power apart,
and by themselves, he now united them in point of
management, and brought the church usurpation and
the army's usurpation together ; the pope to bless the
general in deposing and murdering his master the emperor ; and the general to recognise the pope in dethroning his master Christ Jesus.

From this time forward you are to allow the Devil a

mystical empire in this world ; not an action of moment done without him, not a treason but he has a hand in it, not a tyrant but he prompts him, not a government but he has a ———— in it ; not a fool but he tickles him, not a knave but he guides him ; he has a finger in every fraud, a key to every cabinet, from the divan at Constantinople, to the missisippi in France, and to the South-Sea cheats at ———— ; from the first attack upon the christian world, in the person of the Romish antichrist, down to the bull Unigenitus ; and from the mixture of St. Peter and Confucius in China, to the holy office in Spain ; and down to the Emlins and Dodwells of the current age.

How he has managed, and does manage, and how in all probability he will manage till his kingdom shall come to a period, and how at last he will probably be managed himself, enquire within, and you shall know farther.

236 **THE HISTORY**

Satan carries on his affairs in this world by agitation, &c.

CHAPTER III.

Of the manner of Satan's acting and carrying on his affairs in this world, and particularly of his ordinary workings in the dark, by possession and agitation.

THE Devil being thus reduced to act upon mankind by stratagem only, it remains to enquire how he performs, and which way he directs his attacks; the faculties of man are a kind of a garrison in a strong castle, which as they defend it on the one hand under the command of the reasoning power of man's soul, so they are prescribed on the other hand, and cannot sally out without leave; for the governor of a fort does not permit his soldiers to hold any correspondence with the enemy, without special order and direction. Now the great enquiry before us is, how comes the Devil to a parley with us? How does he converse with our senses, and with the understanding? How does he reach us, which way does he come at the affections, and which way does he move the passions? It is a little difficult to discover this treasonable correspondence, and that difficulty is indeed the Devil's advantage, and, for ought I see, the chief advantage he has over mankind.

It is also a great enquiry here, whether the Devil knows our thoughts or no? If I may give my opinion, I am with the negative; I deny that he knows any thing of our thoughts, except of those thoughts which he puts us upon thinking, for I will not doubt but he has the art to inject thoughts, and to revive dormant thoughts in us: It is not so wild a scheme as some take it to be, that Mr. Milton lays down, to represent the Devil injecting corrupt desires and wandering thoughts into the head of Eve, by dreams, and that he brought her to dream whatever he put into her thoughts, by whispering to her vocally when she was asleep ; and to this end, he imagines the Devil laying himself close to her ear, in the shape of a toad, when she was fast asleep ; I say, this is not so wild a scheme, seeing even now, if you can whisper any thing close to the ear of a person in a deep sleep, so as to speak distinctly to the person, and yet not awaken him, as has been frequently tried, the person sleeping shall dream distinctly of what you say to him ; nay, shall dream the very words you say.

We have then no more to ask, but how the Devil can convey himself to the ear of a sleeping person, and it is granted then that he may have power to make us dream what he pleases : But this is not all, for if he can so forcibly, by his invisible application, cause us to dream what he pleases, why can he not with the same facility prompt our thoughts, whether sleeping or waking ? To dream, is nothing else but to think sleeping ; and we have abundance of deep-headed gentlemen among us, who give us ample testimony that they dream waking.

But if the Devil can prompt us to dream, that is to say, to think, yet if he does not know our thoughts, how then can he tell whether the whisper had its effect ? The answer is plain, the Devil, like the angler, baits the hook, if the fish bite he lies ready to take the advantage, he whispers to the imagination, and then waits to see how it works ; as Naomi said to Ruth, chap. iii. ver. 18.

Sit still, my daughter, until thou know how the matter will fall, for the man will not be at rest until he have finished the thing. Thus when the Devil had whispered to Eve in her sleep, according to Milton, and suggested mischief to her imagination, he only sat still to see how the matter would work, for he knew if it took with her, he should hear more of it; and then by finding her alone the next day, without her ordinary guard her husband, he presently concluded she had swallowed the bait, and so attacked her afresh.

A small deal of craft, and less by far than we have reason to believe the Devil is master of, will serve to discover whether such and such thoughts as he knows he has suggested, have taken place or no; the action of the person presently discovers it, at least to him that lies always upon the watch, and has every word, every gesture, every step we take subsequent to his operation, open to him; it may therefore, for ought we know, be a great mistake, and what most of us are guilty of, to tell our dreams to one another in the morning, after we have been disturbed with them in the night; for if the Devil converses with us so insensibly as some are of the opinion he does, that is to say, if he can hear as far as we can see, we may be telling our story to him indeed, when we think we are only talking to one another.

This brings me most naturally to the important enquiry, whether the Devil can walk about the world invisibly or no? The truth is, this is no question to me; for as I have taken away his visibility already, and have denied him all prescience of futurity to, and have proved he cannot know our thoughts, nor put any force upon persons or actions, if we should take away his invisibility too, we should undevil him quite, to all intents and purposes, as to any mischief he could do; nay, it would banish him the world, and he might even go and seek his fortune somewhere else; for if he could neither be visible or invisible, neither act in public or in private, he could neither have business or being in this sphere, nor could we be any way concerned with him.

The Devil therefore most certainly has a power and liberty of moving about in this world, after some manner or another; this is verified as well by way of allegory, as by way of history, in the scripture itself; and as the first strongly suggests and supposes it to be so, the last positively asserts it; and, not to croud this work with quotations from a book which we have not much to do with in the Devil's story, at least not much to his satisfaction, I only hint his personal appearance to our Saviour in the wilderness, where it is said, *the Devil taketh him up to an exceeding high mountain;* and in another place, *the Devil departed from him.* What shape or figure he appeared in, we do not find mentioned, but I cannot doubt his appearing to him there, any more than I can his talking to our Saviour in the mouths, and with the voices of the several persons who were under the terrible affliction of an actual possession.

These things leave us no room to doubt of what is advanced above, namely, that he (the Devil) has a certain residence, or liberty of residing in, and moving about upon the surface of this earth, as well as in the compass of the atmosphere, vulgarly called the air, in some manner or other: That is the general.

Satan carries on his affairs in this world by agitation, &c.

It remains to enquire into the manner, which I resolve into two kinds;

1. Ordinary, which I suppose to be his invisible motions as a spirit; under which consideration I suppose him to have an unconfined, unlimited, unrestrained liberty, as to the manner of acting; and this either in persons, by possession; or in things, by agitation.

2. Extraordinary; which I understand to be his appearances in borrowed shapes and bodies, or shadows rather of bodies; assuming speech, figure, posture, and several powers, of which we can give little or no account; in which extraordinary manner of appearances, he is either limited by a superior power, or limits himself politically, as being not the way most for his interest or purpose, to act in his business, which is more effectually done in his state of obscurity.

Hence we must suppose the Devil has it very much in his own choice, whether to act in one capacity, or in the other, or in both; that is to say, of appearing and not appearing, as he finds for his purpose: In this state of invisibility, and under the operation of these powers and liberties, he performs all his functions and offices as Devil, as Prince of Darkness, as God of this World, as Tempter, Accuser, Deceiver, and all whatsoever other names of office, or titles of honour he is known by.

Now taking him in this large unlimited, of little limited

state of action, he is well called, the God of this World, for he has very much of the attribute of omnipresence, and may be said, either by himself or his agents, to be every where, and see every thing ; that is to say, every thing that is visible ; for I cannot allow him any share of omniscience at all.

That he rages about every where, is with us, and sometimes in us, sees when he is not seen, hears when he is not heard, comes in without leave, and goes out without noise, is neither to be shut in or shut out, that when he runs from us we cannot catch him, and when he runs after us we cannot escape him, is seen when he is not known, and is known when he is not seen ; all these things, and more, we have knowledge enough about to convince us of the truth of them ; so that, as I have said above, he is certainly walking to and fro through the earth, &c. after some manner or other, and in some figure or other, visible or invisible, as he finds occasion. Now in order to make our history of him complete, the next question before us is, how, and in what manner he acts with mankind ? How his kingdom is carried on, and by what methods he does his business, for he certainly has a great deal of business to do ; he is not an idle spectator, nor is he walking about *incognito*, and clothed in mist and darkness, purely in kindness to us, that we should not be frighted at him ; but it is in policy, that he may act undiscovered, that he may see and not be seen, may play his game in the dark, and not be detected in his roguery ; that he may prompt mischief, raise tempests, blow up coals. kindle strife, embroil nations, use instruments, and not be known to have his

11   2 H

hand in any thing, when, at the same time, he really has a hand in every thing.

Some are of opinion, and I among the rest, that if the Devil was personally and visibly present among us, and we conversed with him face to face, we should be so familiar with him in a little time, that his ugly figure would not affect us at all, that his terrors would not fright us, or that we should any more trouble ourselves about him, than we did with the last great comet in 1678, which appeared so long and so constantly without any particular known event, that at last we took no more notice of it than of the other ordinary stars which had appeared before we or our ancestors were born.

Nor indeed should we have much reason to be frighted at him, or at least none of those silly things could be said of him, which we now amuse ourselves about, and by which we set him up like a scare-crow to fright children and old women, to fill up old stories, make songs and ballads, and in a word, carry on the low prized buffoonery of the common people ; we should either see him in his angelic form, as he was from the original, or if he has any deformities entailed upon him by the supreme sentence, and in justice to the deformity of his crime, they would be of a superior nature, and fitted more for our contempt, as well as horror, than those weak fancied trifles contrived by our antient devil-raisers and devil-makers, to feed the wayward fancies of old witches and sorcerers, who cheated the ignorant world with a devil of their own making, set forth, *in terrorem*, with bat's wings, horns, cloven foot, long tail, forked tongue, and the like.

In the next place, be his frightful figure what it would, and his legions as numerous as the host of heaven, we should see him still, as the prince of devils, though monstrous as a dragon, flaming as a comet, tall as a mountain, yet dragging his chain after him equal to the utmost of his supposed strength ; always in custody of his jailors the angels, his power overpowered, his rage cow'd and abated, or at least aw'd and under correction, limited and restrained ; in a word, we shall see him a vanquished slave, his spirit broken, his malice, though not abated, yet hand-cuffed and overpowered, and he not able to work any thing against us by force ; so that he would be to us but like the lions in the tower, enraged' and locked up, unable to do the hurt he wishes to do, and that we fear, or indeed any hurt at all.

From hence it is evident, that it is not his business to be public, or to walk up and down in the world visibly, and in his own shape ; his affairs require a quite different management, as might be made apparent from the nature of things, and the manner of our actings, as men, either with ourselves or to one another.

Nor could he be serviceable in his generation, as a public person, as now he is, or answer the end of his party who employ him ; and who, if he was to do their business in public, as he does in private, would not be able to employ him at all.

As in our modern meetings for the propagation of impudence and other virtues, there would be no enter- tainment and no improvement for the good of the age, if the people did not all appear in masque, and concealed from the common observation ; so neither could Satan (from whose management those more happy assemblies are taken as copies of a glorious original) perform the usual and necessary business of his profession, if he did not appear wholly in covert, and under needful disguises; how, but for the convenience of his habit, could he cast himself into so many shapes, act on so many different scenes, and turn so many wheels of state in the world, as he has done? As a meer professed devil he could do nothing.

Had he been obliged always to act the meer devil in his own clothes, and with his own shape, appearing uppermost in all cases and places, he could never have preached in so many pulpits, presided in so many councils, voted in so many committees, sat in so many courts, and influenced so many parties and factions in church and state, as we have reason to believe he has done in our nation, and in our memories too, as well as in other nations and in more antient times. The share Satan has had in all the weighty confusions of the times, ever since the first ages of christianity in the world, has been carried on with so much secresy, and so much with an air of cabal and intrigue, that nothing can have been managed more subtlely and closely; and in the same manner has he acted in our times, in order to conceal his interest, and conceal the influence he has had in the councils of the world.

Had it been possible for him to have raised the flames of rebellion and war so often in this nation, as he certainly has done? Could he have agitated the parties on both sides, and inflamed the spirits of three nations, if he had appeared in his own dress, a meer naked devil? It is not the Devil as a devil, that does the mischief, but the Devil in masquerade, Satan in full disguise, and acting at the head of civil confusion and distraction.

If history may be credited, the French court at the time of our old confusions was made the scene of Satan's politics, and prompted both parties in England and in Scotland also to quarrel, and how was it done? Will any man offer to scandalize the Devil so much as to say, or so much as to suggest, that Satan had no hand in it all? Did not the Devil, by the agency of cardinal Richlieu, send 400,000 crowns at one time, and 600,000 at another, to the Scots, to raise an army, and march boldly into England? and did not the same Devil, at the same time, by other agents remit 800,000 crowns to the other party, in order to raise an army to fall upon the Scots? nay, did not the Devil, with the same subtlety send down the archbishop's order to impose the service-book upon the people in Scotland, and at the same time raise a mob against it, in the great church (at St. Giles's)? Nay, did not he actually, in the person of an old woman (his favourite instrument) throw the three-leg'd stool at the service-book, and animate the zealous people to take up arms for religion, and turn rebels for God's sake.

All these happy and successful undertakings, though it is no more to be doubted they were done by the agency of Satan, and in a very surprizing manner too, yet were all done in secret, by what I call possession and injection, and by the agency and contrivance of such instruments, or by the Devil in the disguise of such servants as he found out fitted to be employed in his work, and who he took a more effectual care in concealing of.

But we shall have occasion to touch all this part over again, when we come to discourse of the particular habits and disguises which the Devil has made use of, all along in the world, the better to cover his actions, and to conceal his being concerned in them.

In the mean time, the cunning or artifice the Devil makes use of in all these things is in itself very considerable ; it is an old practice of his using, and he has gone on in divers measures, for the better concealing himself in it ; which measures, though he varies sometimes, as his extraordinary affairs require, yet they are in all ages much the same, and have the same tendency, namely, that he may get all his business carried on by the instrumentality of fools ; that he may make mankind agents in their own destruction, and that he may have all his work done in such a manner as that he may seem to have no hand in it ; nay he contrives so well, that the very name Devil is put upon his opposite party, and the scandal of the black agent lies all upon them.

In order then to look a little into his conduct, let us enquire into the common mistakes about him, see what use is made of them to his advantage, and how far mankind is imposed upon in those particulars, and to what purpose.

CHAPTER IV.

Of Satan's agents or missionaries, and their actings
upon and in the minds of men in his name.

INFINITE advantages attend the Devil in his retired
government, as they respect the management of his interests, and the carrying on his absolute monarchy in the
world ; particularly as it gives him room to act by the
agency of his inferior ministers and messengers, called
on many occasions his angels, of whom he has an innumerable multitude at his command, enough, for aught
we know, to spare one to attend every man and woman
now alive in the world ; and of whom, if we may believe
our second-sight christians, the air is always as full as a
beam of the evening sun is of insects, where they are
ever ready for business, and to go and come as their
great governor issues out orders for their directions.

These, as they are all of the same spirituous quality
with himself, and consequently invisible like him, except as above, are ready upon all occasions to be sent to
and into any such person, and for such purposes, superior limitations only excepted, as the grand Director of
Devils (the Devil properly so called) guides them ; and
be the subject or the object what it will, that is to say, be
the person they are sent to, or into, as above, who it will,
and the business the messenger is to do what it will, they
are sufficiently qualified ; for this is a particular to
Satan's messengers or agents, that they are not like us
humane devils here in the world, some bred up one way

some another, some of one, trade, some of another,
and consequently some fit for some business, some for
another, some good for something, and some good for
nothing, but his people are every one fit for every
thing, can find their way every where, and are a match
for every body they are sent to; in a word, there are
no foolish devils,. they are all fully qualified for their
employment, fit for any thing he sets them about, and
very seldom mistake their errand or fail in the business
they are sent to do.

Nor is it strange at all, that the Devil should have
such a numberless train of deputy devils to act under
him ; for it must be acknowledged he has a great deal of
business upon his hands, a vast deal of work to do,
abundance of public affairs under his direction, and an
infinite variety of particular cases always before him :
For example ;

How many governments in the world are wholly, in his
admistration ? how many divans and great councils under
his direction ? nay, I believe, it would be hard to prove
that there is or has been one council of state in the world
for many hundred years past, down to the year 1713,
(we do not pretend to come nearer home) where the
Devil by himself, or his agents in one shape or another,
has not sat as a member, if not taken the chair.

And though some learned authors may dispute this
point with me, by giving some examples where the
councils of princes have been acted by a better hand,
and where things have been carried against Satan's interests, and even to his great mortification, it amounts to
no more than this ; namely, that in such cases the Devil
has been out-voted ; but it does not argue, but he might

have been present there, and have pushed his interest as far as he could, only that he had not the success he expected; for I do not pretend to say that he has never been disappointed; but those examples are so rare, and of so small signification, that when I come to the particulars, as I shall do in the sequel of this history, you will find them hardly worth naming; and that, take it one time with another, the Devil has met with such a series of success in all his affairs, and has so seldom been baulked; and where he has met with a little check in his politics, has notwithstanding, so soon and so easily recovered himself, regained his lost ground, or replaced himself in another country when he has been supplanted in one, that his empire is far from being lessened in the world, for the last thousand years of the christian establishment.

Suppose we take an observation from the beginning of Luther, or from the year 1420, and call the reformation a blow to the Devil's kingdom, which before that was come to such a height in christendom, that it is a question not yet thoroughly decided whether that medley of superstition and horrible heresies, that mass of enthusiasm and idols called the Catholic Hierarchy, was a church of God or a church of the Devil; whether it was an assembly of saints or a synagogue of Satan : I say, take that time to be the epocha of Satan's declension and of Lucifer's falling from heaven, that is, from the top of his terrestrial glory, yet whether he did not gain in the defection of the Greek church about that time and since, as much as he lost in the reformation of the Roman, is what authors are not yet agreed about, not reckoning what he has regained since of the ground which he had

lost even by the reformation, viz. the countries of the
duke of Savoy's dominion, where the reformation is
almost eaten out by persecution ; the whole Valtoline
and some adjacent countries ; the whole kingdom of
Poland and almost all Hungary ; for since the last war
the reformation, as it were, lies gasping for breath, and
expiring in that country, also several large provinces in
Germany, as Austria, Carinthia, and the whole kingdom of Bohemia, where the reformation once powerfully
planted, received its death's wound at the battle of
Prague, Ann. 1627, and languished but a very little
while, died and was buried, and good king Popery
reigned in its stead.

To these countries thus regained to Satan's infernal
empire, let us add his modern conquests and the encroachments he has made upon the reformation in the
present age, which are, however light we make of them,
very considerable, viz. the electorate of the Rhine and
the Palatinate, the one fallen to the house of Bavaria,
and the other to that of Neuburgh, both popish ; the
dutchy of Deux Ponts fallen just now to a popish branch,
the whole eletorate of Saxony fallen under the power of
popish government by the apostacy of their princes, and
more likely to follow the fate of Bohemia, whenever the
diligent Devil can bring his new project in Poland to
bear, as it is more than probable he will do some time or
other, by the growing zeal as well as power of (that
house of bigots) the house of A————.

But to sum up the dull story ; we must add in the
roll of the Devil's conquests, the whole kingdom of
France, where we have in one year seen, to the immortal
glory of the Devil's politics, that his measures have pre-

vailed to the total extirpation of the Protestant churches without a war ; and that interest, which for 200 years has supported itself in spite of persecutions, massacres, five civil wars and innumerable battles and slaughters, at last received its mortal wound from its own champion Henry IV. and sunk into utter oblivion, by Satan's most exquisite management under the agency of his two prime ministers cardinal Richlieu and Lewis the XIV. whom he entirely possessed.

Thus far we have a melancholy view of the Devil's new conquests, and the ground he has regained upon the reformation, in which his secret management has been so exquisite, and his politics so good, that could he bring but one thing to pass, which by his own former mistake (for the Devil is not infallible) he has rendered impossible, he would bring the Protestant interest so near its ruin, that heaven would be, as it were, put to the necessity of working by miracle to prevent it ; the case is thus.

Antient historians tell us, and from good authority, that the Devil finding it for his interest to bring his favourite mahomet upon the stage, and spread the victorious half-moon upon the ruin of the cross, having with great success, raised first the Saracen empire, and then the Turkish to such a height, as that the name of Christian seemed to be extirpated in those two quarters of the world, which were then not the greatest only, but by far the most powerful, I mean Asia and Africa ; having totally laid waste all those antient and flourishing churches of Africa, the labours of St. Cyprian, Tertullian, St. Augustine, and 670 christian bishops and fathers, who governed there at once, also all the churches of

Smyrna, Philadelphia, Ephesus, Sardis, Antioch, Lao-
dicea, and innumerable others in Pontus, Bithynia, and
the provinces of the Lesser Asia.

The Devil having, I say, finished these conquests so
much to his satisfaction, began to turn his eyes Northward, and though he had a considerable interest in the
whore of Babylon, and had brought his power, by the
subjection of the Roman hierarchy, to a great height,
yet finding the interest of mahomet most suitable to his
devilish purposes, as most adapted to the destruction of
mankind, and laying waste the world, he resolved to
espouse the growing power of the Turk, and bring him
in upon Europe like a deluge.

In order to this, and to make way for an easy conquest, like a true Devil, he worked under-ground, and
sapped the foundation of the christian power, by sowing
discord among the reigning princes of Europe ; that so
envying one another, they might be content to stand still
and look on, while the Turk devoured them one by one,
and at last might swallow them up all.

This devilish policy took to his heart's content ; the
christian princes stood still, stupid, dozing, and unconcerned, till the Turk conquered Thrace, over-run
Servia, Macedonia, Bulgaria, and all the remains of the
Grecian empire, and last the imperial city of Constantinople itself.

Finding this politic method so well answer his ends,
the Devil, who always improves upon the success of his
own experiments, resolved, from that time, to lay a
foundation for the making those divisions and jealousies
of the christian princes immortal ; whereas they were at
first only personal, and founded in private quarrels be-

tween the princes respectively ; such as emulation of one another's glory, envy at the extraordinary valour, or other merit of this or that leader, or revenge of some little affront ; for which notwithstanding, so great was the piety of christian princes in those days, that they made no scruples to sacrifice whole armies, yea; nations, to their piques and private quarrels, a certain sign whose management they were under.

These being the causes by which the Devil first sowed the seeds of mischief among them, and the success so well answering his design, he could not but wish to have the same advantage always ready at his hand ; and therefore he resolved to order it so, that these divisions, which however useful to him, were only personal, and consequently temporary like an annual in the garden, which must be raised anew every season, might for the future be national, and consequently durable and immortal.

To this end it was necessary to lay the foundation of eternal feud, not in the humours and passions of men only, but in the interests of nations : The way to do this was to form and state the dominion of those princes, by such a plan drawn in hell, and laid out from a scheme truly political, of which the Devil was chief engineer ; that the divisions should always remain, being made a natural consequence of the situation of the country, the temper of their people, the nature of their commerce, the climate, the manner of living, or something which should for ever render it impossible for them to unite.

This, I say, was a scheme truly infernal, in which the Devil was as certainly the principal operator, to illustrate great things by small, as ever John of Leyden was of the high Dutch rebellion, or sir John B—t, of the late project, called the South Sea stock. Nor did this contrivance of the Devil at all dishonour its author, or the success appear unworthy of the undertaker; for we see it not only answered the end, and made the Turk victorious at the same time, and formidable to Europe ever after, but it works to this day, the foundation of the divisions remains in all the several nations, and that to such a degree, that it is impossible they should unite.

This is what I hinted before, in which the Devil was mistaken, and is another instance that he knows nothing of what is tò come; for this very foundation of immortal jealousy and discord between the several nations of Spain, France, Germany, and others, which the Devil himself with so much policy contrived, and which served his interests so long, is now the only obstruction to his designs, and prevents the entire ruin of the reformation; for though the reformed countries are very powerful, and some of them, as Great Britain and Prussia are particularly, more powerful than ever; yet it cannot be said that the protestant interests in general are stronger than formerly, or so strong as they were in 1623, under the victorious arms of the Swede; on the other hand, were it possible that the popish powers, to wit, of France, Spain, Germany, Italy, and Poland, which are intirely popish, could heartily unite their interests, and should join their powers to attack the Protestants, the latter would find it very difficult, if not impossible, to defend themselves.

But as fatal as such an union of the popish powers would be, and as useful as it would be to the Devil's cause at this time, not the Devil with all his angels are able to bring it to pass; no, not with all his craft and cunning; he divided them, but he cannot unite them; so that even just as it is with men, so it is with Devils, they may do in an hour what they cannot undo in an age.

This may comfort those faint-hearted christians among us, who cry out of the danger of religious war in Europe, and what terrible things will happen when France, and Spain, and Germany, and Italy, and Poland shall all unite; let this answer satisfy them, The Devil himself can never make France and Spain, or France and the emperor unite; jarring humours may be reconciled, but jarring interests never can: They may unite so as to make peace, though that can hardly be long, but never so as to make conquests together; they are too much afraid of one another, for one to bear that any addition of strength should come to the other. But this is a digression. We shall find the Devil mistaken and disappointed too on several occasions, as we go along.

I return to Satan's interest in the several governments and nations, by virtue of his invisibility, and which he carries on by possession; it is by this invisibility that he presides in all the councils of foreign powers, (for we never mean our own, that we always premise;) and what though it is alledged by the critics, that he does not preside, because there is aways a president; I say, if he is not in the president's chair, yet if he be in the president himself, the difference is not so much; and if he does not vote as a counsellor, if he votes in the councellor it is much the same; and here, as it was in the story of Ahab the king of Israel, as he was a lying spirit in the mouths of all his prophets; so we find him a spirit of some particular evil quality or other, in all the transactions and transactors on that stage of life we call The State.

Thus he was a dissembling spirit in Char. IX. a turbulent spirit in Char. V. emperor; a bigotted spirit of fire and faggot in our queen Mary; an apostate spirit in Hen. IV.; a cruel spirit in Peter of Castile; a revengeful spirit in Ferdinand II; a phaeton in Lewis XIV.; a sardanapalus in C——— II.

In the great men of the world, take them a degree lower than the class of crowned heads, he has the same secret influence; and hence it comes to pass, that the greatest heroes, and men of the highest character for atchievements of glory, either by their virtue or valour, however they have been crowned with victories, and elevated by human tongues, whatever the most consummate virtues or good qualities they have been known by, yet they have always had some devil or other in them, to preserve Satan's claim to them uninterrupted, and prevent their escape out of his hands; thus we have seen a bloody devil in D'Alva; a profligate devil in a Buckingham; a lying, artful, or politic devil in a Richlieu; a treacherous devil in a Mazarin; a cruel, merciless devil in a Cortez; a debauched devil in an Eugene; a conjuring devil in a Luxemburg; and a covetous devil in a M———h: In a word, tell me the man, I'll tell you the spirit that reigned in him.

Nor does he thus carry on his secret management by possession in men of the first magnitude only, but have you not had evidences of it among ourselves? How has he been a lying spirit in the mouths of our prophets, a factious spirit in the heads of our politicians, a profuse

Of Satan's agents, and their actings on the minds of men.

Devil in a B———s, a corrupt Devil in M————, a proud spirit in my lord Plausible, a bullying spirit in my lord Bugbear, a talkative spirit in his grace the d— of Rattle-hall, a scribbling spirit in my lord H—, a runaway spirit in my lord Frightful; and so through a long roll of heroes, whose exceeding, and particular qualifications proclaim loudly what handle the Devil took them by, and how fast he held them; for these were all men of antient fame, I hope you know that.

From men of figure, we descend to the mob, and it is there the same thing; possession, like the plague, is *morbus plebœi;* not a family but he is a spirit of strife and contention among them; not a man but he has a part in him; he is a drunken devil in one, a whoring devil in another, a thieving devil in a third, a lying devil in the fourth, and so on to a thousand, and a hundred thousand, *ad infinitum.*

Nay, even the ladies have their share in the possession; and if they have not the Devil in their heads, or in their tails, in their faces or in their tongues, it must be some poor despicable she-devil that Satan did not think it worth his while to meddle with; and the number of those that are below his operation, I doubt is very small. But that part I have much more to say to in its place.

From degrees of persons, to professions and employments, it is the same; we find the Devil is a true posture-master, he assumes any dress, appears in any shape, counterfeits every voice, acts upon every stage; here he wears a gown, there a long robe; here he wears the jack-boots, there the small sword; is here an enthusiast, there a buffoon; on this side he acts the mountebank, on that side the merry-andrew; nothing comes amiss to

him, from the great mogul to the scaramouch ; the Devil
is in them, more or less, and plays his game so well, that
he makes sure work with them all : He knows where
the common foible lies, which is universal passion, what
handle to take hold of every man by, and how to culti-
vate his interest so, as not to fail of his end, or mistake
the means.

How then can it be denied but that his acting thus *in
tenebris*, and keeping out of the sight of the world, is
abundantly his interest, and that he could do nothing,
comparatively speaking, by any other method ?

What could his public appearance have signified ?
Who would have entertained him in his own proper
shape and person ? Even B——— B——— himself,
though all the world knows him to have a foolish devil
in him, would not have been fool enough to have taken
him into his service, if he had known him : And my lord
Simpleton also, who Satan has set up for a cunning fool,
seems to have it sit much better upon him, now he passes
for a fool of art, than it should have done, if the naked
Devil had come and challenged him for a fool in nature.

Infinite variety illustrate the Devil's reign among the
sons of men ; all which he manages with admirable dexterity, and a slight particular to himself, by the mere
advantage of his present concealed situation, and which
had he been obliged to have appeared in public, had
been all lost, and he capable of just nothing at all, or at
least of nothing more than the other ordinary politicians
of wickedness could have done without him.

Now, authors are much divided as to the manner how
the Devil manages his proper instruments for mischief ;
for Satan has a great many agents in the dark, who

neither have the Devil in them, nor are they much acquainted with him, and yet he serves himself of them, whether of their folly, or of that other frailty called wit, it is all one, he makes them do his work, when they think they are doing their own ; nay, so cunning is he in his guiding the weak part of the world, that even when they think they are serving God, they are doing nothing less or more than serving the Devil ; nay, it is some of the nicest part of his operation, to make them believe they are serving God, when they are doing his work. Thus those who the scripture foretold should persecute Christ's church in the latter days, were to think they do God good service : Thus the inquisition (for example) it may be, at this time, in all the acts of christian cruelty which they are so famous for (if any of them are ignorant enough not to know that they are devils incarnate) they may, for ought we know, go on for God's sake ; torture, murder, starve to death, mangle and macerate, and all for God, and God's catholic church ; and it is certainly the Devil's master-piece to bring mankind to such a perfection of devilism as that of the inquisition is ; for if the Devil had not been in them, could they christen such a hell-fire judicature as the inquisition is, by the name of the Holy Office ? and so in Paganism, how could so many nations among the poor Indians offer human sacrifices to their idols, and murder thousands of men, women, and children, to appease this God of the Air, when he is angry, if the Devil did not act in them under the vizor of devotion ?

But we need not go to America, or to the inquisition, not to paganism, or to popery either, to look for people that are sacrificing to the Devil, or that give their peace-offerings to him, while they are offered upon God's altar ; are not our churches (ay, and meeting-houses too, as much as they pretend to be more sanctified than their neighbours) full of devil worshippers ? Where do his devotees gratulate one another and congratulate him, more than at church ? where, while they hold up their hands, and turn up their eyes towards heaven, they make all their vows to Satan, or at least to the fair devils, his representatives, which I shall speak of in their place.

Do not the sons of God make assignations with the daughters of men, in the very house of worship ? Do not they talk to them in the language of the eyes ? and what is at the bottom of it, while one eye is upon the prayer-book, and the other adjusting their dress ? are they not sacrificing to Venus and Mercury, nay, and the very Devil they dress at ?

Let any man impartially survey the church gestures, the air, the postures and the behaviour ; let him keep an exact roll, and if I do not shew him two devil worshippers for one true saint, then the word saint must have another signification than I ever yet understood it by.

The church (as a place) is the receptacle of the dead, as well as the assembly of the living ; what relates to those below, I doubt Satan, if he would be so kind, could give a better account of than I can ; but as to the superficies, I pretend to so much penetration as to tell you, that there are more spectres, more apparitions always there, than you that know nothing of the matter, may be aware of.

I happened to be at an eminent place of God's most devout worship the other day, with a gentleman of my acquaintance, who, I observed, minded very little the business he ought to come about; first I saw him always busy staring about him, and bowing this way and that way, nay, he made two or three bows and scrapes when he was repeating the responses to the ten commandments, and I assure you, he made it correspond strangely, so that the harmony was not so broken in upon as you would expect it should; thus; Lord, and a bow to a fine lady just come up to her seat, have mercy upon us; ———— three bows to a throng of ladies that came into the next pew all together, and incline ———— then stopped to make a great scrape to my lord ————, our hearts, just then the hearts of all the church were gone off from the subject, for the response was over, so he huddled up the rest in whispers, for God-a-mighty could hear him well enough, he said, nay, as well as if he had spoken as loud as his neighbours did.

After we were come home, I asked him what he meant by all this, and what he thought of it.

How could I help it, said he, I must not be rude.

What, says I, rude to who?

Why, says he, there came in so many she devils, I could not help it.

What, said I, could not you help bowing when you were saying your prayers?

O Sir! says he, the ladies would have thought I had slighted them; I could not avoid it.

Ladies! said I, I thought you called them devils just now.

Ay, ay, devils, said he, little charming devils, but I must not be rude to them however.

Very well, said I, then you would be rude to God-a-mighty, because you could not be rude to the Devil?

Why that is true, said he, but what can we do ? there
is no going to church, as the case stands now, if we must
not worship the Devil a little between whiles.

This is the case indeed, and Satan carries his point
on every hand ; for if the fair speaking world, and the
fair looking world are generally devils, that is to say,
are in his management, we are sure the foul speaking
and the foul doing world are all on his side, and you
have then only the fair doing part of the world that are
out of his class, and when we speak of them, O how few !

But I return to the Devil's managing our wicked part,
for this he does with most exquisite subtilty ; and this
is one part of it (viz.) he thrusts our vices into our
virtues, by which he mixes the clean and the unclean,
and thus by the corruption of the one, poisons and
debauches the other, so that the slave he governs cannot
account for his own common actions, and is fain to be
obliged to his maker, to accept of the heart, without the
hands and feet ; to take, as we vulgarly express it, the
will for the deed, and if heaven was not so good to come
into that half in half service, I do not see but the Devil
would carry away all his servants : Here indeed I
should enter into a long detail of involuntary wickedness,
which in short, is neither more or less than the Devil in
every body, ay, in every one of you (our governors excepted) take it as you please.

What is our language, when we look back with reflection and reproach on past follies ? I think I was
bewitched, I was possessed, certainly the Devil was in
me, or else I had never been such a sot : Devil in you,
sir, ay, who doubts it ; you may be sure the Devil was
in you, and there he is still, and the next time he can

catch you in the same snare, you will be just the same sot that you say you were before.

In short, the Devil is too cunning for us, and manages us his own way; he governs the vices of men by his own methods; though every crime will not make a man a devil, yet it must be owned, that every crime puts the criminal, in some measure, into the Devil's power, gives him a title to the man, and he treats him magisterially ever after.

Some tell us every single man, every individual has a devil attending him, to execute the orders of the (grand signior) Devil of the whole clan; that this attending evil angel, for so he is called, sees every step you take, is with you in every action, prompts you to every mischief, and leaves you to do every thing that is pernicious to yourself; they also allege that there is a good spirit which attends him too, which latter is always accessary to every thing that we do that is good, and reluctant to evil; if this is true, how comes it to pass that those two opposite spirits do not quarrel about it when they are pressing us to contrary actions, one good and the other evil? And why does the evil tempting spirit so often prevail? Instead of answering this difficult question, I shall only tell you, as to this story of good and evil angels attending every particular person, it is a good allegory indeed to represent the struggle in the mind of man, between good and evil inclinations; but to the rest, the best thing I can say of it is, that, I think, it is a fib.

But to take things as they are, and only talk by way of natural consequence, for to argue from nature, is certainly the best way to find out the Devil's story; if there are good and evil spirits attending us, that is to say, a good angel and a devil, then it is no unjust reproach upon any body to say, when they follow the dictates of the latter, the Devil is in them ; or they are devils ; nay, I must carry it farther still, namely, that as the generality and greatest number of people do follow and obey the evil spirit and not the good, and that the predominate power is allowed to be the nominating power ; you must then allow, that in short, the greater part of mankind has the Devil in them, and so I come to my text.

To this purpose give me leave to borrow a few lines of a friend on this very part of the Devil's management.

To places and persons he suits his disguises,
 And dresses up all his banditti,
Who as pick-pockets flock to a country assizes,
 Croud up to the court and the city.

They're at every elbow, and every ear,
 And ready at every call, sir ;
The vigilant scout plants his agents about,
 And has something to do with us all, sir ;

In some he has part, and in some he's the whole,
 And of some (like the vicar of Baddow)
It can neither be said they have body or soul ;
 But only are devils in shadow.

The pretty and witty, are devils in masque,
 The beauties are mere apparitions ;
The homely alone by their faces are known,
 And the good by their ugly conditions.

The beaus walk about like the shadows of men,
    And wherever he leads 'em they follow,
But tak'em and shak'em, there's not one in ten
    But's as light as a feather and hollow.

Thus all his affairs he drives on in disguise,
    And he tickles mankind with a feather :
Creeps in at our ears, and looks out at our eyes,
    And jumbles our senses together.

He raises the vapours and prompts the desires,
    And to ev'ry dark deed holds the candle ;
The passions enflames and the appetite fires,
    And takes ev'ry thing by the handle.

Thus he walks up and down in complete masquerade,
    And with every company mixes,
Sells in every shop, works at every trade,
    And ev'ry thing doubtful perplexes.

How Satan comes by this governing influence in the minds, and upon the actions of men, is a question I am not yet come to, nor indeed does it so particularly belong to the Devil's history, it seems rather a polemic, so it may pass at school among the metaphysics, and puzzle the heads of our masters ; wherefore I think to write to the learned Dr. B——— about it, imploring his most sublime haughtiness, that when his other more momentous avocations of pedantry and pedagogism will give him an interval from wrath and contention, he will set apart a moment to consider human nature devilized, and give us a mathematical anatomical description of it ; with a map of Satan's kingdom in the microcosm of mankind, and such other illuminations as to him and his contemporaries —— and —— &c. in their great wisdom shall seem meet.

CHAPTER V.

Of the Devil's management in the Pagan Hierarchy by omens, entrails, augurs, oracles, and such like pageantry of hell; and how they went off the stage at last by the introduction of true religion.

I HAVE adjourned, not finished, my account of the Devil's secret management by possession, and shall reassume it, in its place; but I must take leave to mention some other parts of his retired scheme, by which he has hitherto managed mankind, and the first of these is by that fraud of all frauds called oracle.

Here his trumpet yielded an uncertain sound for some ages, and like what he was, and according to what he practised from the beginning, he delivered out falshood and delusion by retail: The priests of Apollo acted this farce for him to a great nicety at Delphos; there were divers others at the same time, and some, which to give the Devil his due, he had very little hand in, as we shall see presently.

There were also some smaller, some greater, some more, some less famous places where those oracles were seated, and audience given to the enquirers, in all which the Devil, or some body for him, *permissu superiorum*, for either vindictive or other hidden ends and purposes, was allowed to make at least a pretension to the knowledge of things to come; but, as public cheats generally do, they acted in masquerade, and gave such uncertain and inconsistent responses, that they were obliged to use the utmost art to reconcile events to the prediction, even after things were come to pass.

Here the Devil was a lying spirit, in a particular and extraordinary manner, in the mouths of all the prophets; and yet he had the cunning to express himself so, that whatever happened, the oracle was supposed to have meant as it fell out; and so all their augurs, omens and voices, by which the Devil amused the world, not at that time only, but since, have been likewise interpreted.

Julian the apostate dealt mightily in these amusements, but the Devil, who neither wished his fall, or presaged it to him, evidenced that he knew nothing of Julian's fate; for that, as he sent almost to all the oracles of the East, and summoned all the priests together to inform him of the success of his Persian expedition, they all, like Ahab's prophets, having a lying spirit in them, encouraged him and promised him success.

Nay, all the ill omens which disturbed him, they presaged good from; for example, he was at a prodigious expence when he was at Antioch to buy up white beasts, and white fowls, for sacrifices, and for predicting from the entrails; from whence the Antiochians, in contempt, called him *Victimarius*; but whenever the entrails foreboded evil, the cunning Devil made the priests put a different construction upon them, and promise him good: When he entered into the temple of the

Genii to offer sacrifice, one of the priests dropt down
dead; this, had it had any signification more than a man
falling dead of an apoplectic, would have signified something fatal to Julian, who made himself a brother sacrist
or priest; whereas the priests turned it presently to
signify the death of his colleague, the consul Sallust,
which happened just at the same time, though eight
hundred miles off; so in another case, Julian thought it
ominous that he, who was Augustus, should be named
with two other names of persons, both already dead;
the case was thus, the stile of the emperor was Julianus
Fœlix Augustus, and two of his principal officers were
Julianus and Fœlix; now both Julianus and Fœlix
died within a few days of one another, which disturbed
him much, who was the third of the three names; but
his flattering Devil told him it all imported good to
him, viz. that though Julianus and Fœlix should die,
Augustus should be immortal.

Thus whatever happened, and whatever was foretold,
and how much soever they differed from one another,
the lying spirit was sure to reconcile the prediction and
the event, and make them at least seem to correspond in
favour of the person enquiring.

Now we are told oracles are ceased, and the Devil is
farther limited for the good of mankind, not being allowed to vent his delusions by the mouths of the priests
and augurs, as formerly : I will not take upon me to say
how far they are really ceased, more than they were
before; I think it is much more reasonable to believe
there was never any reality in them at all, or that any
oracle ever gave out any answers but what were the
invention of the priests and the delusions of the Devil; I

have a great many antient authors on my side in this opinion, as Eusebius, Tertullian, Aristotle, and others, who as they lived so near the Pagan times, and when even some of those rites were yet in use, they had much more reason to know, and could probably pass a better judgment upon them; nay Cicero himself ridicules them in the openest manner; again, other authors descend to particulars, and shew how the cheat was managed by the heathen sacrists and priests, and in what enthusiastic manner they spoke; namely, by going into the hollow images, such as the brazen bull and the image of Apollo, and how subtlely they gave out dubious and ambiguous answers; that when the people did not find their expectations answered by the event, they might be imposed upon by the priests, and confidently told they did not rightly understand the oracle's meaning: However, I cannot say but that indeed there are some authors of good credit too, who will have it that there was a real prophetic spirit in the voice or answers given by the oracles, and that oftentimes they were miraculously exact in those answers; and they give that of the Delphic oracle answering the question which was given about Crœsus for an example, viz. what Crœsus was doing at that time? to wit, that he was boiling a lamb and the flesh of a tortoise together, in a brass vessel, or boiler, with a cover of the same metal; that is to say, in a kettle with a brass cover.

To affirm therefore, that they were all cheats, a man must encounter with antiquity, and set his private judgment up against an established opinion; but it is no matter for that; if I do not see any thing in that received

opinion capable of evidence, much less of demonstration,
I must be allowed still to think as I do; others may
believe as they list; I see nothing hard or difficult in the
thing; the priests, who were always historically informed
of the circumstances of the enquirer, or at least something about them, might easily find some ambiguous
speech to make, and put some double *entendre* upon
them, which upon the event solved the credit of the
oracle, were it one way or other; and this they certainly
did, or we have room to think the Devil knows less of
things now than he did in former days.

It is true that by these delusions the priests got infinite
sums of money, and this makes it still probable that they
would labour hard and use the utmost of their skill to
uphold the credit of their oracles; and it is a full discovery, as well of the subtlety of the sacrists, as of the
ignorance and stupidity of the people, in those early
days of Satan's witchcraft; to see what merry work the
Devil made with the world, and what gross things he
put upon mankind: Such was the story of the Dordonian oracle in Epirus, viz. That two pigeons flew out of
Thebes (N. B. it was the Egyptian Thebes) from the
temple of Belus, erected there by the antient sacrists,
and that one of these fled eastward into Lybia, and the
desarts of Africa, and the other into Greece, namely, to
Dordona, and these communicated the divine mysteries
to one another, and afterwards gave mystical solutions
to the devout enquirers; first the Dordonian pigeon
perching upon an oak spoke audibly to the people there,
that the gods commanded them to build an oracle, or
temple, to Jupiter, in that place; which was accord-

ingly done : The other pigeon did the like on the hill in Africa, where it commanded them to build another to Jupiter Ammon or Hammon.

Wise Cicero contemned all this, and, as authors tell us, ridiculed the answer, which, as I have hinted above, the oracle gave to Crœsus, proving that the oracle itself was a liar, that it could not come from Apollo, for that Apollo never spoke latin : In a word, Cicero rejected them all, and Demosthenes also mentions the cheats of the oracles ; when speaking of the oracle of Apollo, he said, *Pithia Philipized;* that is, that when the priests were bribed with money, they always gave their answers in favour of Philip of Macedon.

But that which is most strange to me is, that in this dispute about the reality of oracles, the heathen who made use of them are the people who expose them, and who insist most positively upon their being cheats and impostors, as in particular those mentioned above ; while the christians who reject them, yet believe they did really foretel things, answer questions, &c. only with this difference, that the heathen authors who oppose them, insist that it is all delusion and cheat, and charge it upon the priests ; and the christian opposers insist that it was real, but that the Devil, not the gods, gave the answers ; and that he was permitted to do it by a superior power to magnify that power in the total silencing them at last.

But, as I said before, I am with the heathen here, against the christian writers, for I take it all to be a cheat and delusion :· I must give my reason for it, or I do nothing ; my reason is this, I insist Satan is as blind

in matters of futurity, as we are, and can tell nothing of
what is to come ; these oracles often pretending to pre-
dict, could be nothing else therefore but a cheat formed
by the money-getting priests to amuse the world, and
bring grist to their mill : If I meet with any thing in my
way to open my eyes to a better opinion of them, I
shall tell it you as I go on.

On the other hand, whether the Devil really spake in
those oracles, or set the cunning priests to speak for him;
whether they predicted, or only made the people believe
they predicted ; whether they gave answers which came
to pass, or prevailed upon the people to believe that
was said did come to pass, it was much at one, and fully
answered the Devil's end ; namely, to amuse and delude
the world; and as to do, or to cause to be done, is the
same part of speech, so whoever did it, the Devil's interest was carried on by it, his government preserved, and
all the mischief he could desire was effectually brought
to pass, so that every way they were the Devil's oracles,
that's out of the question.

Indeed I have wondered sometimes why, since by this
sorcery the Devil performed such wonders, that is, played
so many tricks in the world, and had such universal success, he should set up no more of them ; but there might
be a great many reasons given for that, too long to tire
you with at present : It is true, there were not many of
them, and yet considering what a great deal of business
they dispatched, it was enough, for six or eight oracles
were more than sufficient to amuse all the world : The
chief oracles we meet with in history are among the
Greeks and the Romans, viz.

That of Jupiter Ammon, in Lydia, as above.

The Dordonian, in Epirus.

Apollo Delphicus, in the country of Phocis in
Greece.

Apollo Clavius, in Asia Minor.

Seraphis, in Alexandria in Egypt.

Trophomis, in Bæotia.

Sybilla Cumæa, in Italy.

Diana, at Ephesus.

Apollo Daphneus, at Antioch.

Besides many of lesser note, in several other places, as
I have hinted before.

I have nothing to do here with the story mentioned
by Plutarch, of a voice being heard at sea, from some of
the islands called the Echinades, and calling upon one
Thamuz, an Egyptian, who was on board a ship, bid-
ding him, when he came to the Palodes, other islands in
the Ionian seas, tell them there that the great god Pan
was dead ; and when Thamuz performed it, great
groanings, and howlings, and lamentations were heard
from the shore.

This tale tells but indifferently, though indeed it looks
more like a Christian fable, than a Pagan ; because it
seems as if made to honour the Christian worship, and
blast all the Pagan idolatry ; and for that reason I reject
it, the Christian profession needing no such fabulous stuff
to confirm it.

Nor is it true in fact, that the oracles did cease immediately upon the death of Christ ; but as I noted
before, the sum of the matter is this ; the Christian
religion spreading itself universally, as well as mira-

12   2 M

culously, and that too by the foolishness of preaching, into all parts of the world, the oracles ceased ; that is to say, their trade ceased, their rogueries were daily detected ; the deluded people being better taught, came no more after them, and being ashamed, as well as discouraged, they sneaked out of the world as well as they could ; in short, the customers fell off, and the priests, who were the shop-keepers, having no business to do, shut up their shops, broke, and went away ; the trade and the tradesmen were hissed off the stage together ; so that the Devil, who, it must be confessed, got infinitely by the cheat, became bankrupt, and was obliged to set other engines to work, as other cheats and deceivers do, who, when one trick grows stale, and will serve no longer, are forced to try another.

Nor was the Devil to seek in new measures ; for though he could not give out his delusive trash as he did before, in pomp and state, with the solemnity of a temple, and a set of enthusiasts, called priests, who played a thousand tricks to amuse the world, he had then recourse to his old Egyptian method, which indeed was more antient than that of oracles ; and that was by magic, sorcery, familiars, witchcraft, and the like.

Of this we find the people of the South, that is, of Arabia and Chaldea, were the first, from whence we are told of the wise men, that is to say, magicians, were called Chaldeans and Southsayers. Hence also we find Ahaziah, the king of Israel, sent to Baalzebub, the god of Ekron, to enquire whether he should live or die ? This some think was a kind of an oracle, though others think it was only some over-grown magician, who counterfeited himself to be a devil, and obtained upon that idol-hunting age to make a cunning-man of him; and for that purpose he got himself made a priest of Baalzebub, the god of Ekron, and gave out answers in his name. Thus those merry fellows in Egypt, Jannes and Jambres, are said to mimic Moses and Aaron, when they worked the miraculous plagues upon the Egyptians; and we have some instances in Scripture to support this, such as the witch of Endor, the king Manasses, who dealt with the Devil openly, and had a familiar; the woman mentioned Acts xvi. who had a spirit of divination, and who got money by playing the oracle; that is, answering doubtful questions, &c. which spirit, or devil, the apostles cast out.

Now though it is true that the old women in the world have filled us with tales, some improbable, others impossible; some weak, some ridiculous, and that this puts a general discredit upon all the graver matrons, who entertain us with stories better put together; yet, it is certain, and I must be allowed to affirm, that the Devil does not disdain to take into his service many troops of good old women, and old women-men too, who he finds it is for his service to keep in constant pay; to these he is found frequently to communicate his mind, and oftentimes we find them such proficients, that they know much more than the Devil can teach them.

How far our antient friend Merlin, or the grave matron, his (Satan's) most trusty and well-beloved cousin and counsellor, mother Shipton, were commissioned by him to give out their prophetic oracles, and what degree of possession he may have arrived to in them, upon their midnight excursions, I will not undertake to prove; but that he might be acquainted with them both, as well as with several of our modern gentlemen, I will not deny neither.

I confess it is not very incongruous with the Devil's temper, or with the nature of his business, to shift hands ; possibly he found that he had tired the world with oracular cheats ; that men began to be surfeited with them, and grew sick of the frauds which were so frequently detected ; that it was time to take new measures, and contrive some new trick to bite the world, that he might not be exposed to contempt ; or perhaps he saw the approach of new light, which the Christian doctrine bringing with it, began to spread in the minds of men ; that it would out-shine the dim burning ignus fatuus, with which he had so long cheated mankind, and was afraid to stand it, lest he should be mobbed off the stage by his own people, when their eyes should begin to open : That upon this foot he might in policy withdraw from those old retreats, the oracles, and restrain those responces before they lost all their credit ; for we find the people seemed to be at a mighty loss for some time, for want of them, so that it made them run up and down to conjurers, and man-gossips, to brazen heads, speaking calves, and innumerable simple things, so gross that they are scarce fit to be named, to satisfy the itch of having their fortunes told them, as we call it.

Now as the Devil is very seldom blind to his own interest, and therefore thought fit to quit his old way of imposing upon the world by his oracles, only because he found the world began to be too wise to be imposed upon that way ; so on the other hand, finding there was still a possibility to delude the world, though by other instruments, he no sooner laid down his oracles, and the solemn pageantry, magnificent appearances, and other frauds of his priests and votaries, in their temples and shrines; but he set up a new trade, and having, as I have said, agents and instruments sufficient for any business that he could have to employ them in, he begins in corners, as the learned and merry Dr. Brown says, and exercises his minor trumperies by way of his own contriving, listing a great number of new-found operators, such as witches, magicians, diviners, figure-casters, astrologers, and such inferior seducers.

Now it is true, as that doctor says, this was running into corners, as if he had been expelled his more triumphant way of giving audience in form, which for so many ages had been allowed him; yet I must add, that as it seemed to be the Devil's own doing, from a right judgment of his affairs, which had taken a new turn in the world, upon the shining of new lights from the Christian doctrine, so it must be acknowledged the Devil made himself amends upon mankind, by the various methods he took, and the multitude of instruments he employed, and perhaps deluded mankind in a more fatal and sensible manner than he did before, though not so universally.

He had indeed before more pomp and figure put upon it, and he cheated mankind then in a way of magnificence and splendour; but this was not in above eight or ten principal places, and not fifty places in all, public or private; whereas now fifty thousand of his angels and instruments, visible and invisible, hardly may be said to suffice for one town or city; but in short, as his invisible agents fill the air, and are at hand for mischief on every emergence, so his visible fools swarm

in every village, and you have scarce a hamlet or a
town, but his emissaries are at hand for business; and,
which is still worse, in all places he finds business,
nay even where religion is planted and seems to flou-
rish; yet he keeps his ground, and pushes his interest
according to what has been said elsewhere upon the
same subject, that wherever religion plants, the Devil
plants close by it.

Nor, as I say, does he fail of success, delusion
spreads like a plague, and the Devil is sure of votaries; like a true mountebank, he can always bring a
crowd about his stage, and that some time faster than
other people.

What I observe upon this subject is this, that the
world is at a loss for want of the Devil; if it was not so,
what is the reason, that upon the silencing the oracles,
and religion telling them that miracles are ceased, and
that God has done speaking by prophets, they never
enquire whether heaven has established any other or new
way of revelation, but away they ran with their doubts
and difficulties to these dreamers of dreams, tellers of fortunes, and personal oracles to be resolved; as if when
they acknowledge the Devil is dumb, these could speak;
and as if the wicked spirit could do more than the good,
the diabolical more than the divine, or that heaven, having taken away the Devil's voice, had furnished him with
an equivalent, by allowing scolds, termagents, and old
weak and superannuated wretches to speak for him; for
these are the people we go to now in our doubts and
emergencies.

While this blindness continues among us, it is nonsense
to say that oracles are silenced, or the Devil is dumb,

for the Devil gives audience still by his deputies ; only as Jeroboam made priests of the meanest of the people, so he is grown a little humble, and makes use of meaner instruments than he did before ; for whereas the priests of Apollo, and of Jupiter, were splendid in their appearance, of grave and venerable aspect, and sometimes of no mean quality ; now he makes use of scoundrels and rabble, beggars and vagabonds, old hags, superannuated miserable hermits, gypsies and strollers, the pictures of envy and ill luck.

Either the Devil is grown an ill master, and gives but mean wages, that he can get no better servants ; or else common sense is grown very low prized and contemptible ; that such as these are fit tools to continue the succession of fraud, and carry on the Devil's interest in the world ; for were not the passions and temper of mankind deeply pre-engaged in favour of this dark prince, we could never suffer ourselves to accept of his favours by the hands of such contemptible agents as these ! How do we receive his oracles from an old witch of particular eminence, and who we believe to be more than ordinary inspired from hell ; I say, we receive the oracle with reverence ; that is to say, with a kind of horror, with regard to the black prince it comes from, and at the same time turn our faces away from the wretch that mumbles out the answers, lest she should cast an evil eye, as we call it, upon us, and put a devil into us, when she plays the devil before us ? How do we listen to the cant of those worst of vagabonds the gypsies, when at the same time we watch our hedges and hen-roosts for fear of their thieving ?

Either the Devil uses us more like fools than he did

our ancestors, or we really are worse fools than those
ages produced, for they were never deluded by such low
prized devils as we are; by such despicable bridewell
devils, that are fitter for a whipping-post than an altar,
and instead of being received as the voice of an oracle,
should be sent to the house of correction for pick-
pockets.

Nor is this accidental, and here and there one of these
wretches to be seen; but in short, if it has been in other
nations as it is with us, I do not see that the Devil was
able to get any better people into his pay, or at least
very rarely: Where have we seen any thing above a
tinker turn wizard? and where have we had a witch of
quality among us, mother J———gs excepted? and if
she had not been more of something else than a witch, it
was thought she had never got so much money by her
profession.

Magicians, soothsayers, devil-raisers, and such people, we have heard much of, but seldom above the degree of the meanest of the mean people, the lowest of the
lowest rank: Indeed the word Wise Men, which the
Devil would fain have had his agents honoured with,
was used a while in Egypt, and in Persia, among the
Chaldeans, but it continued but a little while, and never
reached so far northward as our country; nor, however
the Devil has managed it, have many of our great men,
who have been most acquainted with him, ever been able
to acquire the title of wise men.

I have heard that in older times, I suppose in good
queen Bess's days, or beyond (for little is to be said here
for any thing on this side of her time) there were some
counsellors and statesmen who merited the character of

wise, in the best sense ; that is to say, good, and wise, as they stand in conjunction ; but as to what has happened since that, or, as we may call it, from that queen's funeral to the late revolution, I have little to say ; but I'll tell you what honest Andrew Marvel said of those times, and by that you may, if you please, make your calculation or let it alone, it is all one.

" To see a white staff-maker, a beggar, a lord,
" And scarce a wise man at a long council-board."

But I may be told this relates to wise men in another constitution, or wise men as they are opposed to fools ; whereas we are talking of them now under another class, namely, as wisemen or magicians, south-sayers, &c. such as were in former times called by that name.

But to this I answer, that take them in which sense you please, it may be the same ; for if I were to ask the Devil the character of the best statesman he had employed among us for many years past, I am apt to think that though oracles are ceased, he would honestly, according to the old ambiguous way, when I asked if they were christians, answer they were (his) privy-counsellors.

It is but a little while ago, that I happened (in conversation) to meet with a long list of the magistrates of that age, in a neighbouring country, that is to say, the men of fame among them ; and it was a very diverting thing to see the judgment which was passed upon them among a great deal of good company ; it is not for me to tell you how many white staves, golden keys, marshals batoons, gordons blue, gordon,rogue and gordon blanc, there were among them ; or by what titles, as dukes,

counts, marquis, abbot, bishop, or justice, they were to
be distinguished ; but the marginal notes I found upon
most of them (being marked with an asterism) as follows.

Such a duke, such eminent offices added to his titles
(* in the margin)——— *No saint*.

Such an arch —— with the title of noble added,
——— *No archangel*.

Such an eminent statesman and prime minister,
——— *No witch*.

Such a ribbon, with a set of great letters added,
——— *No conjurer*.

It presently occured to me, that though oracles were
ceased, and we had now no more double *entendre* in
such a degree as before, yet that ambiguous answers
were not at an end ; and that whether those negatives
were meant so by the writers, or not, it was certain
custom led the readers to conclude them to be satyrs,
that they were to be rung backwards, like the bells when
the town's on fire ; though in short, I durst not read
them backward any where, but as speaking of foreign
people, for fear of raising the Devil I am talking of.

But to return to the subject ; to such mean things is
the Devil now reduced in his ordinary way of carrying
on his business in the world, that his oracles are delivered now by the bellmen and the chimney sweepers, by
the meanest of those that speak in the dark, and if he
operates by them, you may expect it accordingly ; his
agents seem to me as if the Devil had singled them out
by their deformity, or that there was something particular required in their aspect to qualify them for their
employment ; whence it is become proverbial, when our
looks are very dismal and frightful, to say, I look like a

witch; or in other cases to say, as ugly as a witch; in another case to look as envious as a witch; now whether there is any thing particularly required in the looks of the Devil's modern agents, which is assisting in the discharge of their offices, and which make their answers appear more solemn, this the Devil has not yet revealed, at least not to me; and therefore why it is that he singles out such creatures as are fit only to fright the people that come to them with their enquiries, I do not take upon me to determine.

Perhaps it is necessary they should be thus extraordinary in their aspect, that they might strike an awe into the minds of their votaries, as if they were Satan's true and real representatives; and that the said votaries may think when they speak to the witches, they are really talking to the Devil; or perhaps it is necessary to the witches themselves, that they should be so exquisitely ugly, that they might not be surprized at whatever figure the Devil makes when he first appears to them, being certain they can see nothing uglier than themselves.

Some are of the opinion that the communication with the Devil, or between the Devil and those creatures, his agents, has something assimilating in it, and that if they were tolerable before, they are, *ipso facto*, turned into devils by talking with him; I will not say but that a tremor in the limbs, a horror in the aspect, and a surprizing stare in the eyes may seize upon some of them, when they really see the Devil, and that the frequent repetition may make those distortions, which we so constantly see in their faces, become natural to them; by which if it does not continue always upon the countenance, they

can at least, like the posture-masters, cast themselves
into such figures, and frightful dislocations of the lines
and features in their faces, and so assume a devil's face
suitable to the occasion, or as may serve the turn for
which they take it up, and as often as they have any use
for it.

But be it which of these the enquirer pleases, it is all
one to the case in hand ; this is certain, that such deformed devil-like creatures, most of those we call hags
and witches, are alike in their shapes and aspects, and
that they give out their sentences and frightful messages
with an air of revenge for some injury received ; for
witches are famed chiefly for doing mischief.

It seems the Devil has always picked out the most
ugly and frightful old women to do his business ; mother Shipton, our famous English witch or prophetess, is
very much wronged in her picture, if she was not of the
most terrible aspect imaginable ; and if it be true that
Merlin, the famous Welch fortune-teller, was a frightful
figure, it will seem the more rational to believe, if we
credit another story, (viz.) that he was begotten by the
Devil himself, of which I shall speak by itself. But to
go back to the Devil's instruments being so ugly ; it
may be observed, I say, that the Devil has always dealt
in such sort of cattle ; the sybils, of whom so many
strange prophetic things are recorded, whether true or
no is not the question, are (if the Italian painters may
have any credit given them) all represented as very old
women ; and as if ugliness were a beauty to old age,
they seem to paint them out as ugly and frightful as (not
they, the painters) but even as the Devil himself could
make them ; not that I believe there are any original

pictures of them really extant; but it is not unlikely that the Italians might have some traditional knowledge of them, or some remaining notions of them, or particularly that antient sybil named Anus, who sold the fatal book to Tarquin; it is said of her, that Tarquin supposed she doated with age.

I had thoughts indeed here to have entered into a learned disquisition of the excellency of old women in all diabolical operations, and particularly of the necessity of having recourse to them for Satan's more exquisite administration, which also may serve to solve the great difficulty in the natural philosophy of hell; namely, why it comes to pass that the Devil is obliged for want of old women, properly so called, to turn so many antient fathers, grave counsellors both of law and state, and especially civilians or doctors of the law, into old women, and how the extraordinary operation is performed; but this, as a thing of great consequence in Satan's management of human affairs, and particularly as it may lead us into the necessary history, as well as characters of some of the most eminent of these sects among us, I have purposely reserved for a work by itself, to be published, if Satan hinders not, in fifteen volumes in folio, wherein I shall in the first place define, in the most exact manner possible, what is to be understood by a male old woman, of what heterogeneous kind they are produced, give you the monstrous anatomy of the parts, and especially those of the head, which being filled with innumerable globules of a sublime nature, and which being of a fine contexture without, but particularly hollow in the cavity, defines most philosophically that antient paradoxical

saying, viz. being full of emptiness, and makes it very
consistent with nature and common sense.

I shall likewise spend some time, and it must be
labour too, I assure you, when it is done, in determining
whether this new species of wonderfuls, are not derived from that famous old woman Merlin, which I
prove to be very reasonable for us to suppose, because
of the many several judicious authors, who affirm the
said Merlin, as I hinted before, to have been begotten
by the Devil.

As to the deriving his gift of prophesy from the Devil,
by that pretended generation, I shall omit that part,
because, as I have all along insisted upon it, that Satan
himself has no prophetic or predicting powers of his own,
it is not very clear to me that he could convey it to his
posterity, *nil dat quod non habet*.

However, in deriving this so much magnified prophet
in a right line from the Devil, much may be said in
favour of his ugly face, in which it was said he was very
remarkable, for it is no new thing for a child to be like
the father ; but all these weighty things I adjourn for the
present, and proceed to the affair in hand, namely, the
several branches of the Devil's management, since his
quitting his temples and oracles.

CHAPTER VI.

*Of the extraordinary appearance of the Devil, and
particularly of the Cloven-foot.*

SOME people would fain have us treat this tale of the
Devil's appearing with a Cloven-foot with more solemnity, than I believe the Devil himself does ; for Satan,
who knows how much of a cheat it is, must certainly
ridicule it, in his own thoughts, to the last degree ; but
as he is glad of any way to hoodwink the understandings, and bubble the weak part of the world ; so if he
sees men willing to take every scare-crow for a devil, it
is not his business to undeceive them ; on the other
hand, he finds it his interest to foster the cheat, and serve
himself of the consequence : Nor could I doubt but the
Devil, if any mirth be allowed him, often laughs at the
many frightful shapes and figures we dress him up in,
and especially to see how willing we are first to paint
him as black, and make him appear as ugly as we can,
and then stare and start at the spectrum of our own
making.

The truth is, that among all the horribles that we
dress up Satan in, I cannot but think we shew the least
of invention in this of a goat, or a thing with a goat's
foot, of all the rest ; for though a goat is a creature
made use of by our Saviour in the allegory of the day of
judgment, and is said there to represent the wicked rejected party, yet it seems to be only on account of their
similitude to the sheep, and so to represent the just fate

of hypocrisy and hypocrites, and in particular, to form
the necessary antithesis in the story ; for else, our whimsical fancies excepted, a sheep or a lamb has a Cloven-
foot as well as a goat ; nay, if the Scripture be of any
value in the case, it is to the Devil's advantage, for the
dividing the hoof was the distinguishing character or
mark of a clean beast, and how the Devil can be brought
into that number is pretty hard to say.

One would have thought if we had intended to have
given a just figure of the Devil, it would have been more
apposite to have ranked him among the cat kind, and
given him a foot (if he is to be known by his foot) like
a lion, or like a red dragon, being the same creatures
which he is represented by in the text, and so his claws
would have had some terror in them as well as his teeth.

But neither is the goat a true representative of the
Devil at all, for we do not rank the goats among the
subtle or cunning part of the brutes ; he is counted a
fierce creature indeed of his kind, though nothing like
those other abovementioned ; and he is emblematically
used to represent a lustful temper, but even that part does
not fully serve to describe the Devil, whose operation
lies principally another way.

Besides it is not the goat himself that is made use of, it
is the cloven-hoof only, and that so particularly that
the cloven-foot of a ram or a swine, or any other creature, may serve as well as that of a goat, only that
history gives us some cause to call it the goat's foot.

In the next place it is understood by us not as a bare
token to know Satan by, but as if it were a brand upon
him, and that like the mark God put upon Cain, it was
given him for a punishment, so that he cannot get leave

to appear without it, nay cannot conceal it whatever other dress or disguise he may put on ; and as if it was to make him as ridiculous as possible, they will have it be, that whenever Satan has occasion to dress himself in any human shape, be it of what degree soever, from the king to the beggar, be it of a fine lady or of an old woman, (the latter it seems he oftenest assumes) yet still he not only must have this Cloven-foot about him, but he is obliged to shew it too ; nay, they will not allow him any dress, whether it be a prince's robes, a lord Cha——r's gown, or a lady's hoop and long petticoats, but the Cloven-foot must be shewed from under them ; they will not so much as allow him an artificial shoe or a jack-boot, as we often see contrived to conceal a club-foot or a wooden leg ; but that the Devil may be known wherever he goes, he is bound to shew his foot ; they might as well oblige him to set a bill upon his cap, as folks do upon a house to be let, and have it written in capital letters, I am the Devil.

It must be confessed this is very particular, and would be very hard upon the Devil, if it had not another article in it, which is some advantage to him, and that is, that the fact is not true ; but the belief of this is so universal, that all the world runs away with it ; by which mistake the good people miss the Devil many times where they look for him, and meet him as often where they did not expect him, and when for want of this Cloven-foot they do not know him.

Upon this very account I have sometimes thought, not that this has been put upon him by mere fancy, and the cheat of a heavy imagination, propagated by fable and chimney-corner divinity, but that it has been a con-

13 2 O

trivance of his own; and that, in short, the Devil raised
this scandal upon himself, that he might keep his disguise the better, and might go a visiting among his
friends without being known; for were it really so, that
he could go no where without this particular brand of
infamy, he could not come into company, could not dine
with my lord mayor, nor drink tea with the ladies, could
not go to the drawing-r—— at ———, could not have
gone to Fontainbleau to the king of France's wedding,
or to the diet of Poland, to prevent the grandees there
coming to an agreement; nay, which would be still
worse than all, he could not go to the masquerade, nor
to any of our balls; the reason is plain, he would be
always discovered, exposed, and forced to leave the good
company, or which would be as bad, the company
would all cry out, The Devil, and run out of the room as
if they were frighted; nor could all the help of invention
do him any service, no dress he could put on would
cover him; not all our friends at Tavistock-corner could
furnish him with a habit that would disguise or conceal
him, this unhappy foot would spoil it all: Now this
would be so great a loss to him, that I question whether he would carry on any of his most important affairs
in the world without it; for though he has access to
mankind in his complete disguise, I mean that of his
invisibility, yet the learned very much agree in this, that
his corporal presence in the world is absolutely necessary upon many occasions, to support his interest and
keep up his correspondences, and particularly to encourage his friends, when numbers are requisite to carry on
his affairs; but this part I shall have occasion to speak
of again, when I come to consider him as a gentleman of

business in his locality, and under the head of visible apparition ; but I return to the foot.

As I have thus suggested that the Devil himself has politically spread about this notion concerning his appearing with a Cloven-foot, so I doubt not that he has thought it for his purpose to paint this Cloven-foot so lively in the imaginations of many of our people, and especially of those clear-sighted folks who see the Devil when he is not to be seen, that they would make no scruple to say, nay and to make affidavit too, even before Satan himself, whenever he sat upon the bench, that they had seen his worship's foot at such and such a time ; this I advance the rather, because it is very much for his interest to do this, for if we had not many witnesses, *viva voce*, to testify it, we should have had some obstinate fellows always among us, who would have denied the fact, or at least have spoken doubtfully of it, and so have raised disputes and objections against it, as impossible, or at least as improbable ; buzzing one ridiculous notion or other into our ears, as if the Devil was not so black as he was painted, that he had no more a Cloven-foot than a pope, whose apostolical toes have been so often reverentially kissed by kings and emperors ; but now, alas ! this part is out of the question, not the man in the moon, not the groaning board, not the speaking of friar Bacon's brazen-head, not the inspiration of mother Shipton, or the miracles of Dr. Faustas, things as certain as death and taxes, can be more firmly believed : The Devil not have a Cloven-foot ! I doubt not but I could, in a short time, bring you a thousand old women together, that would as soon believe there was no Devil at all ; nay, they will tell you, he could not be a Devil

without it, any more than he could come into the room,
and the candles not burn blue, or go out and not leave a
smell of brimstone behind him.

Since then the certainty of the thing is so well established, and there are so many good and substantial witnesses ready to testify that he has a Cloven-foot, and
that they have seen it too ; nay, and that we have antiquity on our side, for we have this truth confirmed by
the testimony of many ages ; why should we doubt it
any longer ? we can prove that many of our ancestors
have been of this opinion, and divers learned authors
have left it upon record, as particularly that learned
familiarist mother Hazel, whose writings are to be found
in MS. in the famous library at Pye-corner ; also the
admired Joan of Amesbury, the history of the Lanca-
shire witches, and the reverend exorcist of the devils of
London, whose history is extant among us to this day ;
all these and many more may be quoted, and their writings referred to for the confirmation of the antiquity of
this truth ; but there seems to be no occasion for farther
evidence, it is enough, Satan himself, if he did not raise
the report, yet tacitly owns the fact, at least he appears
willing to have it believed, and be received as a general
truth for the reasons above.

But besides all this, and as much a jest as some unbe-
lieving people would have this story pass for, who knows
but that if Satan is empowered to assume any shape or
body, and to appear to us visibly, as if really so shaped;
I say, who knows but he may, by the same authority,
be allowed to assume the addition of the Cloven-foot, or
two or four Cloven-feet, if he pleased ? and why not a
Cloven-foot as well as any other foot, if he thinks fit ?

For if the Devil can assume a shape, and can appear to mankind in a visible form, it may, I doubt not, with as good authority be advanced that he is left at liberty to assume what shape he pleases, and to choose what case of flesh and blood he will please to wear, whether real or imaginary ; and if this liberty be allowed him, it is an admirable disguise for him to come generally with his Cloven-foot, that when he finds it for his purpose, on special occasions to come without it, as I said above, he may not be suspected ; but take this with you as you go, that all this is upon a supposition that the Devil can assume a visible shape, and make a real appearance, which however I do not yet think fit to grant or deny.

Certain it is, the first people who bestowed a Cloven-foot upon the Devil, were not so despicable as you may imagine, but were real favourites of heaven ; for did not Aaron set up the devil of a calf in the congregation, and set the people a dancing about it for a god ? Upon which occasion, expositors tell us, that particular command was given, Levit. xvii. 7. *They shall no more offer their sacrifices unto devils, after whom they have gone a whoring ;* likewise king Jeroboam set up the two calves, one at Dan, and the other at Bethel, and we find them charged afterwards with setting up the worship of devils instead of the worship of God.

After this we find some nations actually sacrificed to the Devil in the form of a ram, and others of a goat ; from which, and that above of the calf at Horeb, I doubt not the story of the Cloven-foot first derived ; and it is plain that the worship of that calf at Horeb is meant in the Scripture quoted above, Levit. xvii. 7. *Thou shalt no more offer sacrifices unto devils :* The original is

Seghnirim ; that is, rough and hairy goats or calves ;
and some think also in this shape the Devil most ordinarily appeared to the Egyptians and Arabians, from
whence it was derived.

Also in the old writings of the Egyptians, I mean
their hieroglyphic writing, before the use of letters was
known, we are told this was the mark that he was known
by ; and the figure of a goat was the hieroglyphic of the
Devil ; some will affirm that the Devil was particularly
pleased to be so represented ; how they came by their
information, and whether they had it from his own
mouth or not, authors have not yet determined.

But be this as it will, I do not see that Satan could have
been at a loss for some extraordinary figure to have
bantered mankind with, though this had not been
thought of ; but thinking of the Cloven-foot first, and
the matter being indifferent, this took place, and easily
rooted itself in the bewildered fancy of the people, and
now it is riveted too fast for the Devil himself to remove
it if he was disposed to try ; but as I said above, it is
none of his business to solve doubts or remove difficulties
out of our heads, but to perplex us with more, as much
as he can.

Some people carry this matter a great deal higher
still, and will have the Cloven-foot be like the great
stone which the Brasilian conjurers used to solve all
difficult questions upon, after having used a great many
monstrous and barbarous gestures and distortions of their
bodies, and cut certain marks or magical figures upon
the stone ; so, I say, they will have this Cloven-foot, be
a kind of a conjuring-stone, and tell us, that in former
times, when Satan drove a greater trade with mankind

in public, than he has done of late, he gave this Cloven-foot as a token to his particular favourites to work wonders with, and to conjure by, and that witches, fairies, hobgoblins, and such things, of which the antients had several kinds, at least in their imagination, had all a goat's leg with a Cloven-foot to put on upon extraordinary occasions; it seems this method is of late grown out of practice, and so like the melting of marble and the painting of glass, it is laid aside among the various useful arts which history tells us are lost to the world; what may be practised in the fairy world, if such a place there be, we can give no particular account at present.

But neither is this all, for other would-be-wise people take upon them to make farther and more considerable improvements upon this doctrine of the Cloven-foot, and treat it as a most significant instrument of Satan's private operation, and that as Joseph is said to divine, that is to say, to conjure by his golden cup which was put into Benjamin's sack, so the Devil has managed several of his secret operations, and possessions, and other hellish mechanisms upon the spirits as well as bodies of men, by the medium or instrumentality of the Cloven-foot; accordingly it had a kind of an hellish inspiration in it, and a separate and magical power by which he wrought his infernal miracles; that the Cloven-foot had a superior signification, and was not only emblematic and significative of the conduct of men, but really guided their conduct in the most important affairs of life; and that the agents the Devil employed to influence mankind, and to delude them and draw them into all the snares and traps that he lays continually for their destruction,

were equipped with this foot in aid of their other powers
for mischief.

Here they read us learned lectures upon the sovereign
operations which the Devil is at present master of, in the
government of human affairs ; and how the Cloven-foot
is an emblem of the true double *entendre* or divided
aspect, which the great men of the world generally act
with, and by which all their affairs are directed ; from
whence it comes to pass that there is no such thing as a
single-hearted integrity, or an upright meaning to be
found in the world ; that mankind, worse than the
ravenous brutes, preys upon his own kind, and devours
them by all the laudable methods of flattery, whine,
cheat and treachery ; crocodile like, weeping over those
it will devour, destroying those it smiles upon, and, in a
word, devours its own kind, which the very beasts refuse,
and that by all the ways of fraud and allurement that
hell can invent ; holding out a cloven divided hoof, or
hand, pretending to save, when the very pretence is
made use of to ensnare and destroy.

Thus the divided hoof is the representative of a
divided double tongue, and heart, an emblem of the
most exquisite hypocrisy, the most fawning and fatally
deceiving flattery ; and here they give us very diverting
histories, though tragical in themselves, of the manner
which some of the Devil's inspired agents have managed
themselves under the especial influence of the Cloven-
foot ; how they have made war under the pretence of
peace, murdered garrisons under the most sacred capitu-
lations, massacred innocent multitudes after surrenders
to mercy.

Of the appearance of the Devil, and of the Cloven-foot.

Again, they tell us the Cloven-foot has been made use of in all treasons, plots, assassinations, and secret as well as open murders and rebellions. Thus Joab under the treason of an embrace, shewed how dexterously he could manage the Cloven-foot, and struck Abner under the fifth rib : Thus David played the Cloven-foot upon poor Uriah, when he had a mind to lie with his wife : Thus Brutus played it upon Cæsar ; and to come nearer home, we have had a great many retrograde motions in this country by this magical implement the foot ; such as that of the earl of Essex's fate, beheading the queen of Scots, and divers other in queen Elizabeth's time : That of the earl of Shrewsbury and sir Thomas Overbury, Gondamor and sir Walter Raleigh, and many others in king James the First's time ; in all which, if the Cloven-foot had not been dexterously managed, those murders had not been so dexterously managed, or the murderers have so well been skreened from justice ; from which and the imprecated justice of heaven unappeased, some have thought the innocent branches of the royal house of Stuart did not fare the better in the ages which followed.

It must be confessed, the Cloven-foot was in its full exercise in the next reign, and the generation that rose up immediately after them, arrived to the most exquisite skill for management of it ; here they fasted and prayed, there they plundered and murdered ; here they raised war for the king, and there they fought against him, cutting throats for God's sake, and deposing both king and kingly government according to law.

Nor was the Cloven-foot unemployed on all sides, for it is the main excellency of this instrument of hell, that

13   2 P

it acts on every side, it is its denominating quality, and is for that reason called a cloven or divided hoof.

This mutilated apparition has been so public in other countries too, that it seems to convince us the Devil is not confined to England only, but that as his empire extended to all the sublunary world, so he gives them all room to see he is qualified to manage them his own way.

What abundant use did that prince of dissemblers, Charles V. make of this foot ? it was by the help of this apparition of the foot that he baited his hook with the city of Milan, and tickled Francis I. of France so well with it, that when he passed through France, and was in that king's power, he let him go, and never got the bait off the hook neither ; it seems the foot was not on king Francis's side at that time.

How cruelly did Philip II. of Spain manage this foot in the murder of the nobility of the Spanish Netherlands, the assassination of the prince of Orange, and at last in that of his own son don Carlos, infant of Spain ? and yet such was the Devil's craft, and so nicely did he bestir his Cloven-hoof, that this monarch died consolated (though impenitent) in the arms of the church, and with the benediction of the clergy too, those second best managers of the said hoof in the world.

I must acknowledge, I agree with this opinion thus far ; namely, that the Devil acting by this Cloven-foot, as a machine, has done great things in the world for the propagating his dark empire among us ; and history is full of examples, besides the little low prized things done among us ; for we are come to such a kind of degeneracy in folly, that we have even dishonoured the Devil, and put this glorious engine the Cloven-foot to such mean uses, that the Devil himself seems to be ashamed of us.

But to return a little to foreign history, besides what has been mentioned above, we find flaming examples of most glorious mischief done by this weapon, when put into the hands of kings and men of fame in the world. How many games have the kings of France played with this Cloven-foot, and that within a few years of one another ? First, Charles IX. played the Cloven-foot upon Gaspar Coligni, admiral of France, when he caressed him, complimented him, invited him to Paris, to the wedding of the king of Navarre, called him father, kissed him, and when he was wounded, sent his own surgeons to take care of him, and yet three days after, ordered him to be assassinated and murdered, used with a thousand indignities, and at last thrown out of the window into the street to be insulted by the rabble ?

Did not Henry III. in the same country, play the Cloven-foot upon the duke of Guise, when he called him to his council, and caused him to be murdered as he went in at the door ? The Guises again played the same game back upon the king, when they sent out a jacobin friar to assassinate him in his tent, as he lay at the siege of Paris.

In a word, this opera of the Cloven-foot has been acted all over the Christian world, ever since Judas betrayed the Son of God with a kiss ; nay, our Saviour says expressly of him, *One of you is a devil;* and the sacred text says in another place, *The Devil entered into Judas.*

It would take up a great deal of time and paper too,

to give you a full account of the travels of this Cloven-foot ; its progress into all the courts of Europe, and with what most accurate hypocrisy Satan has made use of it upon many occasions, and with what success ; but as in the elaborate work of which I just now gave you a specimen, I design one whole volume upon this subject, and which I shall call, The complete history of the Cloven-foot ; I say, for that reason, and divers others, I shall say but very little more to it in this place.

It remains to tell you, that this merry story of the Cloven-foot is very essential to the history which I am now writing, as it has been all along the great emblem of the Devil's government in the world, and by which all his most considerable engagements have been answered and executed ; for as he is said not to be able to conceal this foot, but that he carries it always with him, it imports most plainly, that the Devil would be no devil, if he was not a dissembler, a deceiver, and carried a double *entendre* in all he does or says ; that he cannot but say one thing and mean another, promise one thing and do another, engage and not perform, declare and not intend, and act like a true Devil as he is, with a countenance that is no index of his heart.

I might indeed go back to originals, and derive this Cloven-foot from Satan's primitive state as a cherubim, or a celestial being, which cherubims, as Moses is said to have seen them about the throne of God, in mount Sinai, and as the same Moses, from the original, re-presented them afterwards covering the ark, had the head and face of a man, wings of an eagle, body of a lion, and legs and feet of a calf ; but this is not so much to our present purpose, for as we are to allow that whatever Satan had of heavenly beauty before the fall, he lost it all when he commenced devil ; so to fetch his original so far up, would be only to say, that he retained nothing but the Cloven-foot, and that all the rest of him was altered and deformed, become horrible and frightful as the Devil; but his Cloven-foot, as we now understand it, is rather mystical and emblematic, and describes him only as the fountain of mischief and treason, and the prince of hypocrites, and as such we are now to speak of him.

It is from this original all the hypocritic world copy, he wears the foot on their account, and from this model they act : This made our blessed Lord tell them, *the works of your father ye will do*, meaning the Devil, as he had expressed it just before.

Nor does he deny the use of the foot to the meaner class of his disciples in the world, but decently equips them all upon every occasion with a needful proportion of hypocrisy and deceit ; that they may hand on the power of promiscuous fraud through all his temporal dominions, and wear the foot always about them, as a badge of their professed share in whatever is done by that means.

Thus every dissembler, every false friend, every secret cheat, every bearskin jobber has a cloven-foot, and so far hands on the Devil's interest by the same powerful agency of art, as the Devil himself uses to act when he appears in person, or would act if he was just now upon the spot ; for this foot is a machine which is to be wound up and wound down, as the cause it appears for requires ; and there are agents and engineers to act in it by directions of Satan (the grand engineer) who lies still in his retirement, only issuing out his orders as he sees convenient.

Again, every class, every trade, every shopkeeper, every pedlar, nay, that meanest of tradesmen, that church pedlar the pope, has a cloven-foot, with which he paw wa's upon the world, wishes them all well, and at the same time cheats them ; wishes them all fed, and at the same time starves them ; wishes them all in heaven, and at the same time marches before them directly to the Devil, *a-la-mode de Cloven-foot.*

Nay, the very bench, the ever-living foundation of justice in the world ; how often has it been made the tool of violence, the refuge of oppression, the seat of bribery and corruption, by this monster in masquerade, and that every where (our own country always excepted) ? They had much better wipe out the picture of justice blinded, and having the sword and scales in her hand, which in foreign countries is generally painted over the seat of those who sit to do justice, and place instead thereof, a naked unarmed cloven-hoof, a proper emblem of that spirit that influences the world, and of the justice we often see administered among them ; human imagination cannot form an idea more suitable, nor the Devil propose an engine more or better qualified for an operation of justice, by the influence of bribery and corruption ; it is this magnipotent instrument in the hands of the Devil, which under the closest disguise agitates every passion, bribes every affection, blackens every virtue, gives a double face to words and actions, and to all persons, who have any concern in them, and in a word, makes us all devils to one another.

Indeed the Devil has taken but a dark emblem to be

distinguished by, for this of a goat was said to be a creature hated by mankind from the beginning, and that there is a natural antipathy in mankind against them : Hence the scape goat was to bear the sins of the people, and to go into the wilderness with all that burthen upon him.

But we have a saying among us, in defence of which we must enquire into the proper sphere of action, which may be assigned to this Cloven-foot, as hitherto described : The proverb is this ; Every devil has not a cloven-foot. This proverb, instead of giving us some more favourable thoughts of the Devil, confirms what I have said already, that the Devil raised this scandal upon himself ; I mean, the report that he cannot conceal or disguise his devil's foot, or hoof, but that it must appear, under whatever habit he shews himself ; and the reason I gave holds good still, namely, that he may be more effectually concealed when he goes abroad without it : For if the people were fully persuaded that the Devil could not appear without this badge of his honour, or mark of his infamy, take it as you will ; and that he was bound also to shew it upon all occasions, it would be natural to conclude, that whatever frightful appearances might be seen in the world, if the Cloven-foot did not also appear, we had no occasion to look for the Devil, or so much as to think of him, much less to apprehend he was near us ; and as this might be a mistake, and that the Devil might be there while we thought ourselves so secure, it might on many occasions be a mistake of very ill consequence, and in particular, as it would give the Devil room to act in the dark, and not be discovered, where it might be most needful to know him.

From this short hint, thus repeated, I draw a new thesis, namely, that devil is most dangerous that has no cloven-foot; or, if you will have it in words more to the common understanding, the Devil seems to be most dangerous when he goes without his Cloven-foot.

And here a learned speculation offers itself to our debate, and which indeed I ought to call a council of casuists, and men learned in the Devil's politics, to determine :

Whether is most hurtful to the world, the Devil walking about without his Cloven-foot, or the Cloven-foot walking about without the Devil ?

It is indeed a nice and difficult question, and merits to be well enquired into ; for which reason, and divers others, I have referred it to be treated with some decency, and as a dispute of dignity, sufficient to take up a chapter by itself.

CHAPTER VII.

Whether is most hurtful to the world, the Devil walking about without his Cloven-foot, or the Cloven-foot walking about without the Devil?

IN discussing this most critical distinction of Satan's private motions, I must, as the pulpit gentlemen direct us, explain the text, and let you know what I mean by several dark expressions in it, that I may not be understood to talk (as the Devil walks) in the dark.

1. As to the Devil's walking about.
2. His walking without his Cloven-foot.
3. The Cloven-foot walking about without the Devil.

Now as I study brevity, and yet would be understood too, you may please to understand me as I understand myself, thus:

1. That I must be allowed to suppose the Devil really has an intercourse in, and through, and about this globe, with egress and regress, for the carrying on his special affairs, when, how, and where, to his majesty, in his great wisdom, it shall seem meet; that sometimes he appears and becomes visible, and that, like a mastiff without his clog, he does not always carry his Cloven-foot with him. This will necessarily bring me to some debate upon the most important question of apparitions, hauntings, walkings, &c.

13   2 Q

whether of Satan in human shape, or of human creatures in the Devil's shape, or in any other manner whatsoever.

2. I must also be allowed to tell you that Satan has a great deal of wrong done him by the general embracing vulgar errors, and that there is a Cloven-foot oftentimes without a Devil; or, in short, that Satan is not guilty of all the simple things, no, or of all the wicked things we charge him with.

These two heads well settled will fully explain the title of this chapter, answer the query mentioned in it, and at the same time correspond very well with, and give us a farther prospect into the main and original design of this work, namely, The History of the Devil. We are so fond of, and pleased with the general notion of seeing the Devil, that I am loth to disoblige my readers so much as the calling in question his visibility would do. Nor is it my business, any more than it is his, to undeceive them, where the belief is so agreeable to them; especially since upon the whole it is not one farthing matter, either on one side or on the other, whether it be so or no, or whether the truth of fact be ever discovered or not.

Certain it is, whether we see him or no, here he is, and I make no doubt but he is looking on while I am writing this part of his story, whether behind me, or at my elbow, or over my shoulder, is not material to me, nor have I once turned my head about to see whether he is there or no; for if he be not in the inside, I have so mean an opinion of all his extravasated powers, that it seems of very little consequence to me what shape he takes up, or in what posture he appears ; nor indeed can I find in all my enquiry that ever the Devil appeared (qua Devil) in any of the most dangerous or important of his designs in the world ; the most of his projects, especially of the significant part of them, having been carried on another way.

However, as I am satisfied no body will be pleased if I should dispute the reality of his appearance, and the world runs away with it as a received point, and that admits no dispute, I shall most readily grant the general, and give you some account of the particulars.

History is fruitful of particulars, whether invention has supplied them or not, I will not say, where the Devil is brought upon the stage in plain and undeniable apparition : The story of Samuel being raised by the witch of Endor, I shall leave quite out of my list, because there are so many scruples and objections against that story ; and as I shall not dispute with the Scripture, so on the other hand, I have so much deference for the dignity of the Devil, as not to determine rashly how far it may be in the power of every old (witch) woman, to call him up whenever she pleases, and that he must come, whatever the pretence is, or whatever business of consequence he may be engaged in, as often as it is needful for her to pa wa for half a crown, or perhaps less than half the money.

Nor will I undertake to tell you, till I have talked farther with him about it, how far the Devil is concerned to discover frauds, detect murders, reveal secrets, and especially to tell where any money is hid, and shew folks where to find it ; it is an odd thing that Satan should think it of consequence to come and tell us where such a miser hid a strong box, or where such an old woman buried her chamber pot full of money, the value of all which is perhaps but a trifle, when at the same time he lets so many veins of gold, so many unexhausted mines, nay, mountains of silver, as, we may depend upon it, are hid in the bowels of the earth, and which it would be so much to the good of whole nations to dis-cover, lie still there, and never say one word of them to any body. Besides, how does the Devil's doing things so foreign to himself, and so out of his way, agree with the rest of his character ; namely, shewing a kind of a friendly disposition to mankind, or doing beneficent things ? This is so beneath Satan's quality, and looks so little, that I scarce know what to say to it ; but that which is still more pungent in the case is, these things are so out of his road, and so foreign to his calling, that it shocks our faith in them, and seems to clash with all the just notions we have of him, and of his business in the world. The like is to be said of those little merry turns we bring him in acting with us, and upon us, upon trifling and simple occasions, such as tumbling chairs and stools about the house, setting pots and vessels bottom upward, tossing the glass and crockery ware about, without breaking ; and such like mean foolish things, beneath the dignity of the Devil, who, in my opinion, is rather employed in setting the world with the bottom upward, tumbling kings and crowns about and dashing the nations one against another ; raising tempests and storms, whether at sea, or on shore ; and, in a word, doing capital mischiefs suitable to his nature, and agreeable to his name, Devil; and suited to that circumstance of his condition, which I have fully represented in the primitive part of his exiled state.

But to bring in the Devil playing at push-pin with the world, or like Domitian catching flies, that is to say, doing nothing to the purpose; this is not only deluding ourselves, but putting a slur upon the Devil himself; and, I say, I shall not dishonour Satan so much as to suppose any thing in it: However, as I must have a care too how I take away the proper materials of winter evening frippery, and leave the good wives nothing of the Devil to fright the children with, I shall carry the weighty point no farther. No doubt the Devil and Dr. Faustus were very intimate; I should rob you of a very significant* proverb, if I should so much as doubt it; no doubt the Devil shewed himself in the glass to that fair lady who looked in it to see where to place her patches; but then it should follow too that the Devil is an enemy to the ladies wearing patches, and that has some difficulties in it which we cannot so easily reconcile; but we must tell the story, and leave out the consequences.

But to come to more remarkable things, and in which the Devil has thought fit to act in a figure more suitable to his dignity, and on occasions consistent with himself; take the story of the appearance of Julius Cæsar, or the Devil assuming that murdered emperor, to the great Marcus Brutus, who notwithstanding all the good things said to justify it, was no less than a king-killer and an

---

* As great as the Devil and Doctor Faustus. Vulg. Dr. Foster.

assassinator, which we in our language call by a very good name, and peculiar to the English tongue, a ruffian.

The spectre had certainly the appearance of Cæsar, with his wounds bleeding fresh, as if he had just received the fatal blow ; he had reproached him with his ingratitude, with a *tu Brute ! tu quoque, mi fili :* " What thou, Brutus ! thou, my adopted son !" Now history seems to agree universally, not only in the story itself, but in the circumstances of it ; we have only to observe that the Devil had certainly power to assume, not a human shape only, but the shape of Julius Cæsar in particular.

Had Brutus been a timorous conscience-harried, weak-headed wretch, had he been under the horror of the guilt, and terrified with the dangers that were before him at that time, we might suggest that he was overrun with the vapours, that the terrors which were upon his mind disordered him, that his head was delirious and prepossessed, and that his fancy only placed Cæsar so continually in his eye, that it realized him to his imagination, and he believed he saw him ; with many other suggested difficulties to invalidate the story, and render the reality of it doubtful.

But the contrary, to an extreme, was the case of Brutus ; his known character placed him above the power of all hypochondriacs, or fanciful delusions ; Brutus was of a true Roman spirit, a bold hero, of an intrepid courage ; one that scorned to fear even the Devil, as the story allows : Besides, he gloried in the action ; there could be no terror of mind upon him ; he valued himself upon it, as done in the service of liberty, and the cause of his

country ; and was so far from being frighted at the
Devil in the worst shape, that he spoke first to him, and
asked him, What art thou? and when he was cited to see
him again at Philippi, answered with a gallantry that
knew no fear, Well I will see thee there. Whatever the
Devil's business was with Brutus this is certain, according to all the historians who give us the account of it,
that Brutus discovered no fear ; he did not, like Saul at
Endor, fall to the ground in a swoon, 1 Sam. xxviii. 20.
*Then Saul fell all along upon the earth, and there was
no strength in him, and was sore afraid.* In a word, I
see no room to charge Brutus with being overrun with
the hyppo, or with vapours, or with fright and terror of
mind ; but he saw the Devil, that is certain, and with
eyes open, his courage not at all daunted, his mind
resolute, and with the utmost composure spoke to him,
replied to his answer, and defied his summons to death,
which indeed he feared not, as appeared afterward.

I come next to an instance as eminent in history as the
other ; this was in Char. VI. of France, sirnamed, The
Beloved ; who riding over the forest near Mans, a ghastly
frightful fellow (that is to say, the Devil so clothed in
human vizor) came up to his horse, and taking hold of
his bridle, stopped him, with the addition of these words,
Stop king, whither go you ? You are betrayed ! and
immediately disappeared. It is true, the king had been
distempered in his head before, and so he might have
been deceived, and we might have charged it to the
account of a whimsical brain, or the power of his imagination ; but this was in the face of his attendants, several
of his great officers, courtiers, and princes of the blood

being with him, who all saw the man, heard the words, and immediately, to their astonishment, lost sight of the spectre, who vanished from them all.

Two witnesses will convict a murderer, why not a traitor ? This must be the old gentleman, emblematically so called, or who must it be ? nay, who else could it be ? His ugliness is not the case, though ugly as the Devil, is a proverb in his favour ; but vanishing out of sight is an essential to a spirit, and to an evil spirit in our times especially.

These are some of the Devil's extraordinaries, and it must be confessed they are not the most agreeable to mankind, for sometimes he takes upon him to disorder his friends very much on these occasions, as in the above case of Char. VI. of France ; the king, they say was really demented ever after ; that is, as we vulgarly, but not always improperly, express it, he was really frighted out of his wits. Whether the malicious Devil intended it so, or not, is not certain, though it was not so foreign to his particular disposition if he did.

But where he is more intimate, we are told he appears in a manner less disagreeable, and there he is more properly a familiar spirit ; that is, in short, a Devil of their acquaintance : It is true, the antients understand the word, a familiar spirit, to be one of the kinds of possession ; but if it serves our turn, as well under the denomination of an intimate Devil, or a Devil visitant, it must be acknowledged to be as near in the literal sense and acceptation of the word, as the other ; nay, it must be allowed it is a very great piece of familiarity in the Devil to make visits, and shew none of his disagreeables, not appear formidable, or in the shape of what he is, respectfully withholding his dismal part, in compassion to the infirmities of his friends.

It is true, Satan may be obliged to make different appearances, as the several circumstances of things call for it; in some cases he makes his public entry, and then he must shew himself in his habit of ceremony; in other cases he comes upon private business, and then he appears in disguise; in some public cases he may think fit to be *incog.* and then he appears dressed *a la masque;* so they say he appeared at the famous St. Bartholomew wedding at Paris, where he came in dressed up like a trumpeter, danced in his habit, sounded a levet, and then went out and rung the alarm-bell (which was the signal to begin the massacre) half an hour before the time appointed, lest the king's mind should alter, and his heart fail him.

If the story be not made upon him (for we should not slander the Devil) it should seem, he was not thoroughly satisfied in king Charles IX's steadiness in his cause; for the king, it seems, had relaxed a little once before, and Satan might be afraid he would fall off again, and so prevent the execution : Others say, the king did relent immediately after the ringing the alarm-bell, but that then it was too late, the work was begun, and the rage of blood having been let loose among the people, there was no recalling the order.' If the Devil was thus brought to the necessity of a secret management, it must be owned he did it dexterously; but I have not authority enough for the story, to charge him with the particulars, so I leave it *au croc.*

I have much better vouchers for the story following,

14   2 R

which I had so solemnly confirmed by one that lived in the family, that I never doubted the truth of it. There lived in the parish of St. Bennet Fynk, near the Royal Exchange, an honest poor widow woman, who, her husband being lately dead, took lodgers into her house; that is, she let out some of her rooms in order to lessen her own charge of rent; among the rest, she let her garrets to a working watch-wheel maker, or one some way concerned in making the movements of watches, and who worked for those shop-keepers who sell watches, as is usual.

It happened that a man and woman went up, to speak with this movement maker upon some business which related to his trade, and when they were near the top of the stairs, the garret door where he usually worked being wide open, they saw the poor man (the watch maker, or wheel maker) had hanged himself upon a beam which was left open in the room a little lower than the plaister, or ceiling: Surprized at the sight, the woman stopped, and cried out to the man who was behind her on the stairs, to run up, and cut the poor creature down.

At that very moment comes a man hastily from another part of the room which they upon the stairs could not see, bringing a joint-stool in his hand, as if in great haste, and sets it down just by the wretch that was hanged, and getting up as hastily upon it pulls a knife out of his pocket, and taking hold of the rope with one of his hands, beckoned to the woman and the man behind her with his head, as if to stop and not come up, shewing them the knife in his other hand, as if he was just going to cut the poor man down.

Upon this, the woman stopped awhile, but the man

who stood on the joint-stool continued with his hand and
knife, as if fumbling at the knot, but did not yet cut the
man down; at which the woman cried out again, and the
man behind her called to her, Go up, says he, and help
the man upon the stool! supposing something hindered.
But the man upon the stool made signs to them again to
be quiet, and not come on, as if saying, I shall do it immediately; then he made two strokes with his knife, as if
cutting the rope, and then stopped again; and still the
poor man was hanging, and consequently dying: Upon
this, the woman on the stairs cried out to him, What ails
you? why don't you cut the poor man down? and the
man behind her having no more patience, thrusts her by,
and said to her, let me come, I'll warrant you I'll do it;
and with that runs up and forward into the room to the
man; but when he came there, behold, the poor man
was there hanging; but no man with a knife, or joint-
stool, or any such thing to be seen, all that was spectre
and delusion, in order, no doubt, to let the poor creature
that had hanged himself perish and expire.

The man was so frighted and surprized, that with all
the courage he had before, he dropped on the floor as
one dead, and the woman at last was fain to cut the poor
man down with a pair of scissars, and had much to do to
effect it.

As I have no room to doubt the truth of this story,
which I had from persons on whose honesty I could depend, so I think it needs very little trouble to convince
us who the man upon the stool must be, and that it was
the Devil who placed himself there, in order to finish the
murder of the man who he had, devil-like, tempted
before, and prevailed with to be his own executioner.

Besides, it corresponds so well with the Devil's nature, and with his business, viz. that of a murderer, that I never questioned it; nor can I think we wrong the Devil at all to charge him with it.

> N. B. I cannot be positive in the remaining part of this story, viz. whether the man was cut down soon enough to be recovered, or whether the Devil carried his point, and kept off the man and woman till it was too late; but be it which it will, it is plain he did his devilish endeavour, and stayed till he was forced to abscond again.

We have many solid tales well attested, as well in history as in the reports of honest people, who could not be deceived, intimating the Devil's personal appearance, some in one place, some in another; as also sometimes in one habit or dress, and sometimes in another; and it is to be observed, that in none of those which are most like to be real, and in which there is least of fancy and vapour, you have any mention of the Cloven-foot, which rather seems to be a mere invention of men (and perhaps chiefly of those who had a cloven understanding) I mean a shallow kind of craft, the effect of an empty and simple-head, thinking by such a well-meant, though weak fraud, to represent the Devil to the old women and children of the age, with some addition suited to the weakness of their intellects, and suited to making them afraid of him.

I have another account of a person who travelled upwards of four years with the Devil in his company, and conversed most intimately with him all the while; nay, if I may believe the story, he knew most part of the

time that he was the Devil, and yet conversed with him,
and that very profitably, for he performed many very
useful services for him, and constantly preserved him from
the danger of wolves and wild beasts, which the country
he travelled through was intolerably full of. Where by
the way, you are to understand, that the wolves and bears
in those countries knew the Devil, whatever disguise he
went in ; or that the Devil has some way to fright bears
and such creatures, more than we know of. Nor could
this Devil ever be prevailed upon to hurt him or any of
his company. This account has an innumerable number of diverting incidents attending it ; but they are
equal to all the rest in bulk, and therefore too long for
this book.

I find too upon some more ordinary occasions the
Devil has appeared to several people at their call : This
indeed shews abundance of good humour in him, considering him as a Devil, and that he was mighty com-
plaisant : Nay some, they tell us, have a power to raise
the Devil whenever they think fit ; this I cannot bring
the Devil to a level with, unless I should allow him to
be *servus servorum*, as another devil in disguise calls
himself ; subjected to every old wizard's call ; or that
he is under a necessity of appearing on such or such
particular occasions, whoever it is that calls him ; which
would bring the Devil's circumstances to a pitch of
slavery which I see no reason to believe of them.

Here also I must take notice again, that though I say
the Devil, when I speak of all these apparitions, whether
of a greater or lesser kind, yet I am not obliged to suppose Satan himself in person is concerned to shew himself,
but that some of his agents, deputies and servants, are

sent to that purpose, and directed what disguise of flesh and blood to put on, as may be suitable to the occasion.

This seems to be the only way to reconcile all those simple and ridiculous appearances, which not Satan, but his emissaries (which we old women called imps) sometimes make, and the mean and sorry employment they are put to : Thus fame tells us of a certain witch of quality, who called the Devil once to carry her over a brook where the water was swelled with a hasty rain, and lashed him soundly with her whip for letting her ladyship fall into the water before she was quite over. Thus also, as fame tells us, she set the Devil to work, and made him build Crowland abbey, where there was no foundation to be found, only for disturbing the workmen a little who were first set about it. So it seems another laborious devil was obliged to dig the great ditch cross the country from the Fenn country to the edge of Suffolk and Essex ; which however he has preserved the reputation of, and where it crosses New-Market heath, it is called Devil's Ditch to this day.

Another piece of punishment no doubt it was, when the Devil was obliged to bring the stones out of Wales into Wiltshire, to build Stonehenge : How this was ordered in those days, when it seems they kept Satan to hard labour, I know not ; I believe it must be registered among the antient pieces of art which are lost in the world, such as melting of stone, painting of glass, &c. Certainly they had the Devil under correction in those days ; that is to say, those lesser sorts of devils ; but I cannot think that the muckle thief Devil, as they call him in the North, the grand seignior Devil of all, was ever reduced to discipline. What devil it was that

Dunstan took by the nose with his red hot tongs, I have not yet examined antiquity enough to be certain of, any more than I can what devil it was that St. Francis played so many warm tricks with, and made him run away from him so often : However, this I take upon me to say, in the Devil's behalf, that it could not be our Satan, the arch devil of all devils, of whom I have been talking so long.

Nor is it unworthy the occasion, to take notice that we really wrong the Devil, and speak of him very much to his disadvantage when we say of such a great lord, or of such a lady of quality, I think the Devil is in your grace : No, no, Satan has other business, he very rarely possesses f——ls : Besides, some are far from having the Devil in them, that they are really transmigrated into the very essence of the Devil themselves ; and others again not transmigrated, or assimilated, but in deed and in truth shew us that they are to have mere native devils in every part and parcel of them, and that the rest is only masque and disguise. Thus if rage, envy, pride and revenge can constitute the parts of a devil, why should not a lady of such quality, in whom all those extraordinaries abound, have a right to the title of being a devil really and substantially, and to all intents and purposes, in the most perfect and absolute sense, according to the most exquisite descriptions of devils already given by me or any body else ; and even just as Joan of Arc, or Joan queen of Naples were, who were both sent home to their native country, as soon as it was discovered that they were real devils, and that Satan acknowledged them in that quality.

Nor does my lady D———ss's wearing sometimes a

case of humanity about her, called flesh and blood, at all alter the case ; for so it is evident, according to our present hypothesis, Satan has been always allowed to do, upon urgent occasions ; ay, and to make his personal appearance as such, among even the sons and daughters of God too, as well as among the children of men ; and therefore her grace may have appeared in the shape of a fine lady, as long as she has been supposed to do, without any impeachment of her just claim to the title of devil ; which being her true and natural original, she ought not, nor indeed shall not, by me, be denied her shapes of honour, whenever she pleases to declare for a re-assumption.

And farther, to give every truth its due illustration, this need not be thought so strange ; and is far from being unjust ; her grace (as she, it may be, is now stiled) has not acted, at least that I never heard of, so unworthy her great and illustrious original, that we should think she has lost any thing by walking about the world so many years in apparition : But to give her the due homage of her quality, she has acted as consonant to the essence and nature of devil, which she has such a claim to, as was consistent with the needful reserve of her present disguise.

Nor shall we lead the reader into any mistake concerning this part of our work, as if this was or is meant to be a particular satire upon the D————ss of ————, and upon her only, as if we had no devils among us in the phenomena of fair ladies, but this one : If Satan would be so honest to us as he might be (and it would be very ingenuous in him, that must be acknowleged, to give us a little of his illumination in this case) we should soon be able to unmask a great many notable figures among us to our real surprise.

Indeed it is a point worth our further enquiry, and would be a discovery many ways to our advantage, were we blessed with it, to see how many real devils we have walking up and down the world in masque, and how many hoop-petticoats complete the entire masque that disguises the Devil in the shape of that thing called Woman.

As for the men, nature has satisfied herself in letting them be their own disguise, and in suffering them to act the old women, as old women are vulgarly understood, in matters of council and politics; but if at any time they have occasion for the Devil in person, they are obliged to call him to their aid in such shape as he pleases to make use of *pro hac vice ;* and of all those shapes, the most agreeable to him seems to be that of a female of quality, in which he has infinite opportunity to act to perfection, what part soever he is called in for.

How happy are those people who they say have the particular quality or acquired habit called the second sight ; one sort of whom they tell us are able to distinguish the Devil, in whatever case or outside of flesh and blood he is pleased to put on, and consequently could know the Devil wherever they met him ? Were I blest with this excellent and useful accomplishment, how pleasant would it be, and how would it particularly gratify my spleen, and all that which I, in common with my fellow creatures, carry about me, called ill-nature, to stand in the mall, or at the entrance to any of our assemblies of beauties, and point them out as they pass by, with this particular mark, That's a devil ; that fine

14   2 S

young toast is a devil; there's a devil drest in a new habit for the ball ; there's a devil in a coach and six, *cum aliis.* In short, it would make a merry world among us if we could but enter upon some proper method of such discriminations ; but, Lawr'd, what a hurricane would it raise, if, like ————, who they say scourged the Devil so often, that he durst not come near him in any shape whatever, we could find some new method out to make the Devil unmask, like the angel Uriel, who, Mr. Milton says, had an enchanted spear, with which if he did but touch the Devil, whatever disguise he had put on, it obliged him immediately to start up, and shew himself in his true original shape, mere devil as he was.

This would do nicely ; and as I, who am originally a projector, have spent some time upon this study, and doubt not in a little time to finish my engine, which I am contriving, to screw the Devil out of every body, or any body ; I question not when I have brought it to perfection, but I shall make most excellent discoveries by it ; and besides the many extraordinary advantages of it to human society, I doubt not but it will make good sport in the world too ; wherefore, when I publish my proposals and divide it into shares as other less useful projects have been done, I question not, for all the severe act lately passed against bubbles, but I shall get subscribers enough, &c.

In a word, a secret power of discovering what devils we have among us, and where and what business they are doing, would be a vast advantage to us all ; that we might know among the crowd of devils that walk about streets, who are apparitions, and who are not.

Now you must know, at certain intervals when the old gentleman's illuminations are upon me, and when I have something of an eclaircissement with him, I have some degrees of this discriminating second sight, and therefore it is no strange thing for me to tell a great many of my acquaintance that they are really devils, when they themselves know nothing of the matter : Sometimes indeed I find it pretty hard to convince them of it, or at least they are unwilling to own it, but it is not the less so for that.

I had a long discourse upon this subject one day, with a young beautiful lady of my acquaintance, who the world very much admired ; and as the world judges no farther than they can see, (and how should they, you would say) they took her to be, as she really was, a most charming creature.

To me, indeed, she discovered herself many ways, besides the advantage I had of my extraordinary penetration by the magic powers which I am vested with : To me, I say, she appeared a fury, a satyr, a fiery little fiend as could possibly be dressed up in flesh ; in short, she appeared to me what she really was, a very devil : It is natural to human creatures to desire to discover any extraordinary powers they are possessed of superior to others ; and this itch prevailing on me, among the rest, I was impatient to let this lady know that I understood her composition perfectly well, nay, as well as she did herself.

In order to this, happening to be in the family once for some days, and having the honour to be very intimate with her and her husband too, I took an opportunity on an extraordinary occasion, when she was in the height of

good humour, to talk with her : You must note, that as
I said, the lady was in an extraordinary good humour,
and there had been a great deal of mirth in the family
for some days; but one evening, sir E——— her husband, upon some very sharp turn she gave to another
gentleman, which made all the company pleasant, ran to
her, and with a passion of good humour takes her in his
arms, and turning to me, says he, Jack, this wife of
mine is full of wit and good humour, but when she has a
mind to be smart, she is the keenest little devil in the
world : This was alluding to the quick turn she had
given the other gentleman.

Is that the best language you can give your wife ?
says my lady. O madam, says I, such devils as you,
are all angels; ay, ay, says my lady, I know that, he
has only let a truth fly out that he does not understand :
Look you there now, says sir Edward, could any thing
but such a dear devil as this have said a thing so pointed ?
Well, well, adds he, devil to a lady in a man's arms, is a
word of divers interpretations.   Thus they rallied for a
good while, he holding her fast all the while in his arms,
and frequently kissing her, and at last it went off, all in
sunshine and mirth.

But the next day, for I had the honour to lodge in
the lady's father's house, where it all happened ; I say,
the next day my lady begins with me upon the subject,
and that very smartly, so that at first I did not know
whether she was in jest or earnest : Ay, ay, says she,
you men make nothing of your wives after you have
them, alluding to the discourse with sir Edward the
night before.

Why, madam, says I, we men, as you are pleased to

term it, if we meet with good wives worship them, and make idols of them, what would you have more of us?

No, no, says she, before you have them they are angels, but when you have been in heaven, adds she, and smiled, then they are devils.

Why, madam, says I, devils are angels, you know, and were the highest sort of angels once.

Yes, says she, very smartly, all devils are angels, but all angels are not devils.

But, madam, says I, you should never take it ill to be called devil, you know.

I know! says she, hastily, what do you mean by that?

Why, madam, says I, and looked very gravely and serious, I thought you had known that I knew it, or else I would not have said so, for I would not offend you; but you may depend I shall never discover it, unless you order me to do so for your particular service.

Upon this she looked hard and wild, and bid me explain myself.

I told her, I was ready to explain myself, if she would give me her word, she would not resent it, and would take nothing ill.

She gave me her word solemnly she would not, though like a true devil, she broke her promise with me all at once.

Well however, being unconcerned whether she kept her word or no, I began, by telling her that I had not long since obtained the second sight, and had some years studied magic, by which I could penetrate into many things, which to ordinary perception were invisible, and had some glasses, by the help of which I could see into all visionary or imaginary appearances in a different manner than other people did.

Very well, says she, suppose you can, what's that to me ?

I told her it was nothing to her, any farther than that as she knew herself to be originally not the same creature she seemed to be, but was of a sublime angelic original ; so by the help of my recited art, I knew it too, and so far it might relate to her.

Very fine, says she, so you would make a devil of me indeed.

I took that occasion to tell her, I would make nothing of her but what she was ; that I supposed she knew well enough God almighty never thought fit to make any human creature so perfect and completely beautiful as she was, but that such were also reserved for figures to be assumed by angels of one kind or other.

She rallied me upon that, and told me that would not bring me off, for I had not determined her for any thing angelic, but a mere devil ; and how could I flatter her with being handsome and a devil both at the same time ?

I told her, as Satan, whom we abusively called Devil, was an immortal seraph, and of an original angelic nature, so abstracted from any thing wicked, he was a most glorious being ; that when he thought fit to encase himself with flesh, and walk about in disguise, it was in his power equally with the other angels to make the form he took upon himself be as he thought fit, beautiful or deformed.

Here she disputed the possibility of that, and after charging me faintly with flattering her face, told me the Devil could not be represented by any thing handsome, alleging our constant picturing the Devil in all the frightful appearances imaginable.

I told her we wrong'd him very much in that, and quoted St. Francis, to whom the Devil frequently appeared in the form of the most incomparably beautiful naked woman, to allure him, and what means he used to turn the appearance into a devil again, and how he effected it.

She put by the discourse, and returned to that of angels, and insisted that angels did not always assume beautiful appearances; that sometimes they appeared in terrible shapes, but that when they did not, it was at best only amiable faces, not exquisite; and that therefore it would not hold, that to be handsome, should always render them suspected.

I told her the Devil had more occasion to form beauties than other angels had, his business being principally to deceive and ensnare mankind. And then I gave her some examples upon the whole.

I found by her discourse she was willing enough to pass for an angel, but it was the hardest thing in the world to convince her that she was a devil, and she would not come into that by any means; she argued that I knew her father, and that her mother was a very good woman, and was delivered of her in the ordinary way, and that there were such and such ladies who were present in the room when she was born, and that had often told her so.

I told her that was nothing in such a case as hers; that when the old gentleman had occasion to transform himself into a fine lady, he could easily dispose of a child, and place himself in the cradle instead of it, when the nurse or mother was asleep; nay, or when they were broad awake either, it was the same thing to him; and I quoted Luther to her upon that occasion, who affirms that it had been so. However, I said, to convince her that I knew it, (for I would not have it that she knew it already) if she pleased I would go to my chamber and fetch her my magic looking-glass, where she should see her own picture, not only as it was an angelic picture for the world to admire, but a devil also frightful enough to any body but herself and me that understood it.

No, no, said she, I'll look in none of your conjuring glasses ; I know myself well enough, and I desire to look no otherwise than I am.

No, madam, says I, I know that very well ; nor do you need any better shape than that you appear in, it is most exquisitely fine ; all the world knows you are a complete beauty, and that is a clear evidence what you would be, if your present appearing form was reduced to its proper personality.

Appearing form ! says she, Why, what would you make an apparition of me ?

An apparition ! madam, said I, yes, to be sure ; why you know you are nothing else but an apparition ; and what else would you be, when it is so infinitely to your advantage ?

With that, she turned pale and angry, and then rose up hastily, and looked into the glass, (a large pier-glass being in the room) where she stood surveying herself from head to foot, with vanity not a little.

I took that time to slip away, and running up into my apartment, I fetched my magic glass, as I called it, in which I had a hollow case so framed behind a looking-glass, that in the first she would see her own face only ; in the second, she would see the Devil's

HISTORY OF THE DEVIL

WHERE SHE SAW THE DEVIL INDEED.

Page 199

Drawn by G.M.Brighty.   Engraved by F.Wallis

EXETER,
Publish'd by DAVIES & ELDRIDGE 1815.
and J.WALLIS, Berwick Street, Soho,
LONDON.

face, ugly, and frightful enough, but dressed up
with a lady's head-clothes in a circle, the Devil's
face in the centre, and as it were at a little distance
behind.

I came down again so soon, that she did not think the
time long, especially having spent it in surveying her
fair self; when I returned, I said, Come, madam, do not
trouble yourself to look there, that is not a glass capable
of shewing you any thing ; come, take this glass.

It will shew me as much of myself, says she, a little
scornfully, as I desire to see ; so she continued looking
in the pier-glass ; after some time more (for seeing her a
little out of humour, I waited to see what observations
she would make) I asked her if she had viewed herself to
her satisfaction ? she said she had, and she had seen
nothing of devil about her. Come, madam, said I, look
here ; and with that I opened the looking-glass, and she
looked in it, but saw nothing but her own face ; Well,
says she, the glasses agree well enough, I see no difference ; what can you make of it ? With that I took it a
little away ; Dont you ? says I, then I should be mistaken very much ; so I looked in it myself, and giving
it a turn imperceptible to her, I shewed it her again,
where she saw the Devil indeed, dressed up like a fine
lady, but ugly, and devil-like as could be desired for a
devil to be.

She started, and cried out most horribly, and told me
she thought I was more of a devil than she, for that she
knew nothing of all these tricks, and I did it to fright
her, she believed I had raised the Devil.

I told her it was nothing but her own natural picture,
and that she knew well enough, and that I did not shew

14   2 T

it her to inform her of it, but to let her know that I knew
it too ; that so she might make no pretences of being offended when I talked familiarly to her of a thing of this
nature.

Very well, says she, so I am a real frightful devil, am I ?

O, Madam, says I, don't say am I ? why you know
what you are, don't you ? A devil! ay, certainly ; as sure
as the rest of the world believes you a lady.

I had a great deal of farther discourse with her upon
that subject, though she would fain have beat me off
from it, and two or three times she put the talk off, and
brought something else on ; but I always found means
to revive it, and to attack her upon the reality of her
being a devil, till at last I made her downright angry,
and then she shewed it.

First she cried, told me I came to affront her, that I
would not talk so if sir Ed—— was by ; and that she
ought not to be used so. I endeavoured to pacify her,
and told her I had not treated her with any indecency,
nor I would not ; because while she thought fit to walk
abroad *incog.* it was none of my business to discover her ;
that if she thought fit to tell sir Ed—— any thing of the
discourse, she was very welcome, or to conceal it, (which
I thought the wisest course) she should do just as she
pleased ; but I made no question I should convince sir
Ed—— her husband, that what I said was just, and that
she was really so ; whether it was for her service or no for
him to know it, was for her to consider.

This calmed her a little, and she looked hard at me
for a minute without speaking a word, when on a sudden
she broke out thus : And you will undertake, says she,
to convince sir Ed—— that he has married a devil, will
ye ? A fine story indeed ! and what follows ? why then

it must follow that the child I go with (for she was big with child) will be a devil too, will it? A fine story for sir Ed—— indeed! isn't it?

I don't know that, madam, said I, that is as you order it; by the father's side, said I, I know it will not, but what it may by the mother's side, that is a doubt I can't resolve till the Devil and I talk farther about it.

You and the Devil talk together! says she, and looks rufully at me; why do you talk with the Devil then?

Ay, madam, says I, as sure as ever you did yourself; besides, said I, can you question that? Pray who am I talking to now?

I think you are mad, says she; why you will make devils of all the family, it may be, and particularly I must be with child of a devil, that is certain.

No, madam, said I, it is not certain, as I said before, I question it.

Why you say I am the Devil, the child, you know, has always most of the mother in it, then that must be a devil too, I think, what else can it be? says she.

I can't tell that, madam, said I; that is as you agree among yourselves, this kind does not go by generation; that is a dispute foreign to the present purpose.

Then I entered into a discourse with her of the ends and purposes for which the Devil takes up such beautiful forms as hers, and why it always gave me a suspicion when I saw a lady handsomer than ordinary, and set me upon the search to be satisfied whether she was really a woman or an apparition? a lady or a devil? allowing all along that her being a devil was quite out of the question.

Upon that very foot, she took me up again roundly, and so, says she, you are very civil to me through all

your discourse, for I see it ends all in that, and you take
it as a thing confest, that I am a devil! A very pretty
piece of good usage indeed! says she; I thank you for it.

Nay, madam, says I, do not take it ill of me, for I
only discover to you that I knew it; I do not tell it you
as a secret, for you are satisfied of that another way.

Satisfied of what? says she, that I am a devil? I
think the Devil's in you: And so began to be hot.

A devil! yes, madam, says I, without doubt a mere
devil; take it as you please, I can't help that: And so I
began to take it ill that she should be disgusted at opening such a well known truth to her.

With that she discovered it all at once, for she turned
fury, in the very letter of it; flew out in a passion, railed
at me, curst me most heartily, and immediately disappeared; which you know is the particular mark of a
spirit or apparition.

We had a great deal of discourse besides this, relating
to several other young ladies of her acquaintance, some
of which, I said, were mere apparitions like herself: and
told her which were so, and which not; and the reason why they were so, and for what uses and purposes,
some to delude the world one way, and some another;
and she was pretty well pleased to hear that, but she
could not bear to hear her own true character, which
however, as cunning as she was, made her act the devil at
last, as you have heard; and then vanished out of my
sight.

I have seen her in miniature several times since; but
she proves herself still to be the devil of a lady, for she
bears malice, and will never forgive me, that I would not
let her be an angel; but like a very devil as she is, she
endeavours to kill me at a distance; and indeed the poison

of her eyes (basilisk-like) is very strong, and she has a strange influence upon me ; but I that know her to be a devil strive very hard with myself to drive the memory of her out of my thoughts.

I have had two or three engagements since this, with other apparitions of the same sex, and I find they are all alike, they are willing enough to be thought angels, but the word devil does not go down at all with them : But it is all one, whenever we see an apparition, it is so natural to say we have seen the Devil, that there is no prevailing with mankind to talk any other language. A gentleman of my acquaintance, the other day, that had courted a lady a long time, had the misfortune to come a little suddenly upon her, when she did not expect him, and found her in such a rage at some of her servants, that it quite disordered her, especially a footman : The fellow had done something that was indeed provoking, but not sufficient to put her into such a passion, and so out of herself; nor was she able to restrain herself when she saw her lover come in, but damn'd the fellow, and raged like a fury at him.

My friend did his best to compose her, and begged the fellow's pardon of her, but it would not do ; nay, the poor fellow made all the submissions that could be expected, but it was the same thing : And so the gentleman, not caring to engage himself farther than became him, withdrew, and came no more at her for three days, in all which time she was hardly cool.

The next day my friend came to me, and talking of it in confidence to me, I am afraid, says he, I am going to marry a she devil, and so told me the story ; I took no notice to him, but finding out his mistress, and taking proper measures, with some of my particular skill, I

soon found out that it was really so, that she was a mere
apparition ; and had it not been for that accidental disorder of her passions, which discovered her inside, she
might indeed have cheated any man, for she was a lovely
devil as ever was seen ; she talked like an angel, sung
like a syren, did every thing, and said every thing that
was taking and charming : But what then ? it was all
apparition, for she was a mere devil. It is true, my
friend married her, and though she was a devil without
doubt, yet either she behaved so well, or he was so good,
I never could hear him find fault with her.

These are particular instances ; but alas ! I could run
you a length beyond all those examples, and give you
such a list of devils among the gay things of the town,
that would fright you to think of ; and you would presently conclude, with me, that all the perfect beauties
are devils, mere apparitions ; but time and paper fails,
so we must only leave the men the caution, let them
venture at their peril.   I return to the subject.

We have a great many charming apparitions of like
kind go daily about the world in complete masquerade,
and, though we must not say so, they are in themselves
mere devils, wicked, dangerous, murdering devils, that
kill various ways, some, basilisk-like, with their eyes ;
some syren-like, with their tongues ; all murderers, even
from the beginning : It is true, it is pity these pretty
apparitions should be devils, and be so mischievous as
they are ; but since it is so, I can do no less than to
advertise you of it, that you may shun the Devil in
whatever shape you meet with him

Again, there are some half-devils, they say, like the
sagittarii, half man, half horse, or rather like the satyr,
who, they say, is half devil, half man ; or, like my lord

bishop, who, they say, was half-headed ; whether they mean half-witted or no, I do not find authors agreed about it : But if they had voted him such, it had been as kind a thing as any they could say of him, because it would have cleared him from the scandal of being a devil, or half a devil, for we do not find the Devil makes any alliance with f—ls.

Then as to merry devils, there is my master G——, he may indeed have the Devil in him, but it must be said, to the credit of possession in general, that Satan would have scorned to have entred into a soul so narrow that there was not room to hold him, or to take up with so discording a creature, so abject, so scoundrel, as never made a figure among mankind greater than that of a thief, a morader, moulded up into quality, and a reparee dressed up *a-la-masque*, with a robe and a coronet.

Some little dog-kennel devil may indeed take up his quarters in or near him, and so run into and out of him as his drum beats a call; but to him that was born a devil, Satan, that never acts to no purpose, could not think him worth being possessed by any thing better than a devil of a dirty quality ; that is to say, a spirit too mean to wear the name of devil, without some badge or addition of infamy and meanness to distinguish it by.

Thus what devil of quality would be confined to a P———n, who inheriting all the pride and insolence of his ancestors, without one of their good qualities ; the bully, the Billingsgate, and all the hereditary ill language of his family, without an ounce of their courage ; that has been rescued five or six times from the scandal of a coward, by the bravery, and at the hazard of friends, and never failed to be ungrateful ; that if ever he committed a murder, did it in cold blood, because no body could prove he ever had any hot ; who possessed with a poltroon devil, was always wickeder in the dark, than he durst be by day-light ; and who, after innumerable passive sufferings, has been turned out of human society, because he could not be kick'd or cuff'd either into good manners or good humour.

To say this was a devil, an apparition, or even a half-devil, would be unkind to Satan himself, since though he (the Devil) has so many millions of inferior devils under his command, not one could be found base enough to match him, nor one devil found but what would think himself dishonoured to be employed about him.

Some merry good-for-nothing devils we have indeed, which we might, if we had room, speak of at large, and divert you too with the relation, such as my lady Hatts's devil in Essex, who upon laying a joiner's mallet in the window of a certain chamber, would come very orderly and knock with it all night upon the window, or against the wainscot, and disturb the neighbourhood, and then go away in the morning, as well satisfied as may be ; whereas if the mallet was not left, he would think himself affronted, and be as unsufferable and terrifying as possible, breaking the windows, splitting the wainscot, committing all the disorders, and doing all the damage that he was able to the house, and to the goods in it. And again, such as the drumming-devil in the well at Oundle in Northamptonshire, and such like.

A great many antic devils have been seen also, who seemed to have little or nothing to do, but only to assure us that they can appear if they please, and that there is a reality in the thing called apparition.

As to shadows of devils, and imaginary appearances, such as appear, and yet are invisible at the same time, I had thought to have bestowed a chapter upon them by themselves, but it may be as much to the purpose to let them alone as to meddle with them ; it is said our old friend Luther used to be exceedingly troubled with such invisible apparitions, and he tells us much of them, in what they call his table-talk ; but with master Luther's leave, though the Devil passes for a very great liar, I could swallow many things of his own proper making, as soon as some of those I find in a book that goes by his name, particularly the story of the Devil in a basket, the child flying out of the cradle, and the like.

In a word, the walking devils that we have generally among us, are of the female sex ; whether it be that the Devil finds less difficulty to manage them, or that he lives quieter with them, or that they are fitter for his business than the men, I shall not now enter into a dispute about that ; perhaps he goes better disguised in the fair sex than otherwise : Antiquity gives us many histories of she-devils, such as we can very seldom match for wickedness among the men ; such now as in the text, Lot's daughters, Joseph's mistress, Sampson's Delilah, Herod's Herodias, these were certainly devils, or played the devil sufficiently in their turn ; one male apparition indeed the Scripture furnishes you with, and that is Judas ; for his master says expressly of him, *One of you is a devil ;* not has the Devil, or is possessed of the Devil ; but really is a devil, or is a real devil.

How happy is it, that this great secret comes thus to be discovered to mankind ? Certainly the world has gone on in ignorance a long time, and at a strange rate, that we should have so many devils continually walking about among us in human shape, and we know it not.

Philosophers tell us that there is a world of spirits, and

many learned pieces of guess-work they make at it, representing the world to be so near us, that the air, as they
describe it, must be full of dragons and devils, enough
to fright our imaginations with the very thoughts of
them ; and if they say true, it is our great felicity that
we cannot see any farther into it than we do, which if
we could, would appear as frightful as hell itself ; but
none of those sages ever told us, till now, that half the
people who converse with us are apparitions, especially
of the women ; and among them especially this valuable
part, the woman of figure, the fair, the beautiful, or
patched and painted.

This unusual phænomenon has been seen but a little
while, and but a little way, and the general part of mankind cannot come into the same notions about it ; nay,
perhaps they will all think it strange ; but be it as
strange as it will, the nature of the thing confirms it, this
lower sphere is full of devils ; and some of both sexes
have given strange testimonies of the reality of their pre-
existent devilism for many ages past, though I think it
never came to that height as it has now.

It is true, in former times Satan dealt much in old
women, and those, as I have observed already, very
ugly, ugly as a witch, black as a witch, I look like a
witch, all proverbial speeches, and which testified what
tools it was Satan generally worked with ; and these old
spectres, they tell us, used to ride through the air in the
night, and upon broom-sticks too, all mighty homely
doings ; some say they used to go to visit their grand
seignior the Devil, in those nocturnal perambulations :
But be that as it will, it is certain the Devil has changed
hands, and that now he walks about the world clothed
in beauty, covered with the charms of the lovely, and he

OF THE DEVIL. 339

Of the Cloven-foot walking about the world without the Devil, &c.

fails not to disguise himself effectually by it; for who would think a beautiful lady could be a masque to the Devil? and that a fine face, a divine shape, a heavenly aspect, should bring the Devil in her company, nay, should be herself an apparition, a mere devil.

The enquiry is indeed worth our while, and therefore I hope all the enamoured beaus and boys, all the beauty-hunters and fortune-hunters, will take heed, for I suppose if they get the Devil, they will not complain for want of a fortune; and there is danger enough, I assure you, for the world is full of apparitions, *non rosa sine spinis ;* not a beauty without a devil, the old women spectres, and the young women apparitions; the ugly ones witches, and the handsome ones devils; Lord ha' mercy, and a -|- may be set on the man's door that goes a courting.

CHAPTER VIII.

Of the Cloven-foot walking about the world without the Devil, viz. of witches making bargains for the Devil, and particularly of selling the soul to the Devil.

I HAVE dwelt long upon the Devil in masque as he goes about the world *incog.* and especially without his cloven-foot, and have touched upon some of his disguises in the management of his interest in the world; I must say some of his disguises only, for who can give a full account of all his tricks and arts in so narrow a compass as I am prescribed to?

340   **THE HISTORY**

Of the Cloven-foot walking about the world without the Devil, &c.

But as I said, that every devil has not a cloven-foot, so I must add now for the present purpose, that every cloven-foot is not the Devil.

Not but that wherever I should meet the Cloven-hoof, I should expect that the Devil was not far off, and should be apt to raise the posse against him, to apprehend him; yet it may happen otherwise, that is certain; every coin has its counterfeit, every art its pretender, every whore her admirer, every error its patron, and every day has its devil.

I have had some thought of making a full and complete discovery here of that great doubt which has so long puzzled the world, namely, whether there is any such thing, as secret making bargains with the Devil, and the first positive assurance I can give you in the case, is, that if there is not, it is not his fault, it is not for want of his endeavour, it is plain, if you will pardon me for taking so mean a step, as that of quoting Scripture; I say, it is evident he would fain have made a contract with our Saviour, and he bid boldly (give him his due) namely, all the kingdoms of the world for one bend of his knee: Impudent seraph! To think thy Lord should pay thee homage! How many would agree with him here for a less price! They say, Oliver Cromwell struck a bargain with him, and that he gave Oliver the protectorship, but would not let him call himself king; which stuck so close to that furioso, that the mortification spread into his soul, and it is said, he died of a gangrene in the spleen. But take notice, and do Oliver justice; I do not vouch the story, neither does the bishop say one word of it.

Fame used to say, that the old famous duke of Luxemburg made a magic compact of this kind; nay, I

OF THE DEVIL. 341

Of the Cloven-foot walking about the world without the Devil, &c.

have heard many an (old woman) officer of the troops, who never cared to see his face, declare that he carried the Devil at his back. I remember a certain author of a newspaper in London was once taken up, and they say it cost him 50l. for printing in his news, that Luxemburg was hump-backed. Now if I have resolved the difficulty, namely, that he was not hump'd, only carried the Devil at his back ; I think the poor man should have his 50l. again, or I should have it for the discovery.

I confess, I do not well understand this compacting with such a fellow as can neither write nor read ; nor do I know who is the scrivener between them ; or how the indenture can be executed ; but that which is worse than all the rest is, that in the first place, the Devil never keeps articles ; he will contract perhaps, and they say he is mighty forward to make conditions ; but who shall bind him to the performance, and where is the penalty if he fails? If we agree with him, he will be apt enough to claim his bargain and demand payment ; nay, perhaps before it is due; but who shall make him stand to his.

Besides, he is a knave in his dealing, for he really promises what he cannot perform ; witness his impudent proposal to our Lord, mentioned above, All these kingdoms will I give thee ! Lying spirit ! Why they were none of thine to give, no not one of them ; for the earth is the Lord's and the kingdoms thereof, nor were they in his power any more than in his right : So (I have heard that) some poor dismal creatures have sold themselves to the Devil for a sum of money, for so much cash ; and yet even in that case, when the day of payment came, I never heard that he brought the money or paid the purchase, so that he is a scoundrel in his treaties, for you shall trust for your bargain, but not be able to get your money, and yet for your part, he comes for you to an hour : Of which by itself.

In a word, let me caution you all, when you trade with the Devil, either get the price or quit the bargain ; the Devil is a cunning shaver, he will wriggle himself out of the performance on his side if possible, and yet expect you should be punctual on your side. They tell you of a poor fellow in Herefordshire, that offered to sell his soul to him for a cow, and though the Devil promised, and as they say, signed the writings, yet the poor countryman could never get the cow of him, but still as he brought a cow to him, some body or other came and and challenged it, proving that it was lost or stolen from them ; so that the man got nothing but the name of a Cow-stealer, and was at last carried to Hereford gaol, and condemned to be hanged for stealing two cows, one after the other : The wicked fellow was then in the greatest distress imaginable, he summoned his devil to help him out, but he failed him, as the Devil always will ; he really had not stolen the cows, but they were found in his possession, and he could give no account how he came by them ; at last he was driven to confess the truth, told the horrid bargain he had made, and how the Devil often promised him a cow, but never gave him one, except that several times in the morning early he found a cow put into his yard, but it always proved to belong to some of his neighbours : Whether the man was hanged or no, the story does not relate ; but this part is to my purpose, that they that make bargains with the Devil, ought to make him give security for the performance of covenants, and who the Devil would get to be bound for him I cannot tell, they must look to that who make the bargain : Besides, if he had not had a mind to cheat or baffle the

OF THE DEVIL. 343

Of the Cloven-foot walking about the world without the Devil, &c.

poor man, what need he have taken a cow so near home?
If he had such and such powers as we talk of, and as
fancy and fable furnish for him, could not he have carried a cow in the air upon a broom-stick, as well as an old
woman? Could he not have stole a cow for him in Lin-
colnshire, and set it down in Herefordshire, and so have
performed his bargain, saved his credit, and kept the
poor man out of trouble? So that if the story is true, as
I really believe it is, either it is not the Devil that makes
those bargains, or the Devil has not such power as we
bestow on him, except on special occasions he gets a
permit, and is bid go, as in the case of Job, the Gadarene
hogs, and the like.

We have another example of a man's selling himself
to the Devil, that is very remarkable, and that is in the
Bible too, and even in that, I do not find, what the Devil
did for him, in payment of the purchase price. The
person selling was Ahab, of whom the text says expressly,
*There was none like him, who did sell himself to work
wickedness in the sight of the Lord*, 1 Kings xxi. 20,
and 25. I think it might have been rendered, if not translated, in spite of the Lord, or in defiance of God ; for
certainly that is the meaning of it ; and now allowing me
to preach a little upon this text, my sermon shall be very
short. Ahab sold himself: Who did he sell himself to?
I answer that question by a question : Who would buy
him? who, as we say, would give any thing for him?
and the answer to that is plain also, you may judge of
the purchaser by the work he was to do ; he that buys
a slave in the market, buys him to work for him, and to
do such business as he has for him to do : Ahab was
bought to work wickedness, and who would buy him for
that but the Devil?

I think there is no room to doubt but Ahab sold himself to the Devil ; the text is plain that he sold himself, and the work he was sold to do points out the master that bought him : what price he agreed with the Devil for, that indeed the text is silent in, so we may let it alone, nor is it much to our purpose, unless it be to enquire whether the Devil stood to his bargain or not, and whether he paid the money according to agreement, or cheated him as he did the farmer at Hereford.

Thus buying and selling between the Devil and us, is, I must confess, an odd kind of stock-jobbing, and indeed the Devil may be said to sell the bear-skin, whatever he buys ; but the strangest part is when he comes to demand the transfer ; for as I hinted before, whether he performs or no, he expects his bargain to a tittle : There is indeed some difficulty in resolving how and in what manner payment is made ; the stories we meet with in our chimney-corner histories, and which are so many ways made use of to make the Devil frightful to us and our heirs for ever, are generally so foolish and ridiculous, as, if true or not true, they have nothing material in them, are of no signification, or else so impossible in their nature, that they make no impression upon any body above twelve years old and under seventy ; or else are so tragical that antiquity has fabled them down to our taste, that we might be able to hear them and repeat them with less horror than is due to them.

This variety has taken off our relish of the thing in general, and made the trade of soul-selling, like our late more eminent bubbles, be taken to be a cheat and to have little in it.

However, to speak a little more gravely to it, I cannot say but that since, by the two eminent instances of it

above in Ahab, and in Christ himself, the fact is evidently
ascertained ; and that the Devil has attempted to make
such a bargain on one, and actually did make it with the
other. The possibility of it is not to be disputed ; but
then I must explain the manner of it a little, and bring it
down nearer to our understanding, that it may be more
intelligible than it is ; for as for this selling the soul, and
making a bargain to give the Devil possession by livery
and seisin on the day appointed, that I cannot come into
by any means : no nor into the other part, namely, of
the Devil coming to claim his bargain, and to demand
the soul according to agreement, and upon default of a
fair delivery, taking it away by violence, case and all,
of which we have many historical relations pretty current among us ; some of which, for ought I know, we
might have hoped had been true, if we had not been sure
they were false, and others we had reason to fear were
false, because it was impossible they should be true.

The bargains of this kind, according to the best accounts we have of them, used to consist of two main
articles, according to the ordinary stipulations in all
covenants ; namely,

1. Something to be performed on the Devil's part,
buying.

2. Something to be performed on the man's part,
selling.

1. The Devil's part : This was generally some poor
trifle, for the Devil generally bought good pennyworths,
and oftentimes, like a complete sharper, agreed to give
what he was not able to procure ; that is to say, would
bargain for a price he could not pay, as in the case of
the Hereford man and his cow ; for example, 1. Long
life : This, though the deluded chapman has often had

15   2 X

folly enough to contract for, the Devil never had power
to make good ; and we have a famous story, how true I
know not, of a wretch that sold himself to the Devil on
condition he, Satan, should assure him (1.) That he
should never want victuals ; (2.) That he should never
be cold ; (3.) That he should always come to him when
he called him ; and (4.) that he should let him live one
and twenty years, and then Satan was at liberty to have
him ; that is, I suppose, to take him wherever he could
find him.

It seems, the fellow's desire to be assured of twenty-one
years' life, was chiefly, that during that time, he might
be as wicked as he would, and should yet be sure not to
be hanged, nay, to be free from all punishment ; upon
this foot it is said he commenced rogue, and committed
a great many robberies and other villanous things ; now
it seems the Devil was pretty true to his bargain in
several of those things ; particularly, that two or three
times when the fellow was taken up for petty crimes,
and called for his old friend, he came and frighted the
constables so, that they let the offender get away from
them : But at length having done some capital crime, a
set of constables, or such like officers, seized upon him,
who were not to be frighted with the Devil, in what
shape soever he appeared ; so that they carried him off,
and he was committed to Newgate, or some other prison
as effectual.

Nor could Satan with all his skill unlock his fetters,
much less the prison doors ; but he was tried, convicted,
and executed. The fellow in his extremity, they say,
expostulated with the Devil for his bargain, the term of
twenty-one years it seems not being expired. But the
Devil, it is said, shuffled with him, told him a good

OF THE DEVIL. 347

Of the Cloven-foot, walking about the world without the Devil, &c.

while he would get him out, bid him have patience and stay a little, and thus led him on, till he came as it were within sight of the gallows, that is to say, within a day or two of his execution ; when the Devil cavilled upon his bargain, told him, he agreed to let him live twenty-one years, and he had not hindered him, but that he did not covenant to cause him to live that time ; that there was a great deal of difference between doing and suffering ; that he was to suffer him to live, and that he did ; but he could not make him live when he had brought himself to the gallows.

Whether this story were true or not, for you must not expect we historians should answer for the discourse between the Devil and his chaps, because we were not privy to the bargain : I say, whether it was true or not, the inference is to our purpose several ways.

1. It confirms what I have said of the knavery of the Devil in his dealings, and that when he has stock-jobbed with us on the best conditions he can get, he very seldom performs his bargain.

2. It confirms what I have likewise said, that the Devil's power is limited ; with this addition, that he not only cannot destroy the life of man, but that he cannot preserve it ; in short, he can neither prevent or bring on our destruction.

I may be allowed, I hope, for the sake of the present discourse, to suppose that the Devil would have been so just to this wicked, though foolish creature, as to have saved him from the gallows if he could ; but it seems, he at last acknowledged that it was not in his power ; nay, he could not keep him from being taken and carried

348   THE HISTORY

Of the Cloven-foot, walking about the world without the Devil, &c.

to prison, after he was gotten into the hands of a bold
fellow or two, that were not to be scared with his bluster,
as some foolish creatures had been before.

And how simple, how weak, how unlike any thing of
an angelic nature, was it to attempt to save the poor
wretch, only by little noises and sham appearances, putting out the candles, rushing and jostling in the dark,
and the like! If the Devil was that mighty seraph,
which we have heard of, if he is a god of this world, a
prince of the air, a spirit able to destroy cities and made
havock in the world ; if he can raise tempests and
storms, throw fire about the world, and do wonderful
things, as an unchained devil no doubt could do ; what
need all this frippery ? and what need he try so many
ridiculous ways, by the emptiness, nay, the silly non-
sensical manner, of which, he shews, that he is able to
do no better, and that his power is extinguished ? In a
word, he would certainly act otherwise, if he could.
Sed caret pedibus, he wants power.

How weak a thing is it then, for any man to expect
performance from the Devil ? If he has not power to do
mischief, which is his element, his very nature, and on
many accounts, is the very sum of his desires ; How
should he have power to do good ? how power to deliver
from danger or from death ? which deliverance would be
in itself a good, and we know it is not in his nature to do
good to or for any man ?

In a word, the Devil is strangely impudent, to think
that any man should depend upon him for the performance of an agreement of any kind whatever, when he
knows himself, that he is not able, if he was honest
enough, to be as good as his word.

Come we next to his expecting our performance to

OF THE DEVIL. 349

Of the Cloven-foot, walking about the world without the Devil, &c.

him ; though he is not so just to us, yet, it seems, he
never fails to come and demand payment of us at the
very day appointed : He was but a weak trader in
things of this nature, who having sold his soul to the
Devil, so our old women's tales call the thing, and when
the Devil came to demand his bargain, put it off as a
thing of no force, for that it was done so long ago, he
thought he (the Devil) had forgot it.   It was a better
answer which, they tell us, a Lutheran divine gave the
Devil in the name of a poor wretch, who had sold himself to the Devil, and who was in a terrible fright about
his coming for his bargain, as he might well be indeed,
if the Devil has such a power, as really to come and
take it by force.   The story (if you can hear a serious
one) is this :

The man was in great horror of mind, and the family
feared he would destroy himself, at length they sent for
a Lutheran minister to talk with him, and who after
some labour with him, got out the truth (viz) that he
had sold himself to the Devil, and that the time was
almost expired, when he expected the Devil would come
and fetch him away, and he was sure he would not fail
coming to the time to a minute ; the minister first endeavoured to convince him of the horrid crime, and to bring
him to a true penitence for that part ; and having as he
thought made him a sincere penitent, he then began to
encourage him, and particularly desired of him, that
when the time was come, that the Devil would fetch him
away, he, the minister, should be in the house with him ;
accordingly, to make the story short, the time came, the
Devil came, and the minister was present when the
Devil came ; what shape he was in, the story does not
say ; the man said he saw him, and cried out ; the

minister could not see him, but the man affirming he was in the room, the minister said aloud, ' In the name of the living God, Satan, what comest thou here for ? The Devil answered, I come for my own ; The minister answered, He is not thy own, for Jesus Christ has redeemed him, and in his name I charge thee to avoid and touch him not ;' at which, says the story, the Devil gave a furious stamp (with his Cloven-foot I suppose) went away, and was never known to molest him afterward.

Another story, though it be in itself a long one, I shall abridge (for your reading with the less uneasiness) as follows.

A young gentleman of ———berg, in the elector of Brandenburgh's (now the king of Prussia's) dominions, being deeply in love with a beautiful lady, but something above his fortune, and whom he could by no means bring to love him again, applied himself to an old thing called a witch, for her assistance, and promised her great things, if she could bring the lady to love him, or any how compass her, so as he might have his will of her ; nay, at last he told her he would give up his soul to her, if she would answer his desire.

The old hag, it seems, having had some of his money, had very honestly tried what she could do, but all to no purpose, the lady would not comply ; but when he offered such a great price, she told him, she would consider farther against such a time, and appointed him the next evening.

At the time appointed he comes, and the witch made a long speech to him upon the nicety of the affair ; I suppose to prepare him not to be surprized at what was to come ; for she supposed he was not so very desperately bent as he appeared to be ; she told him it was a thing of very great difficulty ; but as he had made such a great offer, of selling his soul for it, she had an acquaintance in the house, who was better skilled (than she was) in such particular things, and would treat with him farther, and she doubted not but that both together they might answer his end. The fellow it seems was still of the same mind, and told her, he cared not what he pawned or sold, if he could but obtain the lady ; well, says the old hag, sit still a while, and with that she withdraws.

By and by she comes in again with a question in her mouth ; pray, says she, do you seek this lady for a wife, or for a mistress, would you marry her, or would you only lie with her ? The young man told her no, no, he did not expect she would lie with him, therefore he would be satisfied to marry her, but asks her the question ; why truly, says the old hag, my reason is very weighty ; for if you would have her for your wife, I doubt, we can do you no service ; but if you have a mind to lie with her, the person, I speak of, will undertake it.

The man was surprized at that, only he objected that this was a transient or short felicity, and that he should perhaps have her no more ; the old hag bid him not fear, but that if she once yielded to be his whore, he might have her as often as he pleased ; upon this he consents, for he was stark mad for the lady : He having consented, she told him then, he should follow her, but told him, whoever he saw, he must speak to no body but her, till she gave him leave, and that he should not be surprized, whatever happened, for no hurt should befal him ; all which he agreed to, and the old woman going out he followed her.

Being upon this led into another room, where there was but very little light, yet enough to let him see that there was no body in it but himself and the woman, he was desired to sit down in a chair next to a table, and the old woman clapping the door to after her, he asked her why she shut the door, and where was the person she told him of ? At which she answered, there he is, pointing to a chair at a little distance : The young gentleman turning his head, saw a grave kind of a man sitting in an elbow-chair, though he said, he could have sworn there was no body in the chair when the old woman shut the door ; however, having promised not to speak to any body but the old woman, he said not a word.

By and by the woman making abundance of strange gestures and motions, and mumbling over several things which he could not understand, on a sudden a large wicker-chair, which stood by the chimney, removes to the other end of the table, which he sat by, but there was no body in the chair ; in about two minutes after that the chair removed, there appeared a person sitting in that too, who, the room being, as is said, almost dark, could not be so distinguished by the eye, as to see his countenance.

After some while, the first man, and the chair he sat in, moved, as if they had been one body, to the table also ; and the old woman and the two men seemed to talk together, but the young man could not understand any thing they said ; after some time the old witch turned to the young gentleman, told him his request was granted, but not for marriage, but the lady should love and receive him.

The witch then gave him a stick dipt in tar at both

OF THE DEVIL. 353

Of the Cloven-foot walking about the world without the Devil, &c.

ends, and bid him hold it to a candle, which he did, and instead of burning like a stick it burnt out like a torch ; then she bid him break it off in the middle, and light the other end ; he did that too, and all the room seemed to be in a light flame ; then she said, deliver one piece here, pointing to one only of the persons, so he gave the first fire-stick to the first man or apparition ; now says she, deliver the other here, so he gave the other piece to the other apparition, at which they both rose up and spoke to him words, which he said he understood not, and could not repeat, and immediately vanished with the fire-sticks and all, leaving the room full of smoke : I do not remember that the story says any thing of brimstone, or the smell of it, but it says the door continued fast locked, and no body was left in the room but the young gentleman and the witch.

Now the ceremony being over, he asked the witch if the business was done ? She said, yes. Well, but says he, have I sold my soul to the Devil ? Yes, says she, you have, and you gave him possession, when you delivered the two fire-sticks to him. To him ! says he, why, was that the Devil ? Yes, says the old hag. At which the young man was in a terrible fright for a while, but it went off again.

And what is next, says he, when shall I see the lady for whose sake I have done all this ? You shall know that presently, said she, and opening the door, in the next room she presents him with a most beautiful lady, but had charged him not to speak a word to her : She was exactly dressed like, and he presently knew her to be the lady he desired ; upon which he flew to her and clasped her in his arms, but that moment he had her fast, as he thought, in his arms, she vanished out of his sight.

15   2 Y

354 THE HISTORY

Of the Cloven-foot walking about the world without the Devil, &c.

Finding himself thus disappointed, he upbraids the old woman with betraying him, and flew out with ill language at her, in a great rage ; the Devil often deluded him thus, after this, with shews and appearances, but still no performance ; after a while he gets an opportunity to speak with the lady herself in reality, but she was as positive in her denial as ever, and even took away all hopes of his ever obtaining her, which put him into despair ; for now he thought he had given himself up to the Devil for nothing, and this brought him to himself ; so that he made a penitent confession of his crime to some friends, who took great care of him, and encouraged him, and at last furnished him with such an answer as put the Devil into a fright, when he came for the bargain.

For Satan, it seems, as the story says, had the impudence to demand his agreement, notwithstanding he had failed in the performance on his part ; what the answer was I do not pretend to have seen, but it seems it was something like what is mentioned above, viz. that he was in better hands, and that he durst not touch him.

I have heard of another person that had actually signed a contract with the Devil ; and upon a fast kept by some protestant or christian divines, while they were praying for the poor man, the Devil was obliged to come and throw the contract in at the window.

But I vouch none of these stories, there may be much in them, and much use made of them, even whether exactly such in fact, as they are related, or no ; the best use I can make of them, is this, if any wicked desperate wretches have made bargain and sale with Satan, their only way is to repent, if they know how, and that before he comes to claim them ; than batter him with his own guns ; play religion against devilism, and perhaps they may drive the Devil out of their reach ; at least he will not come at them, which is as well.

On the other hand, how many stories have we handed about of the Devil's really coming with a terrible appearance at the time appointed, and powerfully or by violence carrying away those, that have given themselves thus up to him ; nay, and sometimes a piece of the house along with them, as in the famous instance of Sudbury, Anno 1662. It seems he comes with rage and fury upon such occasions, pretending he only comes to take his own, or as if he had leave given him to come and take his goods, as we say, where he could find them, and would strike a terror into all that should oppose him.

The greatest part of the terror we are usually in upon this occasion, is from a supposition, that when this hell-fire contract is once made, God allows the Devil to come and take the wicked creature, how and in what manner he thinks fit, as being given up to him by his own act and deed ; but in my opinion there is no divinity at all in that ; for as in our law we punish a *felo de se*, or self-murderer, because, as the law suggests, he had no right to dismiss his own life ; that he being a subject of the common-wealth, the government claims the ward or custody of him, and so it was not murder only, but robbery, and is a felony against the state, robbing the king of his liege-man, as it is justly called ; so neither has any man a right to dispose of his soul, which belongs to his maker in property and in right of creation : The man then having no right to sell, Satan has no right to buy, or at best he has made a purchase without a title, and consequently has no just claim to the possession.

It is therefore a mistake to say, that when any of us

have been so mad to make such a pretended contract
with the Devil, that God gives him leave to take it as
his due; it is no such thing; the Devil has bought,
what you had no right to sell, and therefore, as an unlawful oath is to be repented of, and then broken; so
your business is to repent of the crime, and then tell the
Devil, you have better considered of it, and that you
won't stand to your bargain, for you had no power to
sell; and if he pretends to violence after that, I am mistaken; I believe the Devil knows better.

It is true, our old mothers and nurses have told us
other things, but they only told us what their mothers
and nurses told them; and so the tale has been handed
down from one generation of old women to another; but
we have no vouchers for the fact other than oral tradition,
the credit of which, I confess, goes but a very little way
with me; nor do I believe it one jot the more for all the
frightful addenda which they generally join to the tale,
for it never wants a great variety of that kind.

Thus they tell us the Devil carried away Dr. Faustus,
and took a piece of the wall of his garden along with
him : Thus at Salisbury the Devil, as it is said, and
publicly printed, carried away two fellows that had
given themselves up to him, and carried away the roof
of the house with them, and the like; all which I believe
my share of; besides, if these stories were really true,
they are all against the Devil's true interest, Satan must
be a fool, which is indeed what I never took him to be
in the main; this would be the way not to encrease the
number of desperadoes, who should thus put themselves
into his hand, but to make himself a terror to them; and
this is one of the most powerful objections I have against
the thing, for the Devil, I say, is no fool, that must be

acknowledged ; he knows his own game, and generally plays it sure.

I might, before I quit this point, seriously reflect here upon our *beau monde*, viz. the gay part of mankind, especially those of the times we live in, who walk about in a composure and tranquillity inexpressible, and yet, as we all know, must certainly have all sold themselves to the Devil, for the power of acting the foolishest things with the greater applause ; it is true, to be a fool is the most pleasant life in the world, if the fool has but the particular felicity, which few fools want, viz. to think themselves wise : The learned say, it is the dignity and perfection of fools, that they never fail trusting themselves ; they believe themselves sufficient and able for every thing ; and hence their want or waste of brains is no grievance to them, but they hug themselves in the satiety of their own wit ; but to bring other people to have the same notion of them, which they have of themselves, and to have their apish and ridiculous conduct make the same impression on the minds of others, as it does on their own ; this requires a general infatuation, and must either be a judgment from heaven, or a mist of hell ; nothing but the Devil can make all the men of brains applaud a fool, and can any man believe, that the Devil will do this for nothing ? no, no, he will be well paid for it, and I know no other way they have to compound with him, but this of bargain and sale.

It is the same thing with rakes and bullies, as it is with fools and beaus ; and this brings me to the subject of buying and selling itself, and to examine what is understood by it in the world ; what people mean by such and such a man selling himself to the Devil : I know the common acceptation of it is, that they make

358   THE HISTORY

Of the Cloven-foot walking about the world without the Devil, &c.

some capitulation for some indulgence in wickedness, on conditions of safety and impunity, which the Devil promises them; though as I said above, he is a bite in that too, for he cannot perform the conditions; however, I say, he promises boldly, and they believe him, and for this privilege in wickedness, they consent, that he shall come and fetch them for his own, at such or such a time.

This is the state of the case in the general acceptation of it; I do not say it is really so, nay it is even an inconsistency in itself; for one would think, they need not capitulate with the Devil to be so, and so, superlatively wicked, and give him such a price for it, seeing, unless we have a wrong notion of him, he is naturally inclined, as well as avowedly willing to have all men be as superlatively wicked as possibly they can, must necessarily be always ready to issue out his licenses gratis, as far as his authority will go in the case; and therefore I do not see why the wretches that deal with him should article with him for a price; but suppose, for argument sake, that it is so, then the next thing is, some capital crime follows the contract, and then the wretch is forsaken, for then the Devil cannot protect him, as he promised; so he is trust up, and like Coleman at the gallows, he exclaims that there is no truth in devils.

It may be true, however, that under the powerful guard and protection of the Devil, men do sometimes go a great way in crime, and that perhaps farther in these our days of boasted morals than was known among our fathers; the only difference that I meet with between the sons of Belial in former days, and those of our ages, seems to be in the Devil's management, not in theirs; the sum of which amounts to this, that Satan seems to act with more cunning, and they with less; for in the former ages of Satan's dominion, he had much business upon his hands, all his art and engines, and engineers also, were kept fully employed to wheedle, allure, betray and circumvent people, and draw them into crimes, and they found him, as we may say, a full employment; I doubt not, he was called the Tempter on that very account; but the case seems quite altered now, the tables are turned; then the Devil tempted men to sin. But now, in short, they tempt the Devil; men push into crimes before he pushes them; they out-shoot him in his own bow, out-run him on his own ground, and, as we say of some hot spurs who ride post, they whip the post-boy; in a word, the Devil seems to have no business now but to sit still and look on.

This, I must confess, seems to intimate some secret compact between the Devil and them; but then it looks, not as if they had contracted with the Devil for leave to sin, but that the Devil had contracted with them, that they should sin so and so, up to such a degree, and that without giving him the trouble of daily solicitation, private management, and artful screwing up their passions, their affections and their most retired faculties, as he was before obliged to do.

This also appears more agreeable to the nature of the thing; and as it is a most exquisite part of Satan's cunning, so it is an undoubted testimony of his success; if it was not so, he could never bring his kingdom to such a height of absolute power as he has done; this also solves several difficulties in the affair of the world's present way of sinning, which otherwise it would be very hard to understand; as particularly how some eminent men of quality among us, whose upper rooms are not extraordinarily well furnished in other cases, yet

360   **THE HISTORY**

Of the Cloven-foot, walking about the world without the Devil, &c.

are so very witty in their wickedness, that they gather
admirers by hundreds and thousands ; who, however
heavy, lumpish, slow and backward, even by nature,
and in force of constitution in better things, yet in their
race devil-wards they are of a sudden grown nimble,
light of foot, and out-run all their neighbours ; fellows
that are as empty of sense as beggars are of honesty, and
as far from brains as a whore is of modesty ; on a sudden
you shall find them dip into polemicks, study Michael
Servetus, Socinus, and the most learned of their disciples ;
they shall reason against all religion, as strongly as a
philosopher ; blaspheme with such a keenness of wit,
and satirise God and eternity, with such a brightness of
fancy, as if the soul of a Rochester or a Hobbs was
transmigrated into them ; in a little length of time more
they banter heaven, burlesque the Trinity, and jest with
every sacred thing, and all so sharp, so ready, and so
terribly witty, as if they were born buffoons, and were
singled out by nature to be champions for the Devil.

Whence can all this come ? how is the change
wrought ? who but the Devil can inject wit in spite of
natural dullness, create brains, fill empty heads, and
supply the vacuities in the understanding ? and will
Satan do all this for nothing ? No, no, he is too wise
for that ; I can never doubt a secret compact, if there is
such a thing in nature ; when I see a head where there
was no head, sense in *posse* where there is no sense in
esse, wit without brains, and sight without eyes, it is all
devil-work : Could G——— write satyrs, that could
neither read Latin or spell English, like old sir William
Read, who wrote a book of optics, which when it was
printed, he did not know which was the right side
uppermost, and which the wrong ?   Could this eminent

OF THE DEVIL. 361

Of the Cloven-foot, walking about the world without the Devil, &c.

uninformed beau turn atheist, and make wise speeches against that being, which made him a fool, if the Devil had not sold him some wit in exchange for that trifle of his, called soul ? Had he not bartered his inside with that son of the morning, to have his tongue tipped with blasphemy, he that knew nothing of a God, but only to swear by him, could never have set up for a wit, to burlesque his providence and ridicule his government of the world.

But the Devil, as he is god of this world, has one particular advantage, and that is, that when he has work to do he very seldom wants instruments ; with this circumstance also, that the degeneracy of human nature supplies him ; as the late king of France said of himself, when they told him what a calamity was like to befal his kingdom by the famine : Well, says the king, then I shall not want soldiers ; and it was so, want of bread supplied his army with recruits ; so want of grace supplies the Devil with reprobates for his work.

Another reason why, I think, the Devil has made more bargains of that kind we speak of, in this age, is, because he seems to have laid by his Cloven-foot : all his old emissaries, the tools of his trade, the engineers which he employed in his mines, such as witches, warlocks, magicians, conjurers, astrologers, and all the hellish train or rabble of human devils, who did his drudgery in former days, seem to be out of work : l shall give you a fuller enumeration of them in the next chapter.

These, I say, seem to be laid aside ; not that his work is abated, or that his business with mankind, for their delusion and destruction, is not the same, or perhaps more than ever ; but the Devil seems to have changed hands ; the temper and genius of mankind is altered, and they

16   2 Z

362   **THE HISTORY**

Of the Cloven-foot, walking about the world without the Devil, &c.

are not to be taken by fright and horror, as they were then : The figures of those creatures was always dismal and horrible, and that is it which I mean by the Cloven-foot ; but now wit, beauty and gay things, are the sum of his craft, he manages by the soft and the smooth, the fair and the artful, the kind and the cunning ; not by the frightful and terrible, the ugly and the odious.

When the Devil for weighty dispatches,
    Wanted messengers cunning and bold,
He passed by the beautiful faces,
    And pick'd out the ugly and old.

Of these he made warlocks and witches,
    To run of his errands by night,
Till the over wrought hag-ridden wretches,
    Were as fit as the Devil to fright.

But whoever has been his adviser,
    As his kingdom encreases in growth ;
He now takes his measures much wiser,
    And trafficks with beauty and youth.

Disguis'd in the wanton and witty ;
    He haunts both the church and the court,
And sometimes he visits the city,
    Where all the best christians resort.

Thus dress'd up in full masquerade,
    He the bolder can range up and down,
For he better can drive on his trade,
    In any one's name than his own.

CHAPTER IX.

Of the tools the Devil works with, viz. witches, wizards or warlocks, conjurers, magicians, diviners, astrologers, interpreters of dreams, tellers of fortunes, and above all the rest, his particular modern privy-counsellors, called wits and fools.

THOUGH, as I have advanced in the foregoing chapter, the Devil has very much changed hands in his modern management of the world, and that instead of the rabble and long train of implements reckoned up above, he now walks about in beaus, beauties, wits and fools; yet I must not omit to tell you that he has not dismissed his former regiments, but like officers in time of peace, he keeps them all in half pay, or like extra-ordinary men at the custom-house, they are kept at a call, to be ready to fill up vacancies, or to employ when he is more than ordinarily full of business; and therefore it may not be amiss to give some brief account of them, from Satan's own memoirs, their performance being no inconsiderable part of his history.

Nor will it be an unprofitable digression, to go back a little to the primitive institution of all these orders, for they are very antient, and I assure you, it requires great knowledge of antiquity, to give a particular of their original; I shall be very brief in it.

In order then to this enquiry, you must know that it was not for want of servants, that Satan took this sort of people into his pay; he had, as I have observed in its place, millions of diligent devils at his call, whatever

business, and however difficult, he had for them to do ;
but as I have said above, that our modern people are
forwarder than even the Devil himself can desire them
to be ; and that they come before they are called, run
before they are sent, and crowd themselves into his service ; so it seems it was in those early days, when the
world was one universal monarchy under his dominion,
as I have at large described in its place.

In those days the wickedness of the world keeping a
just pace with their ignorance, this inferior sort of low-
prized instruments did the Devil's work mighty well ;
they drudged on in his black-art so laboriously, and
with such good success, that he found it was better to
employ them as tools to delude and draw in mankind,
than to send his invisible implements about, and oblige
them to take such shapes and dresses as were necessary
upon every trifling occasion ; which perhaps was more
cost than worship, more pains than pay.

Having then a set of these volunteers in his service,
the true Devil had nothing to do but to keep an exact
correspondence with them, and communicate some needful powers to them, to make them be and do something
extraordinary, and give them a reputation in their business ; and these, in a word, did a great part of, nay
almost all the Devil's business in the world.

To this purpose gave he them power, if we may believe old Glanville, Baxter, Hicks, and other learned
consultors of oracles, to walk invisibly, to fly in the air,
ride upon broom-sticks, and other wooden gear, to interpret dreams, answer questions, betray secrets, to talk
(gibberish) the universal-language, to raise storms, sell
winds, bring up spirits, disturb the dead, and torment
the living, with a thousand other needful tricks to amuse

the world, keep themselves in veneration, and carry on the Devil's empire in the world.

The first nations among whom these infernal practices were found, were the Chaldeans; and that I may do justice in earnest, as well as in jest, it must be allowed that the Chaldeans, or those of them so called, were not conjurers or magicians, only philosophers and studiers of nature, wise, sober, and studious men at first, and we have an extraordinary account of them; and if we may believe some of our best writers of fame, Abraham was himself famous among them for such magic, as sir Walter Raleigh expresses it, *qui contemplatione creaturarum cognovit creatorem.*

Now granting this, it is all to my purpose, namely, that the Devil drew these wise men in, to search after more knowledge than nature could instruct them in; and the knowledge of the true God being at that time sunk very low, he debauched them all with dreams, apparitions, conjurers, &c. till he ruined the just notions they had, and made devils of them all, like himself.

The learned Senensis, speaking of this Chaldean kind of learning, gives us an account of five sorts of them; you will pardon me for being so grave as to go this length back.

1. Chascendin or Chaldeans, properly so called, being astronomers.
2. Asaphim or Magicians, such was Zoroastres and Balaam the son of Beor.
3. Chartumim, or interpreters of dreams and hard speeches, inchanters, &c.
4. Mecasphim, or witches, called at first Prophets, afterwards Malefici, or Venefici, poisoners.

5. Gazarim or Auruspices, and Diviners, such as divined by the entrails of beasts, the liver in particular; mentioned in Ezekiel; or as others, called Augurs.

Now, as to all these, I suppose, I may do them no wrong, if I say, however justifiable they were in the beginning, the Devil got them all into his service, at last, and that brings me to my text again, from which the rest was a digression.

1. The Chascendin or Chaldean astronomers turned astrologers, fortune-tellers, calculators of nativities, and vile deluders of the people, as if the wisdom of the holy God was in them, as Nebuchadnezzar said of Daniel on that very account.

2. The Asaphim or Magi, or Magicians; Sixtus Senensis says, they were such as wrought by covenant with devils, but turned to it from their wisdom, which was to study the practical part of natural philosophy, working admirable effects by the mutual application of natural causes.

3. The Chartumim, from being reasoners or disputers upon difficult points in philosophy, became enchanters and conjurers. So,

4. The Mecasphim or Prophets, they turned to be sorcerers, raisers of spirits, such as wounded by an evil eye, and by bitter curses, and were afterwards famed for having familiar converse with the Devil, and were called Witches.

5. The Gazarim, from the bare observing of the good and bad omens, by the entrails of beasts, flying of birds, &c. were turned to sacrists or priests of the heathen idols and sacrificers.

Thus, I say, first or last the Devil engrossed all the Wise-men of the East, for so they are called ; made them all his own, and by them he worked wonders, that is, he filled the world with lying wonders, as if wrought by these men, when indeed it was all his own, from beginning to the end, and set on foot merely to propagate delusion, impose upon blinded and ignorant men ; the god of this world blinded their minds, and they were led away by the subtilty of the Devil, to say no worse of it, till they became devils themselves, as to mankind ; for they carried on the Devil's work upon all occasions, and the race of them still continue in other nations, and some of them among ourselves, as we shall see presently.

The Arabians followed the Chaldeans in this study, while it kept within its due bounds, and after them the Egyptians ; and among the latter we find that Jannes and Jambres were famous for their leading Pharaoh by their pretended magic performances, to reject the real miracles of Moses ; and history tells us of strange pranks the wise-men, the magicians, and the soothsayers played to delude the people in the most early ages of the world.

But, as I say, now, the Devil has improved himself, so he did then ; for the Grecian and Roman heathen rites coming on, they outdid all the magicians and soothsayers, by establishing the Devil's lying oracles, which, as a master-piece of hell, did the Devil more honour, and brought more homage to him, than ever he had before, or could arrive to since.

Again, as by the setting up the oracles, all the magicians and soothsayers grew out of credit ; so at the ceasing of those oracles, the Devil was fain to go back to the old game again, and take up with the agency of witches, divinations, inchantment and conjurings, as I hinted before, answerable to the four sorts mentioned in the story of Nebuchadnezzar, (viz.) magicians, astrologers, the Chaldeans and the soothsayers : How these began to be out of request, I have mentioned already, but as the Devil has not quite given them over, only laid them aside a little for the present, we may venture to ask what they were, and what use he made of them when he did employ them.

The truth is, I think, as it was a very mean employment for any thing that wears a human countenance to take up, so I must acknowledge, I think, it was a mean low-prized business for Satan to take up with ; below the very Devil ; below his dignity as an angelic, though condemned creature ; below him even as a devil ; to go to talk to a parcel of ugly, deformed, spiteful, malicious old women ; to give them power to do mischief, who never had a will, after they entered into the state of old woman-hood, to do any thing else : Why the Devil always chose the ugliest old women he could find ; whether wizardism made them ugly, that were not so before, and whether the ugliness, as it was a beauty in witchcraft, did not encrease according to the meritorious performance in the black-trade ? These are all questions of moment to be decided (if human learning can arrive to so much perfection) in ages to come.

Some say the evil eye and the wicked look were parts of the enchantment, and that the witches, when they were in the height of their business, had a powerful influence with both ; that by looking upon any person they could bewitch them, and make the Devil, as the Scots express it, ride through them booted and spurred ; and that hence came that very significant saying, To look like a witch.

The strange work which the Devil has made in the world, by this sort of his agents called witches, is such, and so extravagantly wild, that except our hope that most of those tales happen not to be true, I know not how any one could be easy to live near a widow after she was five and fifty.

All the other sorts of emissaries which Satan employs, come short of these ghosts ; and apparitions sometimes come and shew themselves, on particular accounts, and some of those particulars respect doing justice, repairing wrongs, preventing mischief; sometimes in matters very considerable, and on things so necessary to public benefit, that we are tempted to believe they proceed from some vigilant spirit who wishes us well ; but on the other hand, these witches are never concerned in any thing but mischief; nay, if what they do portends good to one, it issues in hurt to many ; the whole tenor of their life, their design in general, is to do mischief, and they are only employed in mischief, and nothing else : How far they are furnished with ability suitable to the horrid will they are vested with, remains to be described.

These witches, it is said, are furnished with power suitable to the occasion that is before them, and particularly that which deserves to be considered as prediction, and foretelling events, which I insist the author of witchcraft is not accomplished with himself, nor can he communicate it to any other : How then witches come to be able to foretel things to come, which, it is said, the Devil himself cannot know, and which, as I have shewn, it is evident he does not know himself, is yet to be determined ; that witches do foretel, is certain, from the witch of Endor, who foretold things to Saul, which he knew

16   3 A

not before, namely, that he should be slain in battle the next day, which accordingly came to pass.

There are, however, and notwithstanding this particular case, many instances wherein the Devil has not been able to foretel approaching events, and that in things of the utmost consequence, and he has given certain foolish or false answers in such cases; the Devil's priests, which were summoned in by the prophet Elijah, to decide the dispute between God and Baal, had the Devil been able to have informed them of it, would certainly have received notice from him, of what was intended against them by Elijah; that is to say, that they would be all cut in pieces; for Satan was not such a fool as not to know that Baal was a non-entity, a nothing; at best a dead man, perished and rotting in his grave; for Baal was Bell or Belus, an antient king of the Assyrian monarchy, and he could no more answer by fire to consume the sacrifice, than he could raise himself from the dead.

But the priests of Baal were left of their master to their just fate, namely, to be a sacrifice to the fury of a deluded people; hence I infer his inability, for it would have been very unkind and ungrateful in him not to have answered them, if he had been able. There is another argument raised here most justly against the Devil, with relation to his being under restraint, and that of greater eminence than we imagine, and it is drawn from this very passage, thus; it is not to be doubted but that Satan, who has much of the element put into his hands, as prince of the air, had a power, or was able potentially speaking, to have answered Baal's priests by fire; fire being in virtue of his airy princi-

pality a part of his dominion; but he was certainly
withheld by the superior hand, which gave him that
dominion, I mean withheld for the occasion only: So in
another case, it was plain that Balaam, who was one of
those sorts of Chaldeans mentioned above, who dealt in
divinations and inchantments, was withheld from cursing
Israel.

Some are of opinion that Balaam was not a witch or a
dealer with the Devil, because it is said of him, or rather
he says it of himself, that he saw the visions of God,
Numb. xxiv. 16. *He hath said, who heard the words
of God, and knew the knowledge of the most High,
which saw the visions of the Almighty, falling into a
trance, but having his eyes open :* Hence they allege
he was one of those magi, which St. Augustin speaks of,
de divinatione, who by the study of nature, and by the
contemplation of created beings, came to the knowledge
of the creature; and that Balaam's fault was, that being
tempted by the rewards and honours that the king promised him, he intended to have cursed Israel; but when
his eyes were opened, and that he saw they were God's
own people, he durst not do it; they will have it therefore, that except, as above, Balaam was a good man, or
at least that he had the knowledge of the true God, and
the fear of that God upon him, and that he honestly
declares this, Numb. xxii. 18. *If Balak would give
me his house full of silver and gold, I cannot go beyond
the word of the Lord my God :* Where though he is
called a false prophet by some, he evidently owns God,
and assumes a property in him, as other prophets did;
my God, and I cannot go beyond his orders : But that
which gives me a better opinion of Balaam than all this
is, his plain prophesy of Christ, chap. xxiv. 17. where

he calls him the star of Jacob, and declares, *I shall see him, but not now, I shall behold him, but not nigh; there shall come a star out of Jacob, and a sceptre shall rise out of Israel, and shall smite the corners of Moab, and destroy all the children of Seth,* all which express not a knowledge only, but a faith in Christ; but I have done preaching, this is all by the by, I return to my business, which is the history.

There is another piece of dark practice here, which lies between Satan and his particular agents, and which they must give us an answer to, when they can, which I think will not be in haste; and that is about the obsequious Devil submitting to be called up into visibility, whenever an old woman has her hand crossed with a white sixpence, as they call it : One would think that instead of these vile things called witches, being sold to the Devil, the Devil was really sold for a slave to them ; for how far soever Satan's residence is off from this state of life, they have power, it seems, to fetch him from home, and oblige him to come at their call.

I can give little account of this, only that indeed so it is ; nor is the thing so strange in itself, as the methods to do it are mean, foolish, and ridiculous ; as making a circle and dancing in it, pronouncing such and such words, saying the Lord's prayer backward, and the like ; now is this agreeable to the dignity of the prince of the air or atmosphere, that he should be commanded forth with no more pomp or ceremony than that of muttering a few words, such as the old witches and he agree about ? Or is there something else in it, which none of us or themselves understand ?

Perhaps, indeed, he is always with those people called witches and conjurers, or at least some of his *camp volant*

HISTORY OF THE DEVIL

DUCKING A WITCH.

Page 229

Drawn by G. M. Brighty.

Engraved by T. Wallis.

EXETER
Published by DAVIES & ELDRIDGE 1815

are always present, and so upon the least call of the wizard, it is but putting off the misty cloak and showing themselves.

Then we have a piece of mock pageantry in bringing those things called witches or conjurers to justice, that is, first to know if a woman be a witch, throw her into a pond, and if she be a witch, she will swim, and it is not in her own power to prevent it; if she does all she can to sink herself it will not do, she will swim like a cork. Then that a rope will not hang a witch, but you must get a withe, a green osier; that if you nail a horse shoe on the sill of the door, she cannot come into the house, or go out, if she be in; these and a thousand more, too simple to be believed, are yet so vouched, so taken for granted, and so universally received for truth, that there is no resisting them without being thought atheistical.

What methods to take to know who are witches, I really know not; but on the other side, I think there are variety of methods to be used to know who are not; W——— G——— esq. is a man of fame, his parts are great, because his estate is so; he has threescore and eight lines of Virgil by rote, and they take up many of the intervals of his merry discourses, he has just as many witty stories to please society; when they are well told, once over, he begins again, and so he lives in a round of wit and learning; he is a man of great simplicity and sincerity; you must be careful not to mistake my meaning as to the word simplicity, some take it to mean honesty, and so do I, only that it has a negative attending it, in his particular case; in a word, W——— G——— is an honest man, and no conjurer; a good character, I think, and without impeachment to his understanding, he may be a man of worth for all that. Take the other

sex, there is the lady H——— is another discovery ;
bless us! what charms in that face! How bright those
eyes! How flowing white her breast! How sweet her
voice! add to all, how heavenly, divinely good her
temper! How inimitable her behaviour! How spotless
her virtue! How perfect her innocence! and to sum up
her character, we may add, the lady H——— is no
witch ; sure none of her beau critics will be so unkind
now as to censure me in those honest descriptions, as if I
meant that my good friend W——— G——— esq. or
my adored angel, the bright, the charming lady H———
were fools ; but what will not those savages, called
critics, do, whose barbarous nature inclines them to
trample on the brightest characters, and to cavil on the
clearest expressions ?

It might be expected of me, however, in justice to my
friends, and to the bright characters of abundance of
gentlemen of this age, who, by the depth of their politics,
and the height of their elevations, might be suspected,
and might give us room to charge them with subterranean
intelligence ; I say, it might be expected that I should
clear up their fame, and assure the world concerning
them, even by name, that they are no conjurers, that
they do not deal with the Devil, at least not by the way
of witchcraft and divination, such as sir T——k, E———
B———, esq. my Lord Homily, Coll. Swagger, Geoffry
Well-with, esq. Capt. Harry Go Deeper, Mr. Wellcome
Woollen, citizen and merchant Tailor of London, Henry
Cadaver, esq. the D—— of Caerfilly, the Marquis of
Sillyhoo, sir Edward Thro' and Thro', bart. and a
world of fine gentlemen more, whose great heads and
weighty understandings have given the world such occasion to challenge them with being at least descended

from the magi, and perhaps engaged with old Satan in his politics and experiments; but I, that have such good intelligence among Satan's ministers of state, as is necessary to the present undertaking, am thereby well able to clear up their characters; and I doubt not, but they will value themselves upon it, and acknowledge their obligation to me, for letting the world know the Devil does not pretend to have had any business with them, or to have enrolled them in the list of his operators; in a word, that none of them are conjurers: Upon which testimony of mine, I expect they be no longer charged with, or so much as suspected of having an unlawful quantity of wit, or having any sorts of it about them, that are contraband or prohibited, but that for the future they pass unmolested, and be taken for nothing but what they are (viz.) very honest worthy gentlemen.

CHAPTER X.

Of the various methods the Devil takes to converse with mankind.

HAVING spoken something of persons, and particularly of such as the Devil thinks fit to employ in his affairs in the world, it comes next of course to say something of the manner how he communicates his mind to them, and by them to the rest of his acquaintance in the world.

I take the Devil to be under great difficulties in his affairs on his part, especially occasioned by the bounds which are set him, or which policy oblige him to set to himself, in his access to the conversing with mankind ; it is evident he is not permitted to fall upon them with force and arms, that is to-say, to muster up' his infernal troops, and attack them with fire and sword ; if he was not loose to act in this manner as he was able, by his own seraphic power to have destroyed the whole race, and even the earth they dwelt upon, so he would certainly, and long ago have effectually done it ; his particular interests and inclinations are well enough known.

But in the next place, as he is thus restrained from violence, so prudentials restrain him in all his other act-ings with mankind ; and being confined to stratagem, and soft still methods, such as persuasion, allurement, feeding the appetite, prompting, and then gratifying corrupt desires, and the like ; he finds it for his purpose not to appear in person, except very rarely, and then in disguise ; but to act all the rest in the dark, under the vizor of art and craft, making use of persons and methods concealed, or at least not fully understood or discovered.

As to the persons whom he employs, I have taken some pains you see to discover some of them ; but the methods he uses with them; either to inform and instruct, and give orders to them, or to converse with other people by them, these are very particular, and deserve some place in our memoirs, particularly as they may serve to remove some of our mistakes, and to take off some of the frightful ideas we are apt to entertain in prejudice of this great manager ; as if he was no more to be matched in his politics, than he would be to be matched in his power, if it was let loose ; which is so much a mistake, that on the contrary, we read of several people that have abused and cheated the Devil, a thing, which I cannot say, is very honest nor just, notwithstanding the old Latin proverb, *Fallere fallentem non est fraus* (which men construe, or rather render, by way of banter upon Satan) it is no sin to cheat the Devil ; which for all that, upon the whole I deny, and allege, that let the Devil act how he will by us, we ought to deal fairly by him.

But to come to the business, without circumlocutions ; I am to enquire how Satan issues out his orders, gives his instructions, and fully delivers his mind to his emissaries, of whom I have mentioned some in the title to chap. IX. In order to this, you must form an idea of the Devil sitting in great state, in open campaign, with all his legions about him, in the height of the atmosphere ; or if you will, at a certain distance from the atmosphere, and above it, that the plan of his encampment might not be hurried round its own axis, with the earth's diurnal motion, which might be some disturbance to him.

By this fixed situation, the earth performing its rotation, he has every part and parcel of it brought to a direct opposition to him, and consequently to his view once in twenty-four hours : The last time I was there, if I remember right, he had this quarter of the world, which we call Christendom, just under his eye ; and as the motion is not so swift, but that his piercing optics can take a strict view of it *en passant ;* for the circumference of it being but twenty-one thousand miles, and its circular motion being full twenty-four hours performing, he has something more than an hour to view every thousand miles, which, to his supernatural penetration, is not worth naming.

As he takes thus a daily view of all the circle, and an hourly view of the parts, he is fully master of all transactions, at least such as are done above board by all mankind ; and then he dispatches his emissaries or aid du camps to every part with his orders and instructions : Now these emissaries, you are to understand, are not the witches and diviners, who I spoke of above, for I call them also emissaries ; but they are all devils, or (as you know they are called) devils' angels ; and these may, perhaps, come and converse personally with the sub-emissaries I mentioned, to be ready for their support and assistance on all occasions of business : These are those devils which the witches are said to raise ; for we can hardly suppose the master-devil comes himself, at the summons of every ugly old woman.

These run about into every nook and corner, wherever Satan's business calls them, and are never wanting to him ; but are the most diligent devils imaginable ; like the Turkish chaiux, they no sooner receive their errand, but they execute it with the utmost alacrity ; and as to their speed, it may be truly written as a motto, upon the head of every individual devil,

Non indiget calcaribus.

These are those, who they tell us our witches, sorcerers, wizards, and such sorts of folks converse freely with, and are therefore called their familiars ; and as they tell us, come to them in human shapes, talk to them with articulate plain voices, as if men, and that yet the said witches, &c. know them to be devils.

History has not yet enlightened us in this part of useful knowledge, or at least not sufficiently for a description of the persons or habits of those sorts of appearances ; as what shapes they take up, what language they speak, and what particular works they perform, so we must

Of the methods the Devil takes to converse with mankind.

refer it to farther enquiry ; but if we may credit history, we are told many famous stories of these appearances ; for example, the famous mother Lakland, who was burnt for a witch at Ipswich, anno 1646, confessed at the time of her execution, or a little before it, that she had frequent conversation with the Devil himself ; that she being very poor, and withal of a devilish, passionate, cruel and revengeful disposition before, used to wish she had it in her power to do such and such mischievous things to some that she hated ; and that the Devil himself, who, it seems, knew her temper, came to her one night as she lay in her bed, and was between sleeping and waking, and speaking in a deep hollow voice, told her ; if she would serve him in some things he would employ her to do, she should have her will of all her enemies, and should want for nothing : That she was much afraid at first, but that he soliciting her very often, bad her not be afraid of him, and still urged her to yield, and as she says, struck his claw into her hand, and though it did not hurt her, made it bleed, and with the blood wrote the covenant, that is to say, the bargain between them. Being asked what was in them, and whether he required her to curse or deny God or Christ ? she said no.

N. B. I do not find she told them whether the Devil wrote it with a pen, or whether on paper or parchment, nor whether she signed it or no, but it seems he carried it away with him. I suppose, if Satan's register were examined, it might be found among the archieves of hell, the rolls of his *acta publica ;* and when his historiographer royal publishes them, we may look for it among them.

Then he furnished her with three devils, to wait upon
her (I suppose) for she confessed they were to be employed in her service; they attended in the shapes of
two little dogs and a mole. The first she bewitched
was her own husband, by which he lay a while in great
misery, and died; then she sent to one captain Beal,
and burnt a new ship of his just built, which had never
been at sea; these and many other horrid things she
did, and confessed; and having been twenty years a
witch, at last the Devil left her, and she was burnt as
she deserved.

That some extraordinary occasions may bring these
agents of the Devil, nay, sometimes the Devil himself,
to assume human shapes, and appear to other people,
we cannot doubt; he did thus in the case of our Saviour
as a tempter, and some think he did so to Manasses as a
familiar, who the Scripture charges with sorcery, and
having a familiar or devil : Fame tells us, that St. Dunstan frequently conversed with him, and finally, took
him by the nose; and so of others.

But in these modern ages of the world, he finds it
much more to his purpose to work under ground, as I
have observed, and to keep upon the reserve; so that
we have no authentic accounts of his personal appearance, but what are very antient or very remote from our
faith, as well as our enquiry.

It seems to be a question that would bear some debating, whether all apparitions are not devils or from
the Devil; but there being so many of those apparitions
which we call spirits, which really assume shapes and
make appearances in the world, upon such accounts as
we know Satan himself scorns to be employed in, that I
must dismiss the question in favour of the Devil; assuring

them, that as he never willingly did any good in his life,
so he would be far from giving himself the trouble of
setting one foot into the world, on such an errand ; and
for that reason we may be assured those certain apparitions, which we are told came to detect a murderer in
Gloucestershire, and others who appeared to prevent the
ruining an orphan for want of finding a deed, that was
not lost, was certainly some other power equally concerned, and not the Devil.

On the other hand, neither will it follow that Satan
never appears in human shape : For though every
apparition may not be the Devil, yet it does not follow
that the Devil never makes an apparition : All I shall
say to it is, as I have mentioned before, that generally
speaking, the Devil finds it more for his purpose, to
have his interest in the world propagated another way ;
namely, in private, and his personal appearances are
reserved for things only of extraordinary consequence,
and, as I may say, of evident necessity, where his
honour is concerned, and where his interest could be
carried on no other way ; not forgetting to take notice
that this is very seldom.

It remains to enquire, what then those things are
which we make so much stir about, and which are called apparitions, or spirits assuming human shapes, and
shewing themselves to people on particular occasions ?
whether they are evil spirits or good ? and though,
indeed, this is out of my way at this time, and does not
relate at all to the Devil's history, yet I thought it not
amiss to mention it ; (1.) Because, as I have said, I do
not wholly exclude Satan from all concern in such
things ; and (2.) Because I shall dismiss the question
with so very short an answer, namely, that we may

determine which are and which are not the Devil's, by
the errand they come upon; every one to his own
business; if it comes of a good errand, you may certainly acquit the Devil of it, conclude him innocent, and
that he has no hand in it; if it comes of a wicked and
devilish errand, you may even take him up upon suspicion, it is ten to one but you find him at the bottom of it.

Next to apparitions, we find mankind disturbed by
abundance of little odd reserved ways which the Devil
is shrewdly suspected of having a hand in, such as
dreams, noises, voices, &c. smells of brimstone, candles
burning blue, and the like.

As to dreams, I have nothing to say in Satan's prejudice at all there; I make no question but he deals very
much in that kind of intelligence, and why should he
not ? We know heaven itself formerly conversed very
often with the greatest of men, by the same method, and
the Devil is known to mimic the methods, as well as the
actions of his maker; whether heaven has not quite left
off that way of working, we are not certain; but we
pretty well know the Devil has not left it, and I believe
some instances may be given where his worship has been
really seen and talked to in sleep, as much as if the person had been awake with his eyes open.

These are to be distinguished too, pretty much by the
goodness or badness of the subject; how often have men
committed murder, robbery, and adultery in a dream,
and at the same time, except an extraordinary agitation
of the soul, and expressed by extraordinary noises in the
sleep, by violent sweating and other such ways, the
head has never been removed from the pillow, or the
body so much as turned in the bed !

Whether in such cases, the soul, with all the passions

and affections, being agitated, and giving their full
assent to the facts, of what kind soever, the man is not as
guilty as if the sins so dream'd of his committing, had
been actually committed ? though it be no doubt to me
but that it is so, yet as it is foreign to the present affair,
and not at all relating to the Devil's history, I leave it
to the reverend doctors of the church, as properly be-
longing to them to decide.

I knew a person who the Devil so haunted with naked
women, fine beautiful ladies in bed with him, and ladies
of his acquaintance too, offering their favours to him,
and all in his sleep ; so that he seldom slept without
some such entertainment ; the particulars are to gross
for my story, but he gave me several long accounts of
his night's amours ; and being a man of a virtuous life
and good morals, it was the greatest surprize to him
imaginable ; for you cannot doubt but that the cunning
Devil made every thing he acted to the life with him,
and in a manner the most wicked ; he owned with grief
to me, that the very first attack the Devil made upon
him, was with a very beautiful lady of his acquaintance,
who he had been really something freer than ordinary
with in their common conversation : This lady he
brought to him in a posture for wickedness, and wrought
up his inclination so high in his sleep, that he, as he
thought, actually went about to debauch her, she not at
all resisting ; but that he waked in the very moment, to
his particular satisfaction.

He was greatly concerned at this part, namely, that
he really gave the consent of his will to the fact, and
wanted to know if he was not as guilty of adultery, as if
he had lain with her ; indeed he decided the question
against himself so forcibly, that I, who was of the same

opinion before, had nothing to say against it ; however, I confirmed him in it, by asking him these questions.

1. Whether he did not think the Devil had the chief hand in such a dream ? He answered, it could certainly be no body else, it must be the Devil.
2. I then asked him what reason the Devil could have for it, if his consent to the fact in sleep had not been criminal ? That is true indeed, says he, I am answered.   But then he asked another question, which, I confess, is not easy to answer, namely, How he should prevent being served so again ?

Nor could all my divinity or his own keep the Devil from attacking him again ; on the other hand, as I have said, he worried him to that degree, that he injured his health, bringing naked women to him, sometimes one, sometimes another, sometimes in one posture of lewdness, sometimes in another, sometimes into his very arms, sometimes with such additions as I am not merry enough, and sometimes such as I am not wicked enough to put into your heads ; the man, indeed, could not help it, and so the Devil was more faulty than he ; but as I hinted to him, he might bring his mind to such stated habit of virtue, as to prevent its assenting to any wicked motion, even in sleep, and that would be the way to put an end to the attempt ; and this advice he relished very well, and practised, I believe, with success.

By this same method, the same Devil injects powerful incentives to other crimes, provokes avarice, by laying a great quantity of gold in your view, and no body present, giving you an opportunity to steal it, or some of it, at the same time, perhaps, knowing your circumstances to be such as that you are at that time in a great want of the money.

I knew another, who being a tradesman, and in great distress for money in his business, dreamed that he was walking alone in a great wood, and that he met a little child with a bag of gold in its hand, and a fine necklace of diamonds on its neck; upon the sight, his wants presently dictated to him to rob the child; the little innocent creature, (just so he dreamed) not being able to resist, or to tell who it was; accordingly he consented to take the money from the child, and then to take the diamond necklace from it too, and did so.

But the Devil, (a full testimony, as I told him, that it was the Devil) not contented with that, hinted to him, that perhaps the child might some time or other know him, and single him out, by crying or pointing, or some such thing, especially if he was suspected and shewed to it, and therefore it would be better for him to kill the child, prompting him to kill it for his own safety, and that he need do no more but twist the neck of it a little, or crush it with his knee; he told me he stood debating with himself, whether he should do so or not; but that in that instant his heart struck him with the word murder, and he entertained a horror of it, refused to do it, and immediately waked.

He told me, that when he waked, he found himself in so violent a sweat as he never had known the like; that his pulse beat with that heat and rage, that it was like a palpitation of the heart to him, and that the agitation of his spirits was such, that he was not fully composed in some hours: Though the satisfaction and joy that attended him when he found it was but a dream, assisted much to return his spirits to their due temperament.

17   3 C

Of the methods the Devil takes to converse with mankind.

It is neither my business or inclination to turn divine here, nor is the age I write to sufficiently grave to relish a sermon, if I was disposed to preach, though they must allow the subject would very well bear it ; but I shall only ask them, if they think this is not the Devil, what they think it is ? If they believe it is the Devil, they will act accordingly I hope, or let it alone, as Satan and they can agree about it.

I should not oblige the Devil over much, whatever I might do to those that read it, if I should enter here upon a debate of interests, (viz) to enquire whether the Devil has not a vast advantage upon mankind this way, and whether it is not much his interest to preserve it ; and if I prove the affirmative, I leave it to you to enquire whose interest it is to disappoint and supplant him.

In short, I take dreams to be the second best of the advantages the Devil has over mankind ; the first, I suppose, you all know (viz.) the treachery of the garrison within ; by dreams he may be said to get into the inside of us without opposition ; here he opens and locks without a key, and like an enemy laying siege to a fortified city, reason and nature, the governor of the city, keep him out by day, and keep the garrison true to their duty : But in the dark he gets in and parleys with the garrison (the affections and passions) debauches their loyalty, stirring them up to disloyalty and rebellion ; so they betray their trust, revolt, mutiny, and go over to the besieger.

Thus he manages his interest, I say, and insinuates himself into the inside of us, without our consent, nay, without our knowledge ; for whatever speculation may do, it is evident demonstration does not assist us to discover which way he gets access to the soul, while the organ tied up, and dozed with sleep, has locked it up from action; that it is so is clear, but how he does it, is a secret which I do not find the antients or moderns have yet made a discovery of.

That devil of a creature, mother Lakland, whose story I mentioned above, acknowledged that the first time the Devil attempted to draw her to be a witch was in a dream, and even when she consented, she said, she was between sleeping and waking; that is, she did not know whether she was awake or asleep, and the cunning Devil it seems was satisfied with her assent given so, when she was asleep, or neither asleep or awake, so taking the advantage of her incapacity to act rationally.

The stories of her bewitching several people, and the manner in which they died, are so formidable and extravagant, that I care not to put any one's faith to the stretch about them, though published by authority, and testified by abundance of witnesses; but this is recorded in particular, and to my purpose, whether from her own mouth or not, I do not say, namely, the description of a witch, and the difference between witches, and those other Satan's acquaintance who act in his name.

1. They have consulted and covenanted with a spirit or devil.
2. They have a deputy devil, sometimes several, to serve and assist them.
3. These they employ as they please, call them by name, and command their appearance in whatever shape they think fit.
4. They send them abroad to or into the persons who they design to bewitch, always torment, and often murder them, as mother Lakland did several.

As to the difference between the several devils that appear, it relates to the office of the persons who employ them ; as conjurers, who seem to command the particular devil that waits upon them with more authority, and raise them and lay them at pleasure, drawing circles, casting figures, and the like ; but the witch, in a more familiar manner, whispers with the Devil, keeps the Devil in a bag or a sack, sometimes in her pocket, and the like, and like Mr. Faux shews tricks with him.

But all these kinds deal much in dreams, talk with the Devil in their sleep, and make other people talk with him in their sleep too ; and it is on this occasion I mention it here ; in short, the Devil may well take this opportunity with mankind, for not half the world that came into his measures would comply, if they were awake ; but of that hereafter.

And yet his thus insinuating himself by dream, does not seem sufficient, in my opinion, to answer the Devil's end, and to carry on his business ; and therefore we must be forced to allow him a kind of actual possession, in particular cases, and that in the souls of some people, by different methods from others ; Luther is of the opinion that the Devil gets a familiarity with some souls just at, or rather before their being embodied ; as to the manner and method how he gets in, that is another question, and may be spoken of by itself ; besides, why may not he, that at Satan's request to enter into the herd of swine, said go, give the same commission to possess a sort of creatures so many degrees below the dignity of the Gaderenian swine, and open the door too ? but as for that, when our Lord said go, the Devil never enquired which way he should get in.

When then I see nations, or indeed herds of nations

set on fire of hell, and as I may say, enflamed by the Devil; when I see towns, parties, factions and rabbles of people visibly possessed; it is enough to me that the great master of the devils has said to him, go; there is no need to enquire which way he finds open, or at what postern gate he gets in; as to his appearing, it is plain he often gets in without appearing, and therefore the question about his appearing still remains a doubt, and is not very easy to be resolved.

In the Scripture we have some light into it, and that is all the help I find from antiquity, and it goes a great way to solve the phænomena of Satan's appearing; what I mean by the Scripture giving some light to it, is this; it is said in several places, and of several persons, God came to them in a dream, Gen. xx. 3. *God came to Abimelech in a dream by night,* Gen. xxxi. 24. *And came to Laban the Syrian in a dream,* Matt. ii. 13. *The angel of the Lord appeared to Joseph in a dream;* short comments are sufficient to plain texts, applying this to my friend when he wanted to be satisfied about the how, relating to his dream (viz.) how he should come to dream such wicked things? I told him, in short, the case was plain, the Devil came to him in a dream by night: How and in what manner he formed the wicked representations, and spread debauched appearances before his fancy, by real whispers and voice, according to Milton, or by what other methods, the learned are not arrived to any certainty about it.

This leads me necessarily to enquire whether the Devil or some of his agents are not always in our company, whether they make any visible appearances or no? For my part I make no question of it, how else could he come at the knowledge of what we do; for as

I can allow him no prescience at all, as for many reasons I have observed already, he must be able to see and know us, and what we are about when we know nothing of him, or else he could know nothing of us and our affairs, which yet we find otherwise ; and this gives him infinite advantage to influence our actions, to judge of our inclinations, and to bring our passions to clash with our reason, as they often do, and get the better of it too.

All this he obtains by his being able to walk about invisible, and see when he is not seen, of which I have spoken already ; hence that most wise and solid suggestion, that when the candles burn blue the Devil is in the room, which great secret in nature, that you may more fully be convinced of its imaginary reality, I must tell you the following story which I saw in a letter directed to a particular friend, take it word for word as in the letter ; because I do not make myself accountable for the facts, but take them *ad referendum*.

Sir,

We had one day, very early in the morning, and for the most part of the day a great deal of rain with a high wind, and the clouds very thick and dark all day.

In the evening the cloudy thick weather continued, though not the rain, when being at a friend's house in —— Lane, London, and several ladies and some gentlemen in the room, besides two or three servants (for we had been eating) the following interlude happened for our entertainment : When the cloth was taken away, two large candles were brought upon the table and placed there, with some bottles and glasses for the gentlemen, who, it seems, were intended to drink and be very merry ; two large wax-candles were also set on another table, the ladies being going to cards, also there were two large candles in sconces over or near the chimney, and one more in a looking glass sconce, on a pier by the window.

With all this apparatus, the company separating sat down, the gentlemen at their table, and the ladies at theirs; to play as above; when after some time the gentleman of the house said hastily to a servant, What a p— ails the candles? and turning to the servant raps out an oath or two, and bid him snuff the candles, for they burnt as if the Devil was in the room.

The fellow going to snuff one of the candles, snuffs it out, at which his master being in a passion the fellow lights it again immediately at the other candle, and then being in a little hurry, going to snuff the other candle snuffed that out too.

The first candle that was re-lighted (as is usual in such cases) burned dim and dull for a good while, and the other being out, the room was much darker than before, and a wench that stood by the ladies table, bawls out to her mistress, Law, madam! the candles burn blue; an old lady that sat by says, Ay Betty! so they do; upon this one of the ladies starts up, Mercy upon us, says she, what is the matter! in this unlucky moment another servant, without orders, went to the great pier sconce, and because, as he thought, he would be sure to snuff the candle well, he offers to take it down, but very unhappily, I say, the hook came out, down falls the sconce, candle and all, and the looking-glass broke all to pieces, with a horrible noise; however, the candle falling out of the sconce did not go out, but lay on the floor burning dully, and as it is usual on such cases, all on one side. Betty cries out again, Law, madam, that candle burns blue, too; the very moment she said this, the foot-

Of the methods the Devil takes to converse with mankind.

man that had thrown down the sconce, says to his fellow
servant that came to his assistance, I think the Devil is in
the candles to night, and away he ran out of the room,
for fear of his master.

The old lady, who, upon the maid Betty's notion of
the candles burning blue, had her head just full of that
old chimney-corner story, the candles burn blue when
the spirits are in the room, heard the footman say the
word devil, but heard nothing else of what he said ;
upon this she rises up in a terrible fright, and cries out
that the footman said the Devil was in the room ; as she
was, indeed, frightened out of her wits, she frighted the
ladies most terribly, and they all starting up together,
down goes the card table, and put the wax-candles out.

Mrs. Betty, that had frighted them all, runs to the
sconce next the chimney, but that having a long snuff,
she cried out it burnt blue too, and she durst not touch it ;
in short, though there were three candles left still burning
in the room, yet the ladies were all so frighted, that they
and the maids too ran out of the parlour screaming like
mad folk. The master in a rage kicked his first man
out of the room, and the second man was run out to
avoid, as I said before, the like, so that no servant was
to be had, but all was in confusion.

The two other gentlemen, who were sitting at the first
table, kept their seats composed and easy enough, only
concerned to see all the house in such a fright ; it was
true, they said, the candles burnt dim and very oddly,
but they could not perceive they burnt blue, except one
of those over the chimney, and that on the table, which
was re-lighted after the fellow had snufft it out.

However, the maid, the old lady and the footman
that pulled down the sconce, all insist that the candles

burnt blue, and all pretended that the Devil was certainly in the room, and was the occasion of it ; and they now come to me with the story, to desire my opinion of it.

This put me upon enquiry into the notion of candles burning blue when spirits are in a room, which upon all the search into things, that I am able to make, amounts to no more than this ; that upon any extraordinary emission of sulphurous or of nitrous particles, either in a close room, or in any not very open place, if the quantity be great, a candle or lamp, or any such little blaze of fire will seem to be, or to burn blue ; and if then they can prove that any such effluvia attends or is emitted from a spirit, then when Satan is at hand it may be so.

But then it is begging the question grossly, because no man can assure us that the Devil has any sulphurous particles about him.

It is true, the candles burn thus in mines and vaults, and damp places ; and it is as true that they will do so upon occasion of very damp, stormy, and moist air, when an extraordinary quantity of vapours are supposed to be dispersed abroad, as was the case when this happened ; and if there was any thing of that in it on that monday night, the candles might, perhaps, burn blue upon that occasion ; but that the Devil was abroad upon any extraordinary business that night, that I cannot grant, unless I have some better testimony than the old lady that heard the footman's out-cry but by halves, or than Mrs. Betty, who first fancied the candles burnt blue ; so I must suspend my judgment till I hear farther.

This story however may solve a great many of those things which pass for apparitions in the world, and which are laid to the Devil's charge, though he really may know nothing of the matter ; and this would bring

17   3 D

me to defend Satan in many things, wherein he may
truly be said to suffer wrongfully ; and if I thought it
would oblige him, I might say something to his advantage this way ; however, I will venture a word or two for
an injured Devil, take it as you will.

First, it is certain, that as this invisibility of the Devil
is very much to our prejudice, so the doctrine of his
visibility is a great prejudice to him, as we make use of it.

By his invisibility he is certainly vested with infinite
advantages against us ; while he can be present with us,
and we know nothing of the matter ; he informs himself
of all our measures, and arms himself in the best and
most suitable manner to injure and assault us, as he can
counteract all our secret concerted designs, disappoint
all our schemes, and, except when heaven apparently
concerns himself to over-rule him, can defeat all our
enterprizes, break all our measures, and do us mischief
in almost every part of our life, and all this, because we
are not privy to all his motions, as he is to ours.

But now for his visibility and his real appearance in
the world, and particularly among his disciples and
emissaries, such as witches and wizards, demonaists, and
the like : Here, I think Satan has a great deal of loss,
suffers manifest injury, and has great injustice done
him ; and, that therefore I ought to clear this matter up
a little, if it be possible, to do justice to Satan, and set
matters right in the world about him, according to that
useful old maxim of setting the saddle upon the right
horse, or giving the Devil his due.

First, as I have said, we are not to believe every idle
head, who pretends even to converse face to face with
the Devil, and who tells us, they have thus seen him,
and been acquainted with him every day : Many of

these pretenders are manifest cheats ; and, however they would have the honour of a private interest in him, and boast how they have him at their beck, can call him this way, and send him that, as they please, raise him and lay him, when and how, and as often as they find for their purpose ; I say, whatever boasts they make of this kind, they really have nothing of truth in them.

Now the injuries and injustice done to the Devil, in these cases, are manifest ; namely, that they entitle the Devil to all the mischief they are pleased to do in the world ; and if they commit a murder or a robbery, fire a house, or do any act of violence in the world, they presently are said to do it by the agency of the Devil, and the Devil helps them ; so Satan bears the reproach, and they have all the guilt ; this is, (1.) a grand cheat upon the world, and (2.) a notorious slander upon the Devil ; and it would be a public benefit to mankind, to have such would-be-devils as these turned inside out; that we might know when the Devil was really at work among us, and when not ; what mischiefs were of his doing, and which were not ; and that these fellows might not slip their necks out of the halter, by con- tinually laying the blame of their wickedness upon the Devil.

Not that the Devil is not very willing to have his hand in any mischief, or in all the mischief that is done in the world ; but there are some low prized rogueries, that are too little for him, beneath the dignity of his operation, and which it is really a scandal to the Devil to charge upon him. I remember the Devil had such a cheat put upon him in East-Smithfield once, where a person pretended to converse with the Devil face to face, and that in open day too, and to cause him to tell for-

tunes, foretel good and evil, &c. discover stolen goods,
tell where they were who stole them, and how to find
them again, nay, and even to find out the thieves ; but
Satan was really slandered in the case, the fellow had
no more to do with the Devil than other people, and
perhaps not so much neither : This was one of those
they called cunning-men, or at least he endeavoured to
pass for such a one, but it was all a cheat.

Besides, what had the Devil to do to detect thieves,
and restore stolen goods ? Thieving and robbing, trick
and cheat, are part of the craft of his agency, and of the
employments which it is his business to encourage ; they
greatly mistake him, who think he will assist any body
in suppressing and detecting such laudable arts and such
diligent servants.

I won't say, but the Devil, to draw these people we
call cunning-men, into a snare, and to push on his
farther designs, may encourage them privately, and in a
manner that they themselves know nothing of, to make
use of his name, and abuse the world about him, till at
last they may really believe they do a deal with the
Devil, when indeed it is only he deals with them, and
they know nothing of the matter.

In other cases he may encourage them in these little
frauds and cheats, and give them leave, as above, to
make use of his name to bring them afterwards, and by
degrees to have a real acquaintance with him ; so bringing the jest of their trade into earnest, till at length
prompting them to commit some great villainy, he
secures them to be his own, by their very fear of his
leaving them to be exposed to the world ; thus he puts
a Jonathan Wild upon them, and makes them be the
very wretches they only pretended to be before : So old

Parsons of Clithroe, as fame tells, was twenty-five years a cunning-man, and twenty-two years a witch; that is to say, for five and twenty years, he was only pretending to deal with the Devil, when Satan and he had no manner of acquaintance, and he only put his leger-de-main upon the people in the Devil's name, without his leave; but at length the Devil's patience being tired quite out, he told the old counterfeit, that in short, he had been his stalking horse long enough, and that now, if he thought fit to enter himself, and take a commission, well and good; and he should have a lease to carry on his trade for so many years more, to his heart's content; but if not, he would expose his knavery to the world, for that he should take away his people's trade no longer; but that he (Satan) would set up another in his room, that should make a mere fool of him, and carry away all his customers.

Upon this, the old man considered of it, took the Devil's counsel, and listed in his pay; so he, that had played his pranks twenty-five years as a conjurer, when he was no conjurer, was then forced really to deal with the Devil, for fear the people should know he did not: Till now he had *ambo dexter*, cheated the Devil on one hand, and the people on the other; but the Devil gained his point at last, and so he was a real wizard ever after.

But this is not the only way the Devil is injured neither, for we have often found people pretend upon him in other cases, and of nearer concern to him a great deal, and in articles more weighty, as in particular, in the great business of possession; it is true this point is not thoroughly understood among men, neither has the Devil thought fit to give us those illuminations about it, as I believe he might do; particularly that great and

important article, is not, for ought I can see, rightly explained ; namely, whether there are not two several
kinds of possession, (viz.) some wherein the Devil possesses us, and some in which we really possess the Devil ;
the nicety of which I doubt this age, with all its penetration, is not qualified to explain, and a dissertation upon
it being too long for this work, especially so near its
conclusion, I am obliged to omit, as I am also all the
practical discourses upon the usefulness and advantages
of real possession, whether considered one way or other
to mankind, all which I must leave to hereafter.

But to come back to the point in hand, and to consider the injustice done to the Devil, in the various turns
and tricks which men put upon him very often in this
one article (viz.) pretending to possession and to have
the Devil in them, when really it is not so ; certainly
the Devil must take it very ill, to have all their demented,
lunatic tricks charged upon him ; some of which, nay
most of which are so gross, so simple, so empty, and so
little to the purpose, that the Devil must be ashamed to
see such things pass in his nam , or that the world
should think he was concerned in them.

It is true, that possession being one of the principal
pieces of the Devil's artifice in his managing mankind,
and in which, with the most exquisite skill, he plays the
devil among us, he has the more reason to be affronted
when he finds himself invaded in this part, and angry
that any body should pretend to possess, or be possessed
without his leave, and this may be the reason, for ought
we know, why so many blunders have been made, when
people have pretended to it without him, and he has
thought fit not to own them in it, of which we have many
examples in history as, in Simon Magus, the devil of

London, the Fair Maid of Kent, and several others, whose history is not worth while to enlarge upon.

In short, possessions, as I have said, are nice things, as it is not so easy to mimic the Devil in that part, as it may be in some other; designing men have attempted it often, but their manner has been easily distinguished, even without the Devil's assistance.

Thus the people of Salem in New-England pretended to be bewitched, and that a black man tormented them by the instigation of such and such, whom they resolved to bring to the gallows : This black man they would have to be the Devil, employed by the person whom they accused for a witch : Thus making the Devil a page or footman to the wizard, to go and torment whoever the said wizard commanded, till the Devil himself was so weary of the foolish part, that he left them to go on their own way, and at last they over-acted the murdering part so far, that when they confessed themselves to be witches, and possessed, and that they had correspondence with the Devil, Satan not appearing to vouch for them, no jury would condemn them upon their own evidence, and they could not get themselves hanged, whatever pains they took to bring it to pass.

Thus you see the Devil may be wronged, and falsely accused in many particulars, and often has been so ; there are likewise some other sorts of counterfeit devils in the world, such as gypsies, fortune-tellers, foretellers of of good and bad luck, sellers of winds, raisers of storms, and many more, some practised among us, some in foreign parts, too many almost to reckon up ; nay I almost doubt whether the Devil himself knows all the sorts of them ; for it is evident he has little or nothing to do with them, I mean not in the way of their craft.

These I take to be interlopers, or with the Guinea mer-
chants' leave, separate traders, and who act under the
screen and protection of Satan's power, but without his
licence or authority ; no doubt these carry away a great
deal of his trade, that is to say, the trade which otherwise
the Devil might have carried on by agents of his own ;
I cannot but say, that while these people would fain be
thought devils, though they really are not, it is but just
they should be really made as much devils as they pretended to be, or that Satan should do himself justice
upon them, as he threatened to do upon old Parsons of
Clithroe abovementioned, and let the world know him.

CHAPTER XI.

*Of divination, sorcery, the black-art, pawawing, and
such like pretenders to devilism, and how far the
Devil is or is not concerned in them.*

THOUGH I am writing the history of the Devil, I
have not undertaken to do the like of all the kinds of
people, male or female, who set up for devils in the world :
This would be a task for the Devil indeed, and fit only
for him to undertake, for their number is and has been
prodigious great, and may, with his other legions, be
ranked among the innumerable.

What a world do we inhabit ! where there is not only
with us a great roaring lying Devil daily seeking whom
of us he may devour, and innumerable millions of lesser
devils hovering in the whole atmosphere over us, nay,

for ought we know, other millions always invisibly moving about us, and perhaps in us, or at least in many of us ; but they have, besides all these, a vast many counterfeit hocus pocus devils ; human devils, who are visible among us, of our own species and fraternity, conversing with us upon all occasions ; who like mountebanks set up their stages in every town, chat with us at every tea-table, converse with us in every coffee-house, and impudently tell us to our faces that they are devils, boast of it, and use a thousand tricks and arts to make us believe it too, and that too often with success.

It must be confessed there is a strong propensity in man's nature, especially the more ignorant part of mankind, to resolve every strange thing, or whether really strange or no, if it be but strange to us, into devilism, and to say every thing is the Devil, that they can give no account of.

Thus the famous doctors of the faculty at Paris, when John Faustus brought the first printed books that had then been seen in the world, or at least seen there, into the city, and sold them for manuscripts, they were surprized at the performance, and questioned Faustus about it ; but he affirming they were manuscripts, and that he kept a great many clerks employed to write them, they were satisfied for a while.

But looking farther into the work, they observed the exact agreement of every book, one with another, that every line stood in the same place, every page a like number of lines, every line a like number of words ; if a word was mis-spelt in one, it was mis-spelt also in all, nay, that if there was a blot in one, it was alike in all ; they began again to muse, how this should be ? in a word, the learned divines not being able to comprehend

17   3 E

the thing (and that was always sufficient) concluded it must be the Devil, that it was done by magic and witch-craft, and that in short, poor Faustus (who was indeed nothing but a mere printer) dealt with the Devil.

> N. B. John Faustus was servant, or journeyman, or compositor, or what you please to call it, to Koster of Harlem, the first inventor of printing ; and having printed the Psalter, sold them at Paris as manuscripts ; because as such they yielded a better price.

But the learned doctors not being able to understand how the work was performed, concluded as above, it was all the Devil, and that the man was a witch ; accordingly they took him up for a magician and a conjurer, and one that worked by the black-art, that is to say, by the help of the Devil ; and in a word, they threatened to hang him for a witch, and in order to it, commenced a process against him in their criminal courts, which made such a noise in the world as raised the fame of poor John Faustus to a frightful height, till at last he was obliged, for fear of the gallows, to discover the whole secret to them.

> N. B. This is the true original of the famous Dr. Faustus or Foster, of whom we have believed such strange things, as that it is become a proverb, As great as the Devil and Dr. Foster : Whereas poor Faustus was no doctor, and knew no more of the Devil than another body.

Thus the magistrates of Bern, in Switzerland, finding

a gang of French actors of puppet-show opened their stage in the town, upon hearing the surprizing accounts which the people gave of their wonderful puppets, how they made them speak, answer questions, and discourse, appear and disappear in a moment, pop up here, as if they rose out of the earth, and down there, as if they vanished, and abundance more feats of art, censured them as demons; and if they had not packed up their trinkets, and disappeared almost as dexterously as their puppets, they had certainly condemned the poor puppets to the flames for devils, and censured, if not otherwise punished their masters. See the count de Rochfort's Memoirs, page 179.

Wonderful operations astonish the mind, especially where the head is not overburthened with brains; and custom has made it so natural to give the Devil either the honour or scandal of every thing, that we cannot otherwise account for, that it is not possible to put the people out of the road of it.

The magicians were, in the Chaldean monarchy, called the wisemen; and though they are joined with the sorcerers and astrologers in the same place, Dan. ii. 4. yet they were generally so understood among those people; but in our language we understand them to be people that have an art to reveal secrets, interpret dreams, foretel events, &c. and that use enchantments and sorceries, by all which we understand the same thing; which now, in a more vulgar way, we express by one general coarse expression, dealing with the Devil.

The Scripture speaks of a spirit of divination, Acts xvi. 16. and a wench that was possessed by this spirit brought her master much gain by soothsaying, that is to say, according to the learned, by oracling or answer-

ing questions ; whence you will see in the margin, that
this soothsaying devil is there called Python, that is,
Apollo, who is often called Python, and who at the
oracle of Delphos gave out such answers and *double
entendres*, as this wench possibly did ; and hence all
those spirits which were called spirits of divination, were
in another sense called Pythons.

Now when the apostle St. Paul came to see this creature, this spirit takes upon it to declare that those men,
meaning St. Paul and Timotheus, were the servants of
the most high God, which shewed unto them the way of
salvation ; this was a good turn of the Devil, to preserve
his authority in the possessed girl ; she brought them
gain by soothsaying, that is to say, resolving difficult
questions, answering doubts, interpreting dreams, &c.
Among these doubts, he makes her give testimony to
Paul and Timotheus, to wheedle in with the new christians, and perhaps (though very ignorantly) even with
Paul and Timotheus themselves, so to give a kind of
credit and respect to her for speaking.

But the Devil, who never speaks truth, but with some
sinister end, was discovered here and detected ; his
flattering recognition not accepted, and he himself un-
kenneled as he deserved ; there the Devil was over-shot
in his own bow again.

Here now was a real possession, and the evil spirits
who possessed her, did stoop to sundry little acts of
servitude, that we could give little or no reason for, only
that the girl's master might get money by her ; but
perhaps this was a particular case, and prepared to
honour the authority and power the apostles had over
evil spirits.

But we find these things carried a great way farther

in many cases, that is to say, where the parties are thus really possessed; namely, the Devil makes agents of the possessed parties to do many things for the propagating his interest and kingdom, and particularly for the carrying on his dominion in the world : But 1 am for the present not so much upon the real possession as the pretended, and particularly we have had many that have believed themselves possessed, when the Devil never believed it of them, and perhaps knew them better ; some of these are really poor devils to be pitied, and are what 1 call *diables imaginaire;* these have notwithstanding done the Devil good service, and brought their masters good gain by soothsaying.

We find possession acknowledged in Scripture to be really and personally the Devil, or according to the text, legion of devils, in the plural. The Devil, or devils rather, which possessed the man among the tombs, is positively affirmed to be the Devil in the Scripture ; all the evangelists agree in calling him so, and his very works shew it ; namely, the mischief he did, as well to the poor creature among the tombs, who was made so fierce, that he was the terror of all the country, as to the herd of swine, and to the country in the loss of them.

I might preach you a lecture here of the Devil's terror upon the approach of our Saviour, the dread of his government, and how he acknowledged that there was a time for his torment, which was not yet come : *Art thou come to torment us before our time ?* It is evident the Devil apprehended that Christ would chain them up before the day of judgment ; and therefore some think the Devil here, being, as it were, caught out of his due bounds, possessing the poor man in such a furious manner, was afraid, and petitioned Christ not to chain him up for it, and as the text says, *They besought him to suffer them to go away,* &c. that is to say, when they say, *Art thou come to torment us before the time ?* the meaning is, they begged he would not cast them into torment before the time, which was already fixed ; but that if he would cast them out of the man, he would let them go away, &c.

The evangelist St. Luke says, *the Devil besought him that he would not command them to go out into the deep :* Our learned annotators think that part is not rightly rendered ; adding, that they do not believe the Devil fears drowning ; but with submission, I believe the meaning is, that they would not be confined to the vast ocean, where no inhabitants being to be seen, they would be effectually imprisoned, and tied down from doing mischief, which would be a hell to them ; as to their going into the swine, that might afford us some allegory ; but I am not disposed to jest with the Scripture, no nor with the Devil neither, farther then needs must.

It is evident the Devil makes use of very mean instruments sometimes, such as the damsel possessed with a spirit of divination, and several others.

I remember a story, how true I know not, of a weak creature next door to an ideot, who was established in the country for an oracle, and would tell people strange things that should be, long before they came to pass ; when people where sick, would tell them whether they should live or die ; if people were married, tell how many children they should have ; and a hundred such things as filled the people with admiration, and they were the easier brought to believe that the girl was possessed ; but then they were divided about her too, and that was the finest spun thread the Devil could work, for he carried a great point in it ; some said she had a good spirit, and some a bad, some said she was a prophetess, and some that she was the Devil.

Now had I been there to decide the question, I should certainly have given it for the latter ; if it were only upon this account, namely, that the Devil has often found fools very necessary agents for the propagating his interest and kingdom, but we never knew the good spirits do so ; on the other hand, it does not seem likely that heaven should deprive a poor creature of its senses, and as it were take her soul from her, and then make her an instrument of instruction to others, and an oracle to declare his decrees by ; this does not seem to be rational.

But as far as this kind of divination is in use in our days, yet I do not find room to charge the Devil with making any great use of fools, unless it be such as he has particularly qualified for his work, for as to ideots and naturals, they are perfectly useless to him ; but a sort of fools called the magi, indeed, we have some reason to think he often works with.

We are not arrived to a certainty yet, in the settling this great point, namely, what magic is ? whether a diabolical art, or a branch of the mathematics ? our most learned *Lexicon Technicum* is of the latter opinion, and gives the magic square and the magic lantern, two terms of art.

The magic square is when numbers in arithmetical proportion are disposed into such parallels or equal ranks as that the sums of each row, as well diagonally as laterally, shall be all equal ; for example, 2, 3, 4, 5, 6, 7, 8, 9, 10 : Place these nine in a square of three, they will directly and diagonally make 18.   Thus,

5	10	3
4	6	8
9	2	7

This he calls the magic square, but gives no reason for the term, nor any account of what infernal operations are wrought by this concurrence of the numbers ; neither do I see that there can be any such use made of it.

The magic lantern is an optic machine, by the means of which are represented, on a wall in the dark, many phantasms and terrible appearances, but no devil in all this, only that they are taken for the effects of magic, by those that are not acquainted with the secret.

All this is done by the help of several little painted pieces of glass, only so and so situated, placed in certain oppositions to one another, and painted with different figures, the most formidable being placed foremost, and such as are most capable of terrifying the spectators ; and by this all the figures may be represented upon the opposite wall, in the largest size.

I cannot but take notice, that this very piece of optic delusion seems too much a-kin to the mock possessions and infernal accomplishments, which most of the possessionists of this age pretend to, so that they are most of them mere phantasms and appearances, and no more ; nor is the spirit of divination, the magic, the necromancing, and other arts which were called diabolical, found to be of any use in modern practice, at least, in these parts of the world ; but the Devil seems to do most of his work himself, and by shorter methods ; for he has so complete an influence among those that he now lists in his service, that he brings all the common affairs of mankind into a narrower compass in his management, with a dexterity particular to himself, and by which he carries on his interest silently and surely, much more to the detriment of virtue and good government, and consequently much more to his satisfaction, than ever he did before.

There is a kind of magic or sorcery, or what else you may please to call it, which, though unknown to us, is yet, it seems, still very much encouraged by the Devil; but this is a great way off, and in countries where the politer instruments, which he finds here, are not to be had; namely, among the Indians of North-America; this is called pawawing, and they have their divines, which they call pawaws or witches, who use strange gestures, distortions, horrid smokes, burnings and scents, and several such things which the sorcerers and witches in antient times are said to use in casting nativities, in philtres, and in determining, or as they pretended, directing the fate of persons; by burning such and such herbs and roots, such as helebore, wormwood, storax, devilwort, mandrake, nightshade, and abundance more such, which are called noxious plants, or the product of noxious plants; also melting such and such minerals, gums, and poisonous things, and by several hellish mutterings and markings over them, the like do these pawaws; and the Devil is pleased, it seems, (or is permitted) to fall in with these things, and as some people think, appears often to them for their assistance upon those occasions.

But be that as it will, he is eased of all that trouble here; he can pawaw here himself, without their aid, and having laid them all aside, he negociates much of his business without ambassadors; he is his own plenipotentiary, for he finds man so easy to come at, and so easy when he is come at, that he stands in no need of secret emissaries, or at least not so much as he used to do.

18   3 F

Upon the whole, as the world, within the compass of a few passed years, is advanced in all kinds of knowledge and arts, and every useful branch of what they knew before improved, and innumerable useful parts of knowledge, which were concealed before, are discovered; why should we think the Devil alone should stand at a stay, has taken no steps to his farther accomplishment, and made no useful discoveries in his way? That he aloue should stand at a stay, and be just the same unimproved Devil that he was before? No, no, as the world is improved every day, and every age is grown wiser and wiser than their fathers; so, no doubt, he has bestirred himself too, in order to an encrease of knowledge and discovery, and that he finds every day a nearer way to go to work with mankind than he had before.

Besides, as men in general seem to have altered their manner, and that they move in a higher and more exalted sphere, especially as to vice and virtue; so the Devil may have been obliged to change his measures, and alter his way of working; particularly, those things which would take in former times, and which a stupid age would come easily into, won't go down with us now: As the taste of vice and virtue alters, the Devil is forced to bait his hook with new compositions; the very thing called temptation is altered in its nature, and that which served to delude our ancestors, whose gross conceptions of things caused them to be manageable with less art, will not do now; the case is quite altered; in some things, perhaps, as I hinted above, we come into the crime with ease, and may be led by a finger; but when we come to a more refined way of sinning, which our ancestors never understood, other and more refined politics must be made use of, and the Devil has been put upon many useful projects and inventions, to make many new discoveries and experiments to carry on his affairs; and to speak impartially, he is strangely improved either in knowledge or experiment, within these few years; he has found out a great many new inventions to shorten his own labour, and carry on his business in the world currently, which he never was master of before, or at least we never knew he was.

No wonder then that he has changed hands too, and that he has left off pawawing in these parts of the world; that we do not find our houses disturbed as they used to be, and the stools and chairs walking about out of one room into another, as formerly; that children do not vomit crooked pins and rusty stub nails, as of old, the air is not full of noises, nor the church-yard full of hobgoblings; ghosts do not walk about in winding-sheets, and the good old scolding wives visit and plague their husbands after they are dead, as they did when they were alive.

The age is grown too wise to be agitated by these dull scare-crow things which their fore-fathers were tickled with; Satan has been obliged to lay by his puppet-shows and his tumblers, those things are grown stale; his morrice-dancing devils, his mountebanking and quacking won't do now; those things, as they may be supposed to be very troublesome to him, (and but that he has servants enough would be chargeable too) are now of no great use in the new management of his affairs.

In a word, men are too much devils themselves, in the sense that I have called them so, to be frighted with such little low-prized appearances as these; they are better acquainted with the old arch-angel than so, and they seem to tell him they must be treated after another manner, and that then, as they are good-natured and tractable, he may deal with them upon better terms.

Hence the Devil goes to work with mankind a much shorter way ; for instead of the art of wheedling and whining, together with the laborious part of tricking and sharping, hurrying and driving, frighting and ter-rifying, all which the Devil was put to the trouble of before ; in short, he acts the grand manner, as the architects call it (I do not know whether our free-masons may understand the word) and therefore I may hereafter explain it, as it is to be diabolically as well as mathe-matically understood.

At present my meaning is, he acts with them immedi-ately and personally by a magnificent transformation, making them mere devils to themselves, upon all needful occasions, and devils to one another too, whenever he (Satan) has need of their service.

This way of embarking mankind in the Devil's parti-cular engagement, is really very modern ; and though the Devil himself may have been long acquainted with the method, and as I have heard, began to practise it towards the close of the Roman empire, when men began to act upon very polite principles, and were capable of the most refined wickedness, and afterwards with some popes, who likewise were a kind of church devils, such as Satan himself could hardly expect to find in the world ; yet I do not find that he was ever able to bring it into practice, at least, not so universally as he does now : But now the case is altered, and men being generally more expert in wickedness than they were formerly, they suffer the smaller alteration of the species, in being transmigrated ; in a word, they turn into devils, without any trouble, either to the Devil or themselves.

This particular would want much the less explanation, could I obtain a licence from sir Hellebore Wormwood, bart. or from my lord Thwartover, baron of
Scoundrel-Hall in the kingdom of Ireland, to write the
true history of their own conduct; and how early, and
above all, how easily they commenced devils, without
the least impeachment of their characters, as wise men,
and without any diminution of that part of their denomination which established them for fools.

How many mad fellows appear among us every day
in the critical juncture of their transmigration, just when
they have so much of the man left as to be known by
their names, and enough of the Devil taken up to settle
their characters? This easiness of the Devil's access to
these people, and the great convenience it is to him in
his general business, is a proof to me that he has no more
occasion for diviners, magicians, sorcerers, and whatever else we please to call those people who were formerly
so great with him; for what occasion has he to employ
devils and wizards to confound mankind, when he is
arrived at such a perfection of art, as to bring men, at
least in these parts of the world, to do it all themselves;
upon this account we do not find any of the old sorcerers
and diviners, magicians or witches appear among us;
not that the Devil might not be as well able to employ
such people as formerly, and qualify them for the employment too, but that really there is no need of them
hereabout, the Devil having a shorter way, and mankind
being much more easily possessed; not the old herd of
swine were sooner agitated, though there were full 2000
of them together: Nature has opened the door, and the
Devil has egress and regress at pleasure, so that the
witches and diviners are quite out of the question.

Nor let any man be alarmed at this alteration, in the case as it stands between mankind and the Devil, and think the Devil having gained so much ground, may in time, by encroachment, come to a general possession of the whole race, and so we should all come to be devils incarnate ; I say, let us not be alarmed, for Satan does not get these advantages by encroachment, and by his infernal power of art, no not at all ; but it is the man himself does it by his indolence and negligence on one hand, and his complaisance to the Devil on the other ; and both ways he, as it were, opens the door to him, beckons him with his very hand to come in, and the Devil has nothing to do but enter and take possession : Now if it be so, and man is so frank to him ; you know the Devil is no fool not to take the advantage when it is offered him, and therefore it is no wonder if the consequences which I have been just now naming follow.

But let no man be discouraged by this, from reassuming his natural and religious powers, and venturing to shut the Devil out ; for the case is plain he may be shut out ; the soul is a strong castle, and has a good garrison placed within to defend it ; if the garrison behave well, and do their duty, it is impregnable, and the cowardly Devil must raise his siege and be gone ; nay, he must fly, or, as we call it, make his escape, lest he be laid by the heels, that is, lest his weakness be exposed, and all his lurking, lying in wait, ambuscade-tricks. This part would bear a great enlargement, but I have not room to be witty upon him, so you must take it in the gross, the Devil lies at blye bush, as our country people call it, to watch your coming out of your hold ; and if you happen to go abroad unarmed he seizes upon and masters you with ease.

Unarmed, you will say, What arms should I take ?

What fence against a flail? What weapons can a man take to fight the Devil? I could tell you what to fight him with, and what you might fright him with, for the Devil is to be frighted with several things besides holy water; but it is too serious for you, and you will tell me I am a preaching and a canting, and the like; so I must let the Devil manage you rather than displease you with talking scripture and religion.

Well, but may not the Devil be fought with some of his own weapons? Is there no dealing with him in a way of human nature? This would require a long answer, and some philosophy might be acted, or at least imitated, and some magic, perhaps; for they tell us there are spells to draw away even the Devil himself; as in some places they nail horse-shoes upon the threshold of the door, to keep him out; in other places old pieces of flint, with so many holes and so many corners, and the like: But I must answer in the negative, I do not know what Satan might be scared at in those days, but he is either grown cunninger since or bolder, for he values none of those things now; I question much whether he would value St. Dunstan and his red hot tongs, if he was to meet him now, or St. Francis or any of the saints, no not the host itself in full procession; and therefore, though you do not care I should preach, yet, in short, if you are afraid he should charge upon you and attack you, if you will not make use of scripture weapons I should have mentioned, and which you may hear of, if you enquire at Eph. vi. 16. you must look for better where you think you can find them.

But to go on with my work, the Devil, I say, is not to be scared with maukins, nor does he employ his old instruments, but does much of his work himself without them.

And yet I must enter a caveat here too against being misunderstood in my saying the Devil stands in no need of agents ; for when I speak so, I am to be taken in a limited sense ; I do not say he needs them no where, but only that he does not need them in those polite parts of the world which I have been speaking of, and perhaps not much here ; but in many remote countries it is otherwise still ; the Indians of America, are particularly said to have witches among them, as well in those countries where the Spaniards and the English, and other nations have planted themselves, as amongst those where the European nations seldom come : For example, the people of Canada, that is, of the countries under the French government of Quebec, the Esquimeaux, and other northern climates, have magicians, wizards and witches, who they call Pilloatas or Pillotoas ; these pretend they speak intimately and familiarly with the Devil, and receive from him the knowledge of things to come ; all which, by the way, I take to be little more than this ; that these fellows being a little more cunning than the rest, think, that by pretending to something more than human, they shall make the stronger impressions on the ignorant people ; as Mahomet amused the world with his pigeon, using it to pick peas out of his ear, and persuaded the people it brought him superior revelations and inspirations from paradise.

Thus these Pillotoas gaining an opinion among the people, behave like so many mountebanks of hell, pretending to understand dark things, cure diseases, practise surgery, physic and necromancy all together ; I will not say, but Satan may pick out such tools to work with, and I believe does in those parts, but I think he has found a nearer way to the wood with us, and that is sufficient to my present purpose.

Of divination, sorcery, the black-art, &c.

Some would persuade me the Devil had a great hand in the late religious breaches in France, among the clergy (viz.) about the pope's constitution *unigenitus*, and that he made a fair attempt to set the pope and the Gallican church together by the ears, for they were all just upon the point of breaking out into a church war, that for ought we know might have gone farther than the Devil himself cared it should ; now I am of the quite contrary opinion, I believe the Devil really did not make the breach, but rather healed it, for fear it should have gone so far among them as to have set them all in a flame, and have opened the door to the return of the hugonots again, which it was in a fair way to have done.

But be it one way or the other, the historical part seems to be a little against me ; for it is certain the Devil both wanted and made use of legions of agents, as well human as infernal, visible and invisible, in that great and important affair, and we cannot doubt but he has innumerable instruments still at work about it.

Like as in Poland, I make no question but the Devil has thousands of his banditti at work at this time, and in another country not far from it, perhaps, preparing matters for the next general diet, taking care to prevent giving any relaxation to the protestants, and to justify the moderate executions at Thorn, to excite a nation to quarrel with every body who are able to fight with no body ; to erect the apostate race of S———y upon a throne which they have no title to, and turn an elective throne into an hereditary, in favour of popery.

I might anticipate all your objections, by granting the busy Devil at this time employing all his agents and instruments (for I never told you they were idle and useless) in striving to enflame the christian world, and

18   3 G

bring a new war to overspread Europe; I might, perhaps, point out to you some of the measures he takes,
the provocatives which his state physicians administer
to the courts and counsellors of princes, to foment and
ferment the spirits, and members of nations, kingdoms,
empires and states in the world, in order to bring these
glorious ends of blood and war to pass; for you cannot
think but he that knows so much of the Devil's affairs,
as to write his history, must know something of all these
matters more than those that do, not know so much as he.

But all this is remote to the present case, for this is no
impeachment of Satan's new methods with mankind, in
this part of the world, and in his private and separate
capacity; all this only signifies that in his more general
and national affairs, the Devil acts still by his old methods; and when he is to seduce or embroil nations, he,
like other conquerors, subdues them by armies, employs
mighty squadrons of devils, and sends out strong detach-
ments with generals and generalissimos to lead them,
some to one part of the world, some to another; some to
influence one nation, some to manage and direct another,
according as business presents, and his occasions require,
that his affairs may be carried on currently, and to his
satisfaction.

If it were not thus, but that the Devil by his new and
exquisite management, of which I have said so much,
had brought mankind in general to be the agents of their
own mischiefs, and that the world were so at his beck,
that he need but command them to go and fight, declare
war, raise armies, destroy cities, kingdoms, countries
and people; the world would be a field of blood indeed,
and all things would run into confusion presently.

But this is not the case at all, heaven has not let go

the government of the creation to his subdued enemy, the Devil; that would overturn the whole system of God, and give Satan more power, than ever he was or will be vested with; when, therefore, I speak of a few forward wretches in our day, who are so warm in their wickedness, that they anticipate the Devil, save him the trouble to tempt, turn devils to themselves, and gallop hellward faster than he drives; I speak of them as single persons, and acting in their own personal and private capacity; but when I speak of nations and kingdoms, there the Devil is obliged to go on in the old road, and act by stratagem, by his proper machinery, and to make use of all his arts, and all his agents, just as he has done in all ages, from the beginning of his politic government to this day.

And if it was not thus too, what would become of all his numberless legions, of which all ages have heard so much, and all parts of the world have had so much fatal experience? They would seem to be quite out of employment, and be rendered useless in the world of spirits, where it is to be supposed they reside; not the Devil himself could find any business for them, which by the way, to busy and mischievous spirits, as they are, would be a hell to them, even before their time; they would be, as it were, doomed to a state of inactivity, which we may suppose was one part of their expulsion from blessedness and the creation of man; or as they were for the surprising interval between the destruction of mankind by the deluge and Noah's coming out of the ark, when indeed they might be said to have nothing at all to do.

But this is not Satan's case, and therefore let me tell you too, that you may not think I treat the case with more levity than I really do, and than I am sure I intend

to do ; though it is too true that our modern and modish
sinners have arrived to more exquisite ways of being
wicked, than their fathers, and really seem, as I have
said, to need no Devil to tempt them ; nay, that they do
Satan's work for him as to others also, and make themselves devils to their neighbours, tempting others to crime
even faster than the Devil desires them, running before
they are sent, and going on the Devil's errands gratis ;
by which means Satan's work is, as to them, done to his
hand, and they may be said to save him a great deal of
trouble ; yet after all, the Devil has still a great deal of
business upon his hands, and as well himself as all his
legions, find themselves a full employment in disturbing
the world, and opposing the glory and kingdom of their
their great Superior, whose kingdom it is their whole
business, however vain in its end, to overthrow and destroy, if they were able, or at least to endeavour it.

   This being the case, it follows of course that the general mischiefs of mankind, as well national and public, as
family mischiefs, and even personal (except as before
excepted) lie all still at the Devil's door, as much as
ever, let his advocates bring him off from it if they can ;
and this brings us back again to the manner of the Devil's
management, and the way of his working by human
agents, or if you will, the way of human devils, working
in affairs of low life, such as we call divination, sorcery,
black-art, necromancy, and the like ; all which I take
to consist of two material parts, and both very necessary
for us to be rightly informed of.

   1. The part which Satan by himself or his inferior
   devils empowers such people to do, as he is in confederacy with here on earth ; to whom he may be

said, like the master of an opera or comedy, to give their parts to act, and to qualify them to act it ; whether he obliges them to a rehearsal in his presence, to try their talents, and see that they are capable of performing, that indeed I have not enquired into.

2. That part which these empowered people do volunteer in beyond their commission, to shew their diligence in the service of their new master, and either (1.) to bring grist to their own mill, and make their market of their employment in the best manner they can ; or (2.) to gain applause, be admired, wondered at, and applauded, as if they were ten times more devils than really they are.

In a word, the matter consists of what the Devil does. by the help of these people, and what they do in his name without him ; the Devil is sometimes cheated in his own business ; there are pretenders to witchcraft and black-art, who Satan never made any bargain with, but who he connives at, because at least they do his cause no harm, though their business is rather to get money, than to render him any service, of which I gave you a remarkable instance before.

But to go back to his real agents, of which I reckon two.

1. Those who act by direction and confederacy, as I have said already many do.

2. Those whom he acts in and by, and they (perhaps) know it not, of which sort history gives us plenty of examples, from Machiavel's first disciple ——— to the famous cardinal Alberoni, and even to some more modern than his eminence, of whom I can say no more till farther occasion offers.

1. Those who act by immediate direction of the Devil and in confederacy with him ; these are such as I mentioned in the beginning of this chapter, whose arts are truly black, because really infernal ; it will be very hard to decide the dispute between those who really act thus in confederacy with the Devil, and those who only pretend to it ; so I shall leave that dispute where I find it ; but that there are, or at least have been, a set of people in the world, who really are of his acquaintance, and very intimate with him ; and though as I have said, he has much altered his schemes and changed hands of late ; yet that there are such people, perhaps of all sorts, and that the Devil keeps up his correspondence with them ; I must not venture to deny that part, lest I bring upon me the whole posse of the conjuring and bewitching crew male and female, and they should mob me for pretending to deny them the honour of dealing with the Devil, which they are so exceeding willing to have the fame of.

Not that I am hereby obliged to believe all the strange things the witches and wizards, who have been allowed to be such, nay, who have been hanged for it, have said of themselves ; nay, that they have confessed of themselves, even at the gallows ; and if I come to have an occasion to speak freely of the matter, I may perhaps convince you that the Devil's possessing power is much lessened of late, and that he either is limited, and his fetter shortened more than it has been, or that he does not find the old way (as I said before) so fit for his purpose as he did formerly, and therefore takes other measures, but I must adjourn that to a time and place by itself : But we are told that there are another sort of people, and perhaps, a great many of them too, in whom and by whom the Devil really acts, and they know it not.

Of divination, sorcery, the black-art, &c.

It would take up a great deal of time and room, too much for this place, so near the close of this work, to describe and mark out the involuntary devils which there are in the world ; of whom it may be truly said, that really the Devil is in them, and they know it not : Now, though the Devil is cunning and managing, and can be very silent where he finds it for his interest not to be known ; yet it is very hard for him to conceal himself, and to give so little disturbance in the house, as that the family should not know who lodged in it ; yet, I say, the Devil is so subtil and so mischievous an agent, that he uses all manner of methods and craft to reside in such people as he finds for his purpose, whether they will or no, and which is more, whether they know it or no.

And let none of my readers be angry or think themselves ill used, when I tell them the Devil may be in them, and may act them, and by them, and they not know it ; for I must add, it may, perhaps, be one of the greatest pieces of human wisdom in the world, for a man to know when the Devil is in him ; and when not ; when he is a tool and agent of hell, and when he is not ; in a word, when he is doing the Devil's work, and under his direction, and when not.

It is true, this is a very weighty point, and might deserve to be handled in a more serious way than I seem to be talking in all this book ; but give me leave to talk of things my own way, and withal, to tell you, that there is no part of this work so seemingly ludicrous, but a grave and well weighed mind may make a serious and solid application of it, if they please ; nor is there any part of this work, in which a clear sight and a good sense may not see that the author's design is, that they should do so ; and as I am now so near the end of my

book, I thought it was meet to tell you so, and lead you
to it as far as I can.

I say, it is a great part of human wisdom to know
when the Devil is acting in us and by us, and when not ;
the next and still greatest part would be to prevent him,
put a stop to his progress, bid him go about his business,
and let him know he should carry on his designs no farther in that manner ; that we will be his tools no longer ;
in short, to turn him out of doors, and bring a stronger
power to take possession ; but this, indeed, is too solid a
subject, and too great to begin with here.

But now, as to the bare knowing when he is at work
with us, I say this, though it is considerable, may be
done, nor is it so difficult : For example, you have no
more to do but look a little into the microcosm of the
soul, and see there how the passions, which are the blood,
and the affections, which are the spirit, move in their
particular vessels ; how they circulate, and in what temper the pulse beats there, and you may easily see who
turns the wheel ; if a perfect calm possesses the soul ; if
peace and temper prevail, and the mind feels no tempests
rising ; if the affections are regular and exalted to virtuous and sublime objects, the spirits cool, and the mind
sedate, the man is in a general rectitude of mind, he may
be truly said to be his own man ; heaven shines upon
his soul with its benign influences, and he is out of the
reach of the evil spirit ; for the Divine Spirit is an influence of peace, all calm and bright, happy and sweet like
itself, and tending to every thing that is good both present and future.

But on the other hand, if at any time the mind is ruffled, if vapours rise, clouds gather, if passions swell the
breast, if anger, envy, revenge, hatred, wrath, strife ; if

these, or any of these hover over you, much more if you feel them within you ; if the affections are possessed, and the soul hurried down the stream to embrace low and base objects ; if those spirits, which are the life and enlivening powers of the soul, are drawn off to parties, and to be engaged in a vicious and corrupt manner, shooting out wild and wicked desires, and running the man headlong into crime, the case is easily resolved, the man is possessed, the Devil is in him ; and having taken the fort, or at least the counterscarp and out-works, is making his lodgment to cover and secure himself in his hold, that he may not be dispossessed.

Nor can he be easily dispossessed when he has got such hold as this ; and it is no wonder, that being lodged thus upon the out-works of the soul, he continues to sap the foundation of the rest, and by his incessant and furious assaults, reduces the man at last to a surrender.

If the allegory be not as just and apposite as you would have it be, you may, however, see by it in a full view, the state of the man, and how the Devil carries on his designs ; nothing is more common, and I believe there are few thinking minds but may reflect upon it in their own compass, than for our passions and affections to flow out of the ordinary channel ; the spirits and blood of the soul to be extravasated, the passions grow violent and outrageous, the affections impetuous, corrupt and violently vicious : Whence does all this proceed ? From heaven we cannot pretend it comes ; if we must not say it is the Devil, whose door must it lie at ? Pride swells the passions ; avarice moves the affections ; and what is pride, and what is avarice, but the Devil in the inside of the man ? ay, as personally and really as ever he was in the herd of swine.

Let not any man then, who is a slave to his passions, or who is chained down to his covetousness, pretend to take it ill, when I say he has the Devil in him, or that he is a devil : What else can it be, and how comes it to pass that passion and revenge so often dispossess the man of himself, as to lead him to commit murder, to lay plots and snares for the life of his enemies, and so to thirst for blood ? How comes this but by the Devil's putting those spirits of the soul into so violent a ferment, into a fever ; that the circulation is precipitated to that degree, and that the man too is precipitated into mischief, and at last into ruin ? it is all the Devil, though the man does not know it.

In like manner avarice leads him to rob, plunder, and destroy for money, and to commit sometimes the worst of violences to obtain the wicked reward. How many have had their throats cut for their money, have been murdered on the highway, or in their beds, for the desire of what they had ? It is the same thing in other articles, every vice is the devil in a man : Lust of rule is the devil of great men, and that ambition is their devil as much as whoring is father ———'s devil ; one has a devil of one class acting him, one another, and every man's reigning vice is a devil to him.

Thus the Devil has his involuntary instruments, as well as those who act in confederacy with him ; he has a very great share in many of us, and acts us, and in us, unknown to ourselves, though we know nothing of it, and indeed, though we may not suspect it ourselves, like Hazael the Assyrian, who when the prophet told him how he would act the Devil upon the poor Israelites, answered with detestation, *Is thy servant a dog that he should do this thing?* and yet he was that dog, and did all those cruel things for all that ; the Devil acting him, or acting in him, to make him wickeder than ever he thought it was possible for him to be.

THE CONCLUSION.

Of the Devil's last scene of liberty, and what may be supposed to be his end, with what we are to understand of his being tormented for ever and ever.

AS the Devil is a prince of the power of the air, his kingdom is mortal, and must have an end ; and as he is called the god of this world, that is, the great usurper of the homage and reverence which mankind ought of right to pay to their maker, so his usurpation also, like the world itself, must have an end : Satan is called the god of the world, as men too much prostrate and prostitute themselves to him, yet he is not the governor of this world ; and therefore the homage and worship he has from the world is an usurpation ; and this will have an end, because the world itself will have an end ; and all mankind, as they had a beginning in time, so must expire and be removed before the end of time.

Since then the Devil's empire is to expire and come to

an end, and that the Devil himself and all his host of devils are immortal seraphs, spirits that are not embodied and cannot die, but are to remain in being ; the question before us next will be, What is to become of him ? What is his state to be ? Whither is he to wander, and in what condition is he to remain to that eternity to which he is still to exist ?

I hope no man will mistake me so much in what I have said as to spirits, which are all flame, not being affected with fire, as if I supposed there was no place of punishment for the Devil, nor any kind of punishment that could affect them ; and so of our spirits also when transformed into flame.

I must be allowed to speak there of that material fire, by which, as by an allegory, all the terrors of an eternal state are represented to us in Scripture, and in the writings of the learned commentators, and by which the pain of sense is described ; this, perhaps, I do not understand as they seem to do, and therefore have said,

When we are all flame (that is all spirit) we shall all fire (that is, all such fire as this) despise. And thus I claim to be understood.

It does not follow from hence, neither do I suggest, or so much as think that infinite power cannot form a something (though inconceivable to us here) which shall be as tormenting, and as unsupportable to a devil, an apostate seraph, and to a spirit, though exalted, unembodied and rarified into flame, as fire would be to other bodies ; in which I think I am orthodox, and do not give the least occasion to an enemy to charge me with prophane speaking, in those words, or to plead for thinking prophanely himself.

Of the Devil's last scene of liberty.

It must be atheistical to the last degree to suggest, that whereas the Devil has been heaping up and amassing guilt ever since the creation of man, encreasing in hatred of God and rebellion against him, and in all possible endeavour to dethrone and depose the Majesty of Heaven; that yet heaven had not prepared, or could not prepare a just penalty for him.; and that it should not all end in God's entire victory over hell, and in Satan's open condemnation : Heaven could not be just to its own glory, if he should not avenge himself upon this rebel, for all his superlative wickedness in his modern as well as antient station; for the blood of so many millions of his faithful subjects and saints whom he has destroyed; and if nothing else offered itself to prove this part, it would appear undoubted to me; but this, I confess, does not belong to Satan's history, and therefore I have reserved it to this place, and shall also be the shorter in it.

That his condition is to be a state of punishment, and that by torment, the Devil himself has owned, and his calling out to our blessed Lord when he cast him out of the furious man among the tombs, is a proof of it, *What have we to do with thee*, and, *Art thou come to torment us before the time ?* Luke viii. 28. where the Devil acknowledges four things, and three of them are directly to my present purpose; and if you won't believe the word of God, I hope you will believe the Devil, especially when it is an open confession against himself.

1. He confessed Christ to be the Son of God (that by the way) and no thanks to him, for that does not want the Devil's evidence.

2. He acknowledges he may be tormented.

3. He acknowledges Christ was able to torment him.

4. He acknowledges that there is a time appointed when he shall be tormented.

As to how, in what manner, and by what means, this tormenting the Devil is to be performed or executed, that I take to be as needless to us as it is impossible to know, and being not at present inclined to fill your heads and thoughts with weak and imperfect guesses, I leave it where I find it.

It is enough to us that this torment of the Devil is represented to us by fire, it being impossible for our confined thoughts to conceive of torment by any thing in the world more exquisite ; whence I conclude, that devils shall at last receive a punishment suitable to their spiritual nature, and as exquisitely tormenting as a burning fire would be to our bodies.

Having thus settled my own belief of this matter, and stated it so, as I think will let you see it is rightly founded, the matter stands thus :

Satan having been let loose to play his game in this world, has improved his time to the utmost ; he has not failed on all occasions to exert his hatred, rage, and malice, at his conqueror and enemy, namely, his Maker ; he has not failed, from principles of meer envy and pride, to pursue mankind with all possible rancour, in order to deprive him of the honour and felicity which he was created for, namely, to succeed the Devil and his angels in the state of glory from which they fell.

This hatred of God and envy at man, having broken out in so many several ways in the whole series of time from the creation, must necessarily have greatly encreased his guilt ; and as heaven is righteous to judge him, must terminate in an encrease of punishment, adequate to his crime, and sufficient to his nature.

Some have suggested, that there is yet a time to come, when the Devil shall exert more rage, and do more mischief than ever yet he has been permitted to do ; whether he shall break his chain, or be unchained for a time, they cannot tell, nor I neither ; and it is happy for my work, that even this part too does not belong to his history ; if ever it shall be given an account of by mankind, it must be after it is come to pass, for my part is not prophesy of foretelling what the Devil shall do, but a history of what he has done.

Thus, good people, I have brought the history of the Devil down to your own times ; I have, as it were, raised him for you, and set him in your view, that you may know him and have a care of him.

If any cunninger men among you think they are able now to lay him again, and so dispose of him out of your sight, that you shall be troubled no more with him, either here or hereafter, let them go to work with him their own way ; you know things future do not belong to an historian, so I leave him among you, wishing you may be able to give no worse an account of him for the time to come, than I have done for the time past.

F I N I S.

Gresswell, Printer, Exeter.